Grace Jennings-Edquist is a journalist at the Australian Broadcasting Corporation, where she writes articles on issues including gender equality and wellbeing for *ABC Everyday*. As a former senior editor at Mamamia Women's Network, Grace has written extensively about women's mental health for an audience of millennial Australian women. Grace's writing has appeared widely online, including in *The Guardian*, *Crikey*, *The Australian*, news.com.au, *New Statesman* and *Ms. Magazine*. She has appeared on radio and television, including on ABC's *The Agony Of…* and is the recipient of a 2018 Michael Gordon Fellowship from the Melbourne Press Club.

A former lawyer with a love of travel, Grace has lived in London, The Hague, Sydney and New York, where she worked for the Financial Times Group. She currently lives in Melbourne with her husband, young daughter and a vegetable garden she occasionally finds time to water. Follow her musings on Twitter: @gracie_je.

The Yes Woman

GRACE JENNINGS-EDQUIST

First published by Affirm Press in 2021
28 Thistlethwaite Street, South Melbourne,
Boon Wurrung Country, VIC 3205
affirmpress.com.au
10 9 8 7 6 5 4 3 2 1

Title: The Yes Woman / Grace Jennings-Edquist, author
ISBN: 9781922400796 (paperback)

A catalogue record for this book is available from the National Library of Australia

Cover design by Alissa Dinallo
Author photograph by Christian Bachelier
Typeset in Adobe Garamond Pro by J&M Typesetting
Proudly printed in Australia by McPherson's Printing Group

For Olive. May you always remember how to say no.

Contents

Chapter 1

This is what a Yes Woman looks like

> No one can do two full-time jobs, and have perfect children and cook three meals and be multi-orgasmic till dawn … Superwoman is the adversary of the women's movement.
>
> – Gloria Steinem[1]

It was only when I found myself in a psych ward, burned out and sleepless, that I realised my inability to say no was making me sick.

I was sitting in group therapy alongside five other frazzled-looking women when it happened. Facing us was a psychologist whose trendy eyeglasses and power suit shoulder pads gave her an air of authority. We were in a deeply unglamorous room, papered with dodgy paintings produced during an art therapy class. It all felt very *Girl, Interrupted* – except, instead of being the sallowly beautiful, Angelina Jolie kind of mental patient, I was an exhausted new mum rocking a soggy maternity bra and bursting into tears at the smallest obstacle.

As a high-achieving perfectionist, I felt quite mortified about being in a psych ward. I thought suffering from burnout was embarrassing – not the kind of thing that happened to fast-moving, multitasking, do-everything-right people like me.

Of course, it was that way of thinking that had landed me in hospital in the first place.

'How many of you have been called perfectionists?' the trendy psychologist asked the room full of women.

I raised my hand. Like a slow-motion Mexican wave, all five other women raised theirs, too.

'How many of you find it hard to put your foot down when others cross your boundaries?' she went on.

All six of us kept our hand in the air.

'How many of you hold yourselves to high standards, and try to be everything to everyone?'

All six hands stayed high.

At that moment, a cartoon lightbulb might as well have flashed next to my uncombed head. You could call it an epiphany.

All six women in that room had different jobs. We all lived in different parts of the state and had come from different cultural backgrounds. We had our own personal mental health histories, of course, and some of us were also battling past traumas and personal issues. Even so, we discovered that we all had a few key traits in common: we hated to disappoint others; we strove to do well in our professional and personal lives; we tried to be 'nice'; and we had trouble saying no when other people – and, hell, society in general – made demands on our time and energy.

And as 'Yes Women', we were stressed out, exhausted, overwhelmed, and resentful.

What is a Yes Woman?

'Yes Woman' is not a clinical term, of course, so you won't find it in the *Diagnostic and Statistical Manual of Mental Disorders*. It's a term I coined to describe my harried state of being prior to burning out – a state I've since recognised in many others, well beyond my original compadres in the mental health unit.

Many people assume that saying yes to others' demands and constantly striving to please is the conscientious thing to do. Some wear it like a badge of honour – proof that they're good, high-achieving people.

One such person is freelance journalist Ainslie, 39, who described to me her own struggle to say no:

> Part of it is genuinely just wanting to be a kind and generous person. I was brought up with manners, and I am someone who tries to take too much on board naturally: with my work, with my volunteering, with my exercise, with my running, it's either all or nothing. Boom or bust. I'd say I try to be high-achieving.

Perhaps you recognise yourself in these words.

Through speaking to dozens of women like Ainslie, I found that the Yes Woman state of mind is indicated by four main traits.

(Ready? Drumroll, please.)

First up, **if you're a Yes Woman, you have a hard time saying no.** You say yes to please others – often, because you fear the alternative might be seen as impolite or selfish. You might also fear that saying no means dropping the ball on an obligation or goal you just *have* to get right (and couldn't *possibly* delegate).

If you're a Yes Woman, you're also a people-pleaser. You tend to put other people's needs first, even when that means pushing your own needs aside and even when, deep down, you don't really want to. And your people-pleasing extends beyond your tendency to say yes: you also care, in a broader sense, about what other people think, and hate the thought of not living up to their expectations. You try to be agreeable, aiming – to borrow a term from psychologist and author Dr Harriet Braiker – to be 'everything to everyone'.[2] You often struggle to put your foot down when others cross your boundaries.

If you're a Yes Woman, you probably have perfectionistic tendencies, too. You not only want to be everything to everybody, you want to do it all *perfectly*. You hold yourself to a high standard and need people to think you have your shit together. Regardless of your career path or seniority level at work, you might have been described as 'ambitious' or 'a wonder woman'; you pride yourself on multitasking and getting things right.

There's a chance you've regarded your perfectionism as a strength, or even used it as the ultimate humblebrag in job interviews: 'My biggest problem is that I always need to make sure my work is just right!' (*Please.*) In fact, as a Yes Woman, you might secretly view your perfectionism as a 'special power' that drives you to constantly strive for more.

If you're a Yes Woman, you're overcommitted and overwhelmed (and over it). Chronically busy, exhausted, pulled in a million different directions and overwhelmed: these are common modes of being, and Yes Women can often feel chronic stress taking a toll on their minds and bodies. Many feel burned out, suffer from anxiety or secretly resent all the self-sacrifice their people-pleasing, yes-ing, perfectionistic ways entail. And while all these experiences are traits or markers of a Yes Woman, they're also *consequences* of, and are exacerbated by, the first three Yes Woman tendencies listed. (I mean, you wouldn't feel so overwhelmed and anxious if you weren't on 'yes' autopilot, and in the business of pleasing everyone to perfection.)

Why not Yes Men?

These Yes Women tendencies aren't exclusive to women, but my strong hunch after that lightbulb moment in the hospital was that women face particular pressures that predispose them to such traits.

It's women who are told, more than men, to be 'nice'. It's women who are expected to put other people's needs first – as carers, partners, mothers and friends. It's women who are taught to seek approval, first and foremost, while men are primarily taught to seek power.[3]

So, it makes sense that women would show more perfectionism and people-pleasing behaviours, which have approval-seeking motivations at their core. And so, it also makes sense that women find themselves in a spiral of stress and overload.

As I got stuck into research for this book – interviewing psychologists and academics, combing through many dozens of books and articles, and surveying more than 200 women across the world – it became clear my hunch was correct: there's a significant gender gap when it comes to 'Yes' tendencies.

Research shows that more women are people-pleasers than men: in one study from the US, more than half of all women identified as people-pleasers, compared to four in ten men.[4] Perfectionism is also more common in women: Australian research has revealed that one-third of women have high scores for perfectionism, compared to just over one-fifth of men.[5] We also – surprise, surprise – struggle to say no: one US research paper from 2014 found that women have more trouble, compared to men, just saying the word 'no' – and experience more guilt when saying it, too.[6]

Women also commonly report feelings of being spread too thin and having too little time to themselves: researchers say that the feeling of being pulled in a million directions – which they call 'role strain' – is felt more commonly by women (and, in particular, mothers) than men.[7] One poll of 2000 mums found that they had an average of just 17 minutes of 'me time' each day, and most of the respondents felt they 'lived their lives entirely for other people'.[8] Women with responsibilities as carers, whether for kids or parents, also feel more time pressure than men,[9] and this also leads to more severe mental health consequences for mothers than fathers.[10]

Role strain is directly linked to stress and anxiety, so it's no surprise that these both show up much more often in women than men, too. Constant, intense stress is reported by a disturbingly large proportion of women: 28 per cent of women report an average stress level of 8–10 on a 10-point scale, versus 20 per cent of men, according to one US survey.[11] Young women report, shockingly, *twice* the levels of daily stress reported by young men.[12] Women are also more likely to report physical symptoms of stress than men.[13]

From the age she hits puberty to the time she turns 50, a woman is almost twice as likely to suffer from an anxiety disorder than a man.[14] The most recent stats from Australia show that anxiety and depression have been diagnosed in 20.1 per cent of women aged 15–34, compared to 11.2 per cent of men. In women aged 35–54, 19.4 per cent had diagnosed depression or anxiety, compared to 13.5 per cent of men.

What's worse, these mental health issues in women seem to be on the rise. Even before COVID-19 wreaked havoc on our mental health, rates of anxiety and depression in women have been skyrocketing, jumping from around 13 per cent to about 20 per cent over the eight years since 2009, Australia's most recent Household, Income and Labour Dynamics in Australia (HILDA) survey shows.[15,16]

And so the stats continue.

It's a bleak picture. Basically, if Shania Twain had written 'Man! I Feel Like a Woman!' in 2020, the title of the song could've been 'Man! I Feel Like a Woman (Worn Out, Spread Too Thin and Stressed to My Eyeballs!)'. Yes Women seem to feel all these stresses particularly acutely, because not only do they push their own needs aside to keep everyone else happy, they also hold themselves to unrelentingly high standards while doing so.

SIDE NOTE: Why this book does more than list practical ways to 'just say no'

Perhaps you picked up this book expecting to find a self-helpy pep talk amounting to being told to 'just say no'. In that case, you may be wondering why I'm also harping on about women's experiences of perfectionism, people-pleasing, and feeling overwhelmed and overcommitted.

My research has found that the difficulties we have with saying no are rooted in much deeper stuff than just individual habits we've cultivated. They're often linked inextricably with the other three tendencies mentioned – people-pleasing, perfectionism, and feeling overwhelmed – and I've found it's more useful to look at the cluster of tendencies as a whole, because they all play into one another.

For example, Yes Women's perfectionism and people-pleasing go hand in hand, because 'both are shame-based strategies', as one therapist, the Austin-based Ann Stoneson of Labyrinth Healing, told me. (Interestingly, researchers have found that women experience shame much more often than men.)[17] This one-two punch of people-pleasing and perfectionism is rooted in a false core belief that 'our value comes from what we do rather than who we inherently are', Stoneson says.[18] In other words, if you're a Yes Woman, you've probably learned you have to earn love or worthiness.

There's another reason I examine four Yes Woman tendencies rather than narrowing my focus to how to 'just say no': these four tendencies are symptomatic of wider cultural forces and gender stereotypes that trap many women into this mode of being. This is a problem that's much bigger than any one of us.

Bottom line: there are other, gender-blind books out there that promise to teach you how to say no or how to become assertive or relax your perfectionism. But without the context of what specific pressures are being faced by women, I believe these books are missing a key ingredient.

Ultimately, we cannot 'self-help' our way to a world that allows us to say no without penalty (to adapt the words of feminist author Soraya Chemaly).[19] So if we're learning to say no, we need to simultaneously work towards changing the bigger picture for women.

What it feels like to be a Yes Woman

So who am I to write a book about how women can better learn to say no?

I'm not a psychologist or a doctor, I'm not a counsellor, and I'm not an Instagram-famous 'wellness guru' (God knows there are enough of those already). I am, however, a journalist who's written about gender and wellbeing for years, covering everything from perfectionism, loneliness, and body image to sexual abuse and harassment. As a journalist, I've interviewed experts, compiled their best advice for overcoming Yes Woman behaviour, researched the way that behaviour affects women specifically, and served all those insights up to you here – *voila!* – in a handy little package.

More importantly, perhaps, I know what it's like to be a Yes Woman – because I used to be one.

A year ago, I looked like I had my act together. If you clicked onto my Instagram, you'd think my life was a montage of satisfying career accolades and wholesome moments with my baby daughter and doting husband. Oh, and you'd think my hair was always spot-on.

There's one photo that shows me, back to the camera, at the beach holding my daughter up for a kiss. She's giggling cutely into my shoulder, and my bikini appears to fit surprisingly well considering I gave birth just a few weeks prior. The sun is highlighting my blonde topknot, and laid out before me is a crystal-clear rock pool.

It's idyllic, and it's – frankly – bullshit.

When I posted that image on social media, a friend sent me a private message saying, 'You make parenting look so easy!' What she didn't know from glancing at that photo is how much of a nervous wreck I was when posing for it.

I'd always been a people-pleasing, perfectionistic type, and when I became a mum in 2019, I approached motherhood with the drive and rigour with which I'd typically approached all other realms of my life. I wanted to be an ideal parent. I researched the best methods for sleep training, vocabulary development, and sustainable nappy practices.

I also wanted to be a strong career woman, so I kept the old parts of my life spinning: attending industry talks to stay on top of the latest news, reading through my work inbox while on maternity leave, and listening to podcasts to stay abreast of world news.

I wanted to look good while doing all this, so I got stuck into a diet and exercise regimen that, with some help from breastfeeding, had me back below my pre-baby weight in a couple of months.

At the beach that day, I'd cast my partner, Ben, in the role of 'Instagram husband', imploring him to take at least a dozen photos of me and the baby (which, I'm embarrassed to say, I then reviewed, cropping out all sign of my stretchy, squooshy post-pregnancy waist before posting to social media).

Intent on staying on top of my friendships, family relationships and other networks, I also agreed to an endless stream of requests and invitations because I couldn't bear the thought of disappointing anyone.

I remember being offered tickets to a show when my daughter was ten days old. Wanting to still feel like 'the old me' – sociable and artsy – and to prove (to whom? I can't even remember) that I could be a 'cool mum', I accepted. So my husband and I settled my daughter to sleep at my in-laws' place nearby, then set off to the show. I even wore lippie.

When we arrived at the theatre, I had to ask for new seats on the ground floor because I was still recovering from my caesarean section and couldn't hobble up the stairs. Was that a sign I wasn't ready to be out and about? I dismissed the thought. *Recovery is for suckers!* Then, halfway through the show, I ducked into the ladies' room and sobbed because I missed the sight of my daughter's tiny hands. (*I'm not hormonal,* you're *hormonal!*)

Would I have been happier if I'd stayed at home and rested while my daughter slept? Almost certainly. I knew, even then, that I should probably slow down. But it wasn't the only ridiculous thing I agreed to do as a new mum. So the yes-es kept coming.

Would I email an old friend back with advice on how to navigate a big career transition? *Yes!*

Could I drive over to my uncle's side of town for a catch-up, even though it was in the middle of baby's bedtime? *Yes!*

Could I help a friend go shopping for her newly renovated home? *Yes!*

I'd been a Yes Woman my entire adult life, but the added responsibilities of parenthood brought it to a head. I became chronically overcommitted: late for appointments; forgetful; always double-booked because I was so frazzled. At night I struggled to sleep, or knocked myself out with a sleeping pill, only to wake up at 3am terrified that I'd forgotten something on my to-do list, had failed to respond to an email, or was embarrassingly overdue for a hair appointment.

I didn't realise it at the time, but my preoccupation with presenting myself in a certain way – sans weakness or vulnerability – was draining me. My drive to succeed in different areas of my life might sound like a blessing, but it had become a millstone. Somewhere along the way, I'd forgotten that I was allowed to actually do things for myself and enjoy my life. So, ironically, with each thing I tried to do 'right', I became more stressed out and miserable.

That's how, the day after I took that photo on the beach – four months after I became a mum – the pressures weighing on me came to a head.

I'd developed fantasies of depositing my daughter with her dad for a week and running away to a five-star resort, where my phone would magically deactivate and I wouldn't have to write back to anyone's text messages. I sobbed to my mum: 'I'm so fucking exhausted I just want to walk into the ocean so I can get a break.'

I wasn't actually depressed or suicidal, but I was so … *very* … tired. I was burned out, and my anxiety was off the charts.

So I checked into the aforementioned ugly suburban mental hospital (which went by the gentle euphemism 'mother and baby unit').[20] Unappealing though the venue might have been, my stay there was the first stretch of free time I'd had in what felt like years. I spent four days doing not very much at all. I read. I adjusted my medication (and, to this day, remain on Zoloft for my generalised anxiety disorder). I wrote. I attended group therapy.

And I had my 'aha' moment, about how saying yes was making me sick.

At one point during my recovery, I asked a psychiatrist if I might have attention deficit hyperactivity disorder (ADHD), after reading that people with that condition often feel 'driven by a motor' and struggle with forgetfulness, irritability and constant lateness. The psychiatrist's response? I didn't tick enough of the diagnostic criteria to make a formal diagnosis of ADHD.

'It's more likely,' he said, 'that you're simply very, very stressed because you're in great demand and pulled in too many directions.' Memory and attention can be the first things to go when a person is living in a heightened state of stress, he added.

After my four-day stay in the mother and baby unit, I checked myself out and scribbled down a few thoughts that soon turned into the start of a book – the one you're holding in your hands or flicking through on your device.

The ambition behind this book is simple: to help you reclaim your time and energy by learning how to gracefully say no – without feeling guilty.

But writing this story isn't just about encouraging others to stop the perfectionistic, people-pleasing act; it's also proof that I've stopped being a Yes Woman myself. My old self would never have written about her mental health. She was too busy pretending to be perfect on Instagram.

❦

If you're a Yes Woman, hopefully you haven't got to the point where you have to spend time in a mental health unit, but I'll bet you're still suffering a slew of ill-effects from your habit of saying yes to everybody's demands.

Perhaps being rushed or hassled has become your default state, like it had for me right before my burnout. You might have physical symptoms of stress: headaches or backaches; a 'nervous stomach'; a tight chest; skin rashes; sleep problems; and feeling 'wired but tired' are common symptoms identified by women who try to be everything to everyone.[21]

Maybe your symptoms are milder but every so often you find yourself asking, 'Why the hell did I say yes to this?' and feel a familiar weariness and resentment that you didn't stick up for yourself. You might worry that you're not giving the best of yourself to the ones you care about most. Maybe you're checking your phone when your spouse is trying to tell you about their day, or ignoring your best friend's calls because you said you'd help out at the world's dullest work function.

You may have spent a very – exhaustingly – long time trying to hide your struggle from the world. That's because central to the Yes Woman psyche is the desire to appear 'together'. Many of us feel a bit like a duck who seems to be calmly gliding across the lake but whose legs are peddling away furiously underwater. Chances are you've had people comment that you're a 'superwoman' and you 'always have it together'. But under the surface, you're a frantic ball of stress. You might feel you're slipping into quicksand, battling a nagging feeling that there isn't enough of you to go around.

Despite these difficulties, if you're a Yes Woman, you seem to be on 'yes' autopilot.

Sometimes it's a direct question you're answering: *yes to helping an acquaintance with a favour. Yes to a colleague's fun-run donation tin. Yes to driving your friends to the airport. Yes to volunteering for a committee at work. Yes to allowing a friend you haven't been close to since high school 'pick your brain' for work.*

Other times it's a 'silent' yes – a tacit agreement to comply with unspoken expectations: *yes to trying that new fasting diet. Yes to being a strong and effective leader at work. Yes to planning the next family holiday. Yes to wearing the latest style of shoe, even though they cause blisters straight from hell. Yes to planning a fancy catered party for your kid's birthday. Yes to straightening or curling or cutting your hair. Yes to worrying about whether your new colleague likes you. Yes to watching the new Netflix show everyone's talking about. Yes to navigating the stock market. Yes to doing all this while being glamorous and attractive (but not too sexy).*

Exhausting, isn't it?

If none of this sounds like you, feel free to put this book down – or, hey, pass it on to a sister or friend who might benefit. Not all women are Yes Women: it would be wrong, and offensive, to suggest that. But it's obvious these traits are widespread, and they're not restricted to women from any one background.

I also don't expect you to recognise yourself in every aspect of my own story – you may have had very different experiences based on race, sexuality, disability or any number of other factors. But what's remarkable about this Yes Woman phenomenon is how broad a range of people have experienced it. The more-than-200 women I surveyed for this project represent a wide range of age groups, sexualities, levels of education, gender experiences, geographic locations and ethnic groups. Across the board, what women told me is that they are pressed for time, struggle to deal with boundary-violators in their lives, and feel pressured to say yes to things for which they don't have the time or energy.

Chen, a Melbourne-based queer bookstore owner in her early 30s, told me she often feels 'a sense of duty as well as guilt' when her mother asks her to babysit a much younger sibling. Despite wanting to say no, 'I typically cave and babysit to suit her needs,' Chen told me.

Jess, a lawyer in her 20s living in New York, was lumped with extra work – but with no raise, promotion or title change – after her manager left without immediately being replaced. 'Then my new manager started to ask me to do administrative work, and trying to frame it as a good opportunity in a very condescending way,' she told me. Jess accepted the extra work because she felt put on the spot, but secretly felt indignant.

Shoshanna, a Canberra-based writer in her late 60s, was asked by a poet she hardly knew to look at some writing he was struggling with. She agreed, and gave him feedback on his work. 'Then he asked me to look at the rewrite,' she said. Despite feeling he was asking too much, Shoshanna felt awkward about shrugging off his request.

Aida, a stay-at-home mum in her early 40s from regional Victoria, described feeling pressured to help an injured friend. 'I took her to emergency, stayed with her, then next day went back to clean her apartment on my own,' Aida told me. 'She was quite demanding and direct about what I should do. I just dealt with it by being there, but never really admitted that I felt unappreciated.'

The scenarios described by Chen, Jess, Shoshanna and Aida are, individually, irritating but not unbearable. The problem is that Yes Women find themselves constantly struggling to field these demands – and the cumulative effect can be an exhausting sense that everyone 'wants a piece of you'.

Whether it was a colleague, an acquaintance, a friend or a family member putting on the pressure, all the women I surveyed told me they often feel drained by the expectation they'll say yes in the name of 'being nice'.

It robs them of their time and energy. It draws their focus away from their true passions and priorities. And it's undermining their power.

What this book is about (and how it works)

If you haven't noticed yet, this book has unashamedly feminist leanings. It's not just a practical handbook on how to draw boundaries but also a call to arms for women to take back their power, time and energy in a world that demands we say yes to other people's priorities.

This is not a book about sex, consent and sexual assault – although they are crucially important conversations. (Women already do say no in these contexts, but that 'no' is not respected.)

This is also not a book about 'doing it all' – and it's certainly not a book about how 'doing it all' is bad for women. The hackneyed debate about whether women should 'do it all' only ever really referred to women working *and* having children.[22] The pressures explored in this book are broader than that, encompassing a wide range of roles that women are expected to fulfil in the 21st century: from friend, to partner, worker, community organiser and boss.

I'm also not interested in the 'Can women really do it all?' trope because some conservative commentators and men's rights activists use it to argue that if women are so stressed this must mean that feminism has failed – that it would be easier and better for everyone if we reverted back to a time when women remained at home and men brought home the bacon.

I argue the opposite: we need *more*, not less, progress on redefining gender roles.

Finally, this is not a book about blaming women for their Yes Woman tendencies. If you struggle to say no, it's not your fault. I point the finger of blame primarily at a society that, through the enforcement of rigid gender roles, teaches us from the moment we gain consciousness to be 'good' and compliant at all costs.

This book is about how women can stop spending time and energy on things they don't *want* to do in the first place. It's about how women can live happier lives by resisting the stifling pressure to be agreeable.

♣

That's a lot of ground to cover, so this is how the book will play out.

First we'll dig into how we become Yes Women – and why that state of being is a problem. The factors that contribute to our Yes Woman ways are many and varied, but my research suggests they can be broadly grouped into six categories.

The first factor is **gender roles**, because it's clear that the way women are taught by society to be agreeable and self-sacrificing has a lot to do with how some of us become perfectionists and people-pleasers. The other five factors that contribute to Yes Woman tendencies are our parents and **upbringing**; our temperament or **personality**; a predisposition to anxiety or other **mental health issues**; the **feeling of being an outsider**; and **rushing to get things done** before gendered expectations around caring responsibilities come into play. These last five influences tend to apply to some Yes Women, but not others.

We'll spend some time looking at each of these factors, so you'll be able to see in detail how certain personality traits (conscientiousness and neuroticism, anyone?) are more closely correlated with Yes Woman behaviour; how impostor syndrome can be linked to the feeling of being an outsider; and the way childhood environments – having perfectionistic parents who valued achievements, or a traumatic, chaotic or unsafe childhood – can prime girls to become Yes Women. Then we'll move on to peep at the facts about how saying yes undermines us, and take a look at the price we pay – both individually, and as a collective of women – for saying yes all the time.

After that, *it's all about you, baby*. Here's your chance to spot your unique combo of Yes Woman tendencies. We'll figure out whether you're a Yes Woman – and, if so, whether you've got it bad. We'll also look at myths you might have swallowed (anyone else always assumed that 'busy is best'?) and challenge them. We'll work out what you actually *want* – because, often, Yes Women have been pushing aside their own needs for so long that they have trouble identifying what they actually want or need.

At which point, it'll be time to dive into those practical, 'here's exactly what to do and say' bits you've been waiting for – with the scripts, tips and strategies you'll need to unlearn your Yes Woman tendencies, and the exact words you can use to politely decline everything from professional requests to coffee dates and toddlers' birthday parties – and I'll also give you permission to 'take back' your previous yes-es (hallelujah, this trick is a life-changer).

We will also unpack strategies and techniques to dodge irksome asks, invitations and favours in specific scenarios – from friends asking for favours, to overbearing relatives and overstepping parents, to dating and relationships (including the load at home). We'll take a close look at saying no in your career, as well as in some other big, juicy situations where the pressure to put other people's needs first, and do it all perfectly, looms large – from motherhood, to eco-guilt, to expectations around beauty. Each chapter looks at the challenges that you, my dear reader, might face in trying to make changes in your life.

Finally, we'll look at how throwing away our Yes Woman

tendencies sits within the wider context of feminism. Learning how to say no isn't a magic bullet for women's liberation and happiness. It's not that simple – there are structures of power (hello, patriarchy and capitalism) that are heavily invested in women saying yes to things that sap their time and energy: working for less pay, looking after the domestic sphere so men can run the world, buying into the latest trends, or wearing undies that wedge all the way up our bums because they look sexy. As long as those structures are in place, women will be taught to, and sometimes coerced into, smiling, nodding, and saying yes to the crushing demands they face.

Without underplaying the importance of structural change, there's another way we can try to make things better for women: by starting with changes in our own individual lives. If enough of us change the way we individually think and behave, we can contribute to a broader movement that, across the world, is challenging these expectations and pressures more systemically. The personal is political, as second-wave feminists said – so I'll take a closer look at how we can join together in pushing for these larger changes.

♣

Before we proceed, brace yourself: learning how to say no might involve undoing a lifetime of indoctrination about what it means to be a woman – by our parents, the media, and our teachers, coaches and bosses.

We live in a world that tells women not to offend others and not to stand up for themselves, so this is not going to be easy. Nothing good is.

But it's worth the work: once you start saying no without feeling guilty, you'll feel liberated, you'll notice that others respect you more and place a greater value on your time, and you'll feel you have taken back your power, time and energy.

In a world that teaches girls to grow into Yes Women, that's a radical feat.

Chapter 2

(Not) born this way: how culture makes us Nice

In order to learn to say 'no', you must first understand why you so often say 'yes'.

– Brenda Dolieslager, psychologist[1]

I watched with dismay as the scene at the playground unfolded.

As a tiny girl of three waddled towards the slide, a bigger boy roughly shouldered her out of the way. The little girl's face crumbled, and she reached towards the queue-jumping boy to bat him away.

'Hey! Be nice,' called her mother, swooping in to restrain the girl before she made contact. 'We don't hit! Be a good girl and share,' the woman continued, red-faced with embarrassment. 'And the slide is wet anyway. You don't want to get damp.'

As the woman mumbled her apologies and bundled her defeated daughter off the play equipment, the older boy whooped and hollered down the slide without a second glance. His dad, standing nearby, shrugged with a what-can-you-do expression. 'My son's not very good at waiting his turn,' he remarked lackadaisically.

Nobody checked in with the shoved little girl. Nobody cautioned the older boy. Nobody told him to be nice. And when he misbehaved, it was explained away as a natural attribute.

My annoyance lingered for hours afterwards, as my thoughts intermittently returned to the little girl's disgruntled face and trembling bottom lip. Just like that girl at the playground, I thought, haven't many of us been taught to be deferential, to be 'nice', since we were tiny? And when these messages about being a 'good girl' start coming so early, is it any wonder that so many of us fall into the trap of bottling up our own needs and putting other people first?

When I spoke to experts and dug into the research about how cultural norms dictate gender roles, I discovered that, just as I had expected, the stifling pressure to be agreeable does contribute to the tendency to say 'yes' (as well as to perfectionism, people-pleasing and ultimately feeling overcommitted and stressed to the gills).

In fact, the way girls are socialised according to strict gender norms is so core to the Yes Woman way of being that I've dedicated this entire chapter to it.

Good as gold and twice as Nice: we're raised (not born) to be agreeable

'Overall the main thing that I always tried to be was just – a good girl.'

These are the words of singer-songwriter Taylor Swift in the documentary *Miss Americana*,[2] but they could just as well have been spoken by me, or any Yes Woman.

'My entire moral code as a kid and now is a need to be thought of as good,' Swift explains. 'Do the right thing, do the good thing.'

It's little wonder that Swift, and every Yes Woman I've encountered, grew up with 'be good' at the very core of their moral identity. We've been taught to be good, to be 'nice' – to avoid being unruly or confrontational at all costs – since infancy.

These cultural forces are nothing new, of course: women have long faced societal pressures to be compliant, self-sacrificing, and primarily devoted to caring for family. As Queensland-based clinical and coaching psychologist and *Crappy to Happy* podcast host Cass Dunn put it when I interviewed her: 'Women particularly are subjected to all those messages about needing to keep people happy, being polite, being told our value is in being liked more so than being respected – all that kind of gender conditioning that we receive.' Until very recently, those expectations were codified in law: married women can't work; women can't vote because they should be confined to the home; women can't access abortion in order to control the size of their families. Today, many laws have evolved (thank you, feminist forebears). Many of us around the world are now free to work outside the home, and, in theory at least, to control our fertility, and have a voice in politics. These are undoubtedly enormous wins.

But even in the 2020s, old attitudes and gender stereotypes still shadow women, making it clear that we're expected to carry the emotionally attuned, self-sacrificing roles in various arenas of our lives. The result? We now face the difficulty of undertaking many more roles simultaneously than our mothers and grandmothers did – and all the while, the same old tune of 'be a nice girl now, dear' plays in the background.

♣

Perhaps you're thinking, But aren't women just naturally nicer?

Well, no – but they can certainly appear that way. Personality studies tend to show that women score higher on traits like 'agreeable', 'nurturing' and 'altruistic'. In one 1994 study, women scored especially high on what researchers called 'tender-mindedness' (those soft and fuzzy little brains of ours!).[3] In 2007, when a research team from Europe asked more than 17,000 people across the world to fill out personality questionnaires, they found that women indeed scored higher on agreeableness, and also on the warmth and gregariousness facets of extraversion.[4] Studies have also found that women are better at decoding non-verbal signals of emotion.[5] So by the time they're adults, women appear more agreeable, more compliant, and less directly assertive than their menfolk, and they often give off the appearance of being 'nice'.

For a long time, historians, law-makers and scientists (typically white men) have claimed that these tendencies to be 'nice' and touchy-feely are rooted in biology. They've tried to 'prove' that women are better suited to caring roles in the home, while men go out to work. Some have argued that, even as foetuses or babies, there are physiological differences that gear males and females differently. One well-known example: Simon Baron-Cohen, a British clinical psychologist and University of Cambridge professor, created a study in which newborn babies were shown a mobile and a human face, to see whether the girls preferred the face (said to signal an interest in human relationships and emotions).[6] The study found that baby girls looked at the human face slightly longer than the mobile, while boys looked at the mobile slightly longer than the face.

Baron-Cohen and his peers used those findings to claim that women's brains are simply wired for emotions, while men are 'systematisers', with mathematical brains best geared for leadership. *'Big strong men are geared to rule the world!'* Baron-Cohen claimed. (I paraphrase, but you get the gist.)

The methodology of that study has been heavily criticised and dismissed elsewhere, and a sizeable body of scientific literature flat-out contradicts Baron-Cohen's results, suggesting that male and female infants respond equally to people and objects.[7] Ultimately, researchers have come to varying conclusions about the extent of the brain's impact on gender traits, but crucially, one key belief supporting the idea of a distinctly 'female brain' – that the hippocampus, a part of the brain that helps connect emotions to the senses, is larger in females than in males – was largely debunked in a 2015 meta-analysis that looked at findings from 76 published papers involving more than 6000 healthy people. The study found that there were no, or minimal, differences in size of the hippocampus.[8]

In other words, many experts now believe we're all born with similar brains, but women are trained into niceness by cultural expectations about what it means to be a girl or woman. Long story short: we raise babies differently based on the biological sex they are born with – and this helps determine how they behave as they grow up.

So while it's true that women score higher on 'agreeable' and 'empathetic' traits when tested, let's not buy into the myth that niceness (or 'Niceness', as I'll call it throughout this book, because it really is 'Nice' with a capital 'N') comes naturally to all women.

SIDE NOTE: The problem with 'Nice'

'What's wrong with encouraging women to smile and practice selflessness?' you might well be thinking. Isn't it just nice to be Nice?

Let me be clear: kindness and generosity of spirit are wonderful traits in any person. I think all kids should be raised with those traits. But there's a key difference between being Nice and being truly kind. As Soraya Chemaly adeptly puts it: 'Nice is something you do to please others, even if you have no interest, desire, or reason to. Kindness, on the other hand, assumes that you are true to yourself first.'[9]

The Niceness I address in this book is a trait that society deems compulsory for women but not men. It's a form of politeness and self-sacrifice that, as girls, we are taught we must engage in – even if it doesn't come from the heart. Even if it harms us.

Some might also argue that I'm being sexist by taking such issue with Niceness and these other traits associated with femininity. To which I remind them: if we accept that there's no evidence that women are inherently 'Nicer' than men, then labelling women 'naturally Nice' can actually be seen as a form of sexism – albeit a type of sexism that looks and sounds polite. We might even call it 'benevolent sexism', to use a term coined by psychologists Peter Glick and Susan Fiske in the 90s.[10] Insisting women are naturally 'Nicer', self-sacrificing and demure isn't as overtly prejudiced as out-and-out hostile sexism – but it nevertheless serves to maintain the patriarchy by justifying traditional gender roles, Glick and Fiske argue.

Framing Niceness as 'natural' for women gives men a great excuse to be the powerful leaders making the hard calls. They can tell themselves it's only reasonable for them to rule, while women stay at home being carers in society ('They're naturally great at that!'). This mindset has been compared by academics to the paternalistic colonial mindset known as 'the white man's burden'. Just as some white colonial men spoke of this alleged duty to care for and 'civilise' the indigenous subjects whose territories they invaded,[11] so do some benevolent sexists think of women as sweet, weaker, lesser beings who must be protected and controlled.

(This brings to mind an ex-boyfriend of mine, who used to stand in front of the TV news when it showed footage of war zones or car crashes. 'I don't want you to have to see such unpleasant things,' he explained. Never mind that I was studying television journalism at the time!)

In short: Nice and kind are not the same thing, and it's not a compliment to say that women are just Nicer than men. If women always acted Nice not because they were trained to by society but because they were just inherently kind and generous, then pleasing others wouldn't feel like a burden – it'd be a pleasure, right?

If Niceness was natural, we wouldn't crack under the pressure of being Yes Women.

And if being Nice was in my nature, I wouldn't have ended up in hospital, completely frazzled and burnt out from trying to be Nice to everyone. All. The. Damn. Time.

How gender roles teach girls to be Nice

'It's a girl!' proclaims the doctor.

'It's a girl!' reads the balloon by the maternity bed.

'It's a girl!' declare the dozens of cards – covered in flowers and unicorns and diamantes – sent to the parents.

As the tiny new being pops shoutily into the world, she's blithely unaware that gender is a thing at all. But by the time that baby girl takes her first breath, society has already determined a colour-coded layout for her life. She's assigned a gender identity at birth – female – on the basis of her biological sex, which immediately forms the basis of the roles, attributes and responsibilities assigned to her by society, and perhaps also her family. (A proper analysis of the impact of compulsory cis-heteronormativity – the way society assumes we are all cisgendered and straight, and the harm that this can cause – requires more knowledge than I have, so I'll leave that to the experts, some of whom I've listed in the resources section at the end of this book.)

To borrow a thought from researcher and author Brené Brown: from the moment she is born, society projects onto a little girl immediate expectations – that she will be cute and attractive; she will grow up, get married, become a mother, have natural parenting skills, and be a loving family member.[12]

For those of us born biologically female, the doctor's cry of 'it's a girl!' is the start of a social mechanism known as 'girling', as American philosopher Judith Butler once wrote.[13] As girls, we are not only expected to convey and display a social gender that coordinates with the labelled sex, we're also expected to communicate and display emotions that align with the named social gender.[14] In other words, as children, we learn to regard 'feelings' as feminine, and we learn to associate being female with caring for others, keeping the peace, and self-sacrifice.

Here's one common example of how this 'girling' happens: I was shopping for my baby daughter at a large chain store the other day and I noticed the messages printed on the clothing were all variations on a theme.

'Lovely!' screamed one tiny pink t-shirt.

'Mummy's little helper,' read another.

'Happy and I know it,' smirked another.

'Sugar and spice and all things nice,' said another.

My daughter is only a few months old, but before she can even read, she and other little girls are being marketed the message: 'Be compliant, be Nice; you're there to make the world more pleasant for others', as British writer Kate Long once noted in a Twitter thread that went viral.[15]

Those messages are echoed by toys marketed to girls. Even at 6 to 12 months old, the 'girls' aisle of toy stores are packed with 'toys of the home' (dolls and cooking sets), which typically focus on nurturing others. Boys' toys, by comparison, are overwhelmingly 'toys of the world' (machines and transportation vehicles).[16]

At just 10 months old, babies have developed the ability to make mental notes regarding what goes along with being male or female.[17] By the age of five, children already have gender stereotypes in their heads.[18] By six, boys and girls agree that girls tend to be Nicer than boys – and that boys are more likely to be 'Really, really smart'.[19]

When I interviewed Hobart-based psychologist Dr Kimberley Norris for this book, she told me that this kind of socialisation plays a huge role in the people-pleasing that underlies Yes Woman behaviour. 'Young children don't question the messages they receive from adults, from the media,' says Norris, who is also a professor of clinical psychology at The University of Tasmania. 'They develop this pattern of behaviour quite early on and it just gets reinforced.'

These kinds of messages about what it means to be a girl versus a boy are sometimes taught explicitly: your grandmother telling you to be a good girl and help with the dishes while your brother languishes on the couch, for example. Or rules at all-girl schools teaching students that they must be Nice to everyone: share, be a good listener, be loyal and not let people down, as Irish writer and actor Stefanie Preissner recalls from her own childhood in her book *Can I Say No?*[20] The rules at the local boys' school were simpler, she recalls: no biting, no kicking; wash your hands after using the toilet.

Other messages are 'caught'. They're the inadvertent memos we pick up, like watching your mum – and not your dad – buy Christmas gifts for the extended family every year.[21] We notice that when boys and girls raise their hands in class at the same rate, boys get called on more than girls by a factor of at least eight. (Meanwhile, when girls are called on, they get corrected more than boys.)[22]

So we lower our voices, and we're praised for being well-behaved little girls. It feels good. We let a friend borrow our favourite toy and, because we're praised for our generosity, we learn to keep lending out our things.

As girls, we're also taught to have a different relationship with space and the use of our bodies. Girls are taught that much of their value comes from being small and cute: even as newborn babies, little girls are more often described as 'weak' and 'delicate', whereas boys are more frequently described as 'strong', and 'well coordinated'.[23] As American political theorist and socialist feminist Iris Marion Young famously wrote, girls come to take up less space by what they do, and by what they do not do; girls come to restrict themselves by restructuring how they use their bodies.[24] So while men 'man-spread', women are more likely to sit with elbows tucked in and legs crossed. And just like the little girl at the playground, we're taught early on to restrict our movements so that we don't get our dresses damp or dirty; meanwhile, boys wear no-fuss shorts and comfortable shoes made for running and exploring.

All this is a long way of saying that girls are taught that they're meant to keep their voices, their bodies and their needs discreetly tucked away.

These messages can be amplified for girls and women of colour, who are often taught, as *Good Black News* founder Lori Lakin Hutcherson put it, 'not to make a fuss, speak out or rock the boat. To just "deal with it", lest more trouble follow (which, sadly, it often does).'[25]

Indeed, girls from certain diverse cultural backgrounds can suffer the effects of the 'Niceness' expectation more acutely. Young women from collectivist cultures, which emphasise the needs and goals of the group over the desires of each individual, may face greater expectations to be quiet and submissive. According to London-based psychotherapist and author of *Emotional Sensitivity* Imi Lo, in East Asian cultures, including those in China, Japan, Vietnam, Korea, Taiwan, Singapore and Malaysia, for women in particular 'there are many unwritten rules.'

'Asian women are celebrated for their compliance, adaptability, gentleness and youthful sweetness,' Lo writes in an essay about 'non-conforming Asian women'. 'They are taught to play the femme fatale, the dutiful daughters, and the charming wife, but not to be assertive or ambitious in their career.'[26]

Ultimately, in all sorts of cultures across the world, little girls learn that they are meant to self-sacrifice. And as American lawyer and author of *The H-Spot: The Feminist Pursuit of Happiness* Jill Filipovic writes, they learn that girls and women are meant to give:

> We give birth, we give life, we give milk created in our own bodies. We give up – food, ambition, money, fun. We sometimes give up our children. When we have sex with men, we're 'giving it up'. We give up our names. We are told to give until it hurts, and then give more.[27]

The requirement that women give is no small matter – it's a central dynamic of misogyny, as feminist philosopher and author Kate Manne says. Under the white patriarchal order in which we live, 'women are obligated to give, not to ask, and are expected to feel indebted and grateful, rather than entitled', Manne explains. 'This is especially the case with respect to characteristically moral goods: attention, care, sympathy, respect, admiration, and nurturing.'[28]

'But I wasn't raised to be a doormat!'

If you live in modern-day Australia, all this talk of training girls to be gentle little wallflowers might sound ludicrous. Isn't this the 2020s? Don't most parents have high hopes of their daughters being strong, independent career women?

Maybe your own parents were ahead of the curve – as mine were – and raised you to believe you could do anything a man does. If that rings true for you, you might be tempted to toss this book aside with a derisive snort: 'This retrograde BS doesn't apply to me!'

But regardless of your upbringing, it's unlikely you were shielded completely from traditional expectations that girls be 'Nice'. Research shows that even in families where the parents consider themselves equitable on the gender front, these kinds of gendered messages can persist.[29]

Sociologist Emily Kane, author of *The Gender Trap*, has found that these messages can take root even before a child is born – even among progressive, modern families. She interviewed a diverse group of parents in a not particularly conservative part of America about their preferences for sons or daughters before they became parents – and found that where parents had wanted daughters, it was often because daughters were expected to provide more emotional closeness. As one white, upper-middle-class, lesbian mother told Kane:

> I envisioned that a daughter would be sweet, a great companion in old age ... a girl would never forget your birthday, would be much more emotionally connected.[30]

For another example of how even the most egalitarian-minded parent can fall into this trap, we can look to the work of New York-based sociologist Dr Barbara Katz Rothman, whose work includes examining birth and midwifery through a feminist lens. Rothman conducted a study in which a group of expectant mothers described the movement of the foetus. She found that pregnant women who didn't know the sex of their children described the baby's kicks in similar terms – but when the mothers knew the baby's sex, they used gender-stereotyped language: boys' kicks were deemed 'strong' and 'vigorous', while girls' were 'not terribly active'.[31]

Before a baby girl has taken her first breath, she's cocooned in preconceived notions, in other words. Canadian-born British philosopher, psychologist and writer Cordelia Fine points out in her book *Delusions of Gender* that this phenomenon is backed by a body of research showing how implicit associations – including gender stereotypes – influence our behaviour and decisions, even without us realising it.[32]

The bottom line: even if you were raised by forward-thinking parents, there's a good chance some of this societal gendering around 'Niceness' crept in anyway. This stuff is pervasive as heck, people.

Nice and queer: LGBTQI Yes Women

Can LGBTQI folks be Yes Women? Hell yes.

Admittedly, while most research into people-pleasing, perfectionism and the tendency to say yes hasn't collected data on the respondents' sexuality (or whether they identified as cisgender, transgender, agender or non-binary, for that matter) the findings of one study published in 2020 suggest that lesbian women are less likely to be perfectionists than straight women, and the same study found that bisexual women are less likely to be perfectionists than both straight women and lesbian women.[33]

But, extrapolating from that study, it's not as simple as saying that lesbian, bisexual or queer women are less likely to be Yes Women. Far from it. Sexuality is, of course, one piece of a large number of overlapping factors that shape who we are – women of any sexuality can be perfectionistic people-pleasers who say yes on autopilot. And what's more, in one of the first surveys I carried out while researching this book, a full 25 per cent of respondents said they identified as LGBTQI. Some explained that, for them, the sexuality- or gender-based discrimination they'd experienced had distinctly played into their Yes Woman ways.

Taylor, a 27-year-old trans non-binary person who uses 'they/them' pronouns, told me they had to start learning to say no as part of the process of coming out. 'When I started talking about wanting to change my name or my pronouns, my therapist said, "I'll be honest with you, the trans people-pleaser has a more difficult time at the start,"' Taylor says.

Coming out is, after all, saying no to the assumptions society has about your gender or sexuality. And it's saying it repetitively, to everyone you meet.

'You don't just say, "No, that's not my name and these are my pronouns." You have to say that again and again, for the rest of your life, to people who you talk to at dinner parties and interviews and everywhere else,' explains Taylor. 'You're saying, "No, your idea of me might not line up with who I am."'

Taylor says that, while this idea of continually saying no to society's heteronormative assumptions can be intimidating, it's also been a great learning curve.

'Compulsory heterosexuality is people-pleasing, because you're acting in a certain way, in a way that you've been told,' Taylor says. 'In my experience, the trans non-binary people I know are some of the most authentic people that I know, because they have to move through things that cis or hetero people might not have to ask themselves.'

Another member of the LGBTQI community who's struggled with Yes Woman tendencies is Stace, a 28-year-old bisexual architect from Sydney: 'I grew up telling the lie "I'm not bisexual", and honestly I think it made me put a lot of time and energy into hiding my own wants.'[34] She goes on, 'I spent years in this pattern of lying to others – and to myself – by trying to wear the right thing and looking the perfect way … Even since I've come out now and my friends and family are supportive, it's still such an ingrained pattern of mine to strive to make others like or accept me.'

Then there's Allie, a 34-year-old nurse from Brisbane. She tells me that before coming out as a lesbian, she suffered profoundly under the 'Niceness' expectation – perhaps more so than her straight counterparts. In the minds of her high school classmates, Allie says that 'lesbian' meant loud, unkempt and outspoken. She feared coming out would mean she would be thought unfeminine – not 'nice, cute or demure like a lady,' as she put it.

These fears – which she describes as 'a fearful flavour of shame' – were a strong factor in choosing to deny her sexuality until her late teens. They also drove her to try to be 'extra nice' – a strategy she used 'to head off' what she 'thought people would assume' about her once she came out.

Allie ultimately found that her sexuality helped her transcend heteronormative expectations around beauty ideals. So while she initially felt her sexuality fuelled her Yes Woman tendencies, it helped her rise above her people-pleasing ways in the end.

'My closest friends were always very, very attractive in that straight, pretty, sorority-girl kind of way, so I grew up assuming that's what I had to look like as a woman,' Allie explains. 'When I realised I was a lesbian and came out, it was like this weight lifted off me. Suddenly nobody expected me to do the hair-colouring and the eyelashes and all the other stuff my straight friends spend their time on to please men or society or whatever. Now I just dress how I feel.'

♣

The trans experience is particularly interesting in this context. Transgender women haven't been subject to the earliest moments of the 'girling' processes – the process that starts with the doctor's cry of 'it's a girl!' – because their gender identity differs from the sex assigned to them at birth. However, societal expectations can nevertheless powerfully effect trans women.

Diversity trainer, educator, speaker and occasional performer Sally Goldner AM – a co-founder of Transgender Victoria – tells me she noticed those societal expectations come to bear on her soon after she announced herself as a woman. 'There was this sense of mansplaining,' she says. 'It was as if, suddenly, I lost my knowledge' – so men felt they had to start explaining things to her in a way they hadn't previously.[35]

Psychotherapist and counsellor Grace Lee, who works with trans, gender diverse and non-binary clients, and is a trans woman herself, has remarked on this phenomenon, too. 'I think trans women do have the experience [before coming out] of being able to take up space and being dominant and heard and all those things, and then finding that once they've transitioned they're not acknowledged as being able to take up as much space,' Melbourne-based Lee tells me, adding that trans women can feel they have to 'be more acquiescent' after transitioning.

Ben Barres, a transgender man and neuroscientist at the Stanford University School of Medicine in California, described a similar experience – in reverse – of feeling taken more seriously as a man than a woman. 'People who don't know I am transgender treat me with much more respect. I can even complete a whole sentence without being interrupted by a man,' Barres wrote in an article for *Nature*.[36] He recalls hearing an audience member remark, following his transition, 'Ben Barres gave a great seminar today, but then his work is much better than his sister's.' There was, of course, no sister – the audience member just took Barres less seriously when perceiving him as a woman.[37]

♣

There isn't one 'LGBTQI Yes Woman story' of course – gender identity and expression is far from simple, and these are merely some examples of the way things can go. Nevertheless, the experiences of women from the LGBTQI community show that the 'be a Nice girl' expectation is far-reaching and can be hard to overcome, even for (and sometimes especially for) those who've confronted gender expectations head-on.

The price of stepping out of the 'good girls' line

So far, this chapter has explored how girls are encouraged to become Yes Women. Much of the time, this is a process of positive reinforcement: it's the Nice girls who are worshipped as love interests in blockbuster movies. They're the self-sacrificing mums getting hugged by strong sons on breakfast cereal commercials. They're the lovely media darlings – the Bachelorettes, the (early) Taylor Swifts, the breakfast television sidekicks.

But with that carrot of social reward also comes a stick for the women who refuse, even in tiny ways, to subjugate their own needs.[38] That stick is aggression towards, and exclusion of, women who step out of the 'obedient women's line'.[39]

The very real consequences for women who are not seen as caring and demure include hurtful labels used to keep women quiet – 'nasty', 'loudmouth', 'bitch' – and public shaming, as well as racist stereotypes such as 'angry Black women', online trolling, and even physical violence. The fear of these consequences is a tune that plays, ever so softly, in the background of many everyday interactions – and it's a powerful part of what turns some girls into Yes Women.

In other words, we fear the negative responses we might receive if we express what we need, want and feel. So, all too often, we remain silent. When a creepy bloke on the street yells out something vulgar, we 'grin and bear it'. When we're riled up, we go out of our way to seem calm and to contain ourselves. When someone treats us poorly, we couch our concerns in light, breezy, non-confrontational terms.

We suppress our anger. We remain silent. We say 'yes'.

♣

Picture this: you're in a team meeting at work, about to present a great new idea you've come up with. Out of nowhere, a male colleague – who you'd run your idea past, for feedback – presents the idea as his own. Do you speak up, calling him out for passing off your idea as his own?

Many women wouldn't – and it's not because they're pushovers. It's because women are simply aware of the reality that we are all too often shamed as loudmouthed or pushy when we speak out. Just as we're admonished as little girls to use 'Nicer' voices three times more often than boys are,[40] gendered expectations about whose voices should be heard continue into adolescence and then adulthood.

In the workforce, women who are seen as 'too' ambitious or 'too' confident – who speak up – bump up against the 'Nice girl' female stereotype. Often, they are penalised for those behaviours for which men are rewarded: when women express anger at work, they are viewed as less competent, less powerful and less likely to be paid a high salary; when men express anger at work, meanwhile, both male and female evaluators judge them to be powerful, competent and worthy of a high salary.[41]

At work, women are also expected to give of themselves more than men. In one study, employees were asked to help colleagues finish a task. When the men didn't engage in this 'helping behaviour', those who were asked to rate them – both male and female – didn't mark them down. When the women didn't help their colleagues, however, they were severely marked down.[42] On the other side of the coin, when the men helped, the judges rated them very highly; the women who helped got no benefit, though.[43]

Studies also show that when men talk, people see them as powerful, while when women talk, people see them as incompetent and unsuited for leading, as Caryl Rivers and Rosalind C Barnett have pointed out.[44]

Have you seen that famous *Punch* cartoon that shows a group of workmates drawn sitting around a table? The boss is saying, 'That's an excellent suggestion, Miss Triggs. Perhaps one of the men here would like to make it.'[45] It was drawn in 1988, but it's still funny – because it's true.

That double-standard is something most professional women can relate to, even today.

♣

Women in politics are particularly vulnerable to these sorts of double standards. More than 80 per cent of women parliamentarians across the globe have been targeted by some sort of psychological violence, according to a 2016 global survey from the Inter-Parliamentary Union.[46]

Here in Australia, the treatment of former Australian Prime

Minister Julia Gillard throughout her term as PM gives a good indication of the kind of labelling and shaming women politicians are subject to. Gillard was called a bitch, a witch; her choice not to have children saw her labelled 'barren'; and when her father, John, died, conservative shock jock Alan Jones suggested that he had 'died of shame'.[47]

Similarly, in the US, presidential candidate Hillary Clinton was often described as more hostile, irritable, less competent, and unlikeable – 'the kiss of death for a class of people expected to maintain social connections', as Soraya Chemaly wrote in her powerful book about women and anger, *Rage Becomes Her*.[48] Clinton's critics, including Donald Trump, often also expressed their dislike of her in terms of disgust – which, as Kate Manne says, is a particularly powerful misogynistic way of describing women 'because it sticks, and because it makes us want to keep our distance from its object'.[49]

If women in politics get into a debate, it's a 'catfight'.[50] If the women are young and attractive (and even if they're not) their sexual life is often turned into a matter of public spectacle – and they're sometimes even 'slut-shamed'. For instance, there was the case of Australian Greens Senator Sarah Hanson-Young, who was defamed by Senator David Leyonhjelm and told to 'stop shagging men'. (Hanson-Young later successfully sued for defamation, saying the victory was for women who had been 'made to stay silent'.)[51]

This kind of harassment can drive some women in politics or other leadership roles to people-pleasing behaviour, says Senator Larissa Waters, a senator for Queensland, a former lawyer, and a member of the Australian Greens. 'There is an unspoken rule that women in leadership roles are expected to not only be competent and trustworthy, but caring and likeable,' she tells me. 'Too often, that leads to us agreeing to take on more work to seem like a team player, someone who doesn't think themselves above helping out.' (This can also play into many women in leadership positions experiencing impostor syndrome, she adds – but we'll explore that later.)

♣

It's not just women in politics or leadership roles who are vulnerable to these attacks, of course. In a world where social media makes anonymous trolling so easy, the threat of being attacked for voicing your opinion looms large for any of us who use the internet, causing many of us to think twice before posting online. Facebook and Twitter have become tools of call-out culture, which leaves little room for mistakes – and can leave some women too afraid to speak up at all. Afraid of being 'cancelled' – and putting our reputations and even careers on the line – many women obsess about getting their status updates, opinions or shared links 'right'.

Social media is not evil – it has many upsides, including its potential to amplify previously marginalised voices. But it's a double-edged sword: as Canadian-Australian author, presenter, journalist and former model Tara Moss wrote, having an opinion as a woman online now comes with gendered abuse, almost inevitably:

> Speak out against rape and murder … get rape and death threats. Speak out against inequality and have your 'f*ckability' rating assessed by trolls, who presumably think this is the only use for a woman.[52]

Online abuse is more common for women who face multiple oppressions as a result of their race, sexuality, class, disability or because they are transgender, as a report from Gender Equity Victoria has made clear. These women are 'even more at risk of online abuse, and their experiences of gender-based harassment are intensified by these aspects of identity', the report tells us.[53]

For example, Aboriginal and Torres Strait Islander people are disproportionately targeted by image-based sexual abuse.[54] The podcast *Pretty for an Aboriginal*, hosted by Indigenous Australian writers and actors Nakkiah Lui and Miranda Tapsell, has reflected that this may be the case because, as an Aboriginal woman, 'Historically you're on the bottom rung, you're not meant to talk up,' as one podcast guest put it.[55]

The way that sexism and racism manifest in Black women's lives to create intersecting forms of oppression is so common and distinct that it has its own name: 'misogynoir'. A label coined by African American feminist scholar Moya Bailey,[56] misogynoir describes how when Black[57] women express anger, they often experience a double-whammy of abuse. They're not only hit with labels often directed at emotional women across the board ('bitch' or 'hysterical') – they're also branded with racist stereotypes about Black women being angry.

Remember when tennis legend Serena Williams lost the US open and cartoonist Mark Knight drew a cartoon of the sports star mid-tantrum, stomping on her tennis racquet? That's an example of misogynoir here in Australia. Along with sexism, the cartoon lobbed in racist stereotypes, and The National Association of Black Journalists accused Knight's depiction of being 'unnecessarily sambo-like'[58] (a reference to the racist Jim Crow caricatures of the 19th century).[59]

Whether you're a woman of colour or not, whether you're in politics or sports or you're an office worker or a stay-at-home mum, to various degrees we are mocked and ridiculed if we display anger or put ourselves first – and these hurtful stereotypes are often used to keep us quiet.

SIDE NOTE: Has 'Niceness' served us as a tool of survival?
There's an argument that, historically, being Nice and gaining others' approval may have felt like a lifeline for women. In generations past, we 'couldn't protect our own safety through physical, legal or financial means. We couldn't defend ourselves through a kick or a punch, nor could we rely on the law if our safety was threatened,' author Tara Mohr writes in her book *Playing Big*.[60] 'For millennia, we could ensure our survival by complying with what was approved

of or desired by those with greater power. Being likeable, or at least acceptable, to stronger, more powerful people was a survival strategy.'

This is why disapproval feels unsafe to many women: for generations, it was life-threatening. It remains life-threatening to women who live under oppressive regimes or in violent homes, Mohr adds.[61]

But some would argue that remaining quiet, agreeable and Nice hasn't kept us safe at all.

Writer and civil rights activist Audre Lorde, in a powerful paper arguing for women to transform their silence into language and action, famously said: 'your silence will not protect you'.[62] In Lorde's view, speaking and sharing what's most important is necessary – partly as a way of pressing for political change alongside other women.[63]

When 'Nice' isn't actually nice: women police gender roles, too

'Oh, you're putting your kid into childcare at six months old? You're so brave!' said the woman in the park, a gleam in her eye. 'I'm going to wait until my daughter's two, personally, but that's my own silly obsession with making sure she doesn't feel abandoned!'

Spoken with a smile, there was no way I could challenge this mother's well-concealed barb without coming off as defensive. I let it slide – because it can be particularly difficult to challenge this kind of passive-aggressive comment.

In my experience as a mother, it's often women like this mum at the park who judge and attack other women's choices most harshly. And often, it's choices about caregiving, self-sacrifice, appearance and other gendered expectations that are most subject to scrutiny.

So let's be clear: it's not only men who enforce society's unspoken gender rules. While gender roles around Niceness do serve patriarchal ends, in ways I explored earlier, some women certainly judge and shame other women who step outside society's mandated 'Nice' and caring stereotype.

❦

Why do we women police each other like this?

Sometimes, we're projecting our own anxieties about the difficult choices we make as women. We see other women make different choices to us, and wonder if we're 'doing womanhood right':

> If she's going back to work when her baby is six months old, does that mean I'm not ambitious enough in my career?
>
> If she's going cosmetics-free, does that mean I'm ridiculous for going all-out with the fake tan?
>
> If she's breastfeeding her two-year-old, does that mean I've short-changed my own kid by weaning earlier?

In some cases, it's because women have internalised those gender stereotypes themselves. They come to believe that they really do have these self-sacrificing, agreeable traits from birth – and that they're fulfilling nature's own path in supporting men in their working roles, looking after the children, and generally being pretty, caring, Nice little homemakers. Buying into these ideas, some police other women – turning on those who eschew gender norms about self-sacrifice by choosing not to have kids, for example. (Which is ironic, because shaming other women that way is, really, the opposite of being truly 'Nice'.)

As we've seen above, when women police other women, they don't tear into them directly. That would violate the cultural script. Because society demands that we, as women, put on a 'Nice face', we only have cultural consent to express disagreement or aggression in sneaky, backhanded ways. Author Rachel Simmons explained this modus operandi in her book *Odd Girl Out*,[64] but I believe it applies to fully grown women, too.

Just like the mum at the park, women and girls often wrap aggression and judgement into polite-sounding jibes; back-handed compliments; kiss-kick comments; subtle modes of exclusion; passive-aggressive notes; dirty looks.

I'm all for the sisterhood, but wow – some women are experts at throwing grenades wrapped up in sweet-sounding sentiments.

'I wish I was confident enough to wear such curve-hugging jeans!' a boyfriend's ex once squealed at me as she embraced me into a perfumed, passive-aggressive hug. And remember Regina George from *Mean Girls*? She'd compliment a classmate's jewellery with 'that's adorable' as a coded way of saying 'that's hideous and you're very uncool'.

This form of indirect, Nice-seeming aggression can feel near-impossible to challenge. It's a bit like gaslighting: you know you're being mistreated, but if you say as much, you're 'overreacting'.

All this is to say that women certainly aren't always Nice – and they certainly play a part in policing gender roles, just as men do. They just do it in a different way: in a culture that prohibits out-and-out aggression among girls, other women might put on a performance of 'Niceness', at least to your face.

In the end, gender stereotypes about women's 'Niceness' can help coerce us into seeming agreeable at all costs. In a society where this Niceness is policed by men and women alike, Yes Women sometimes say yes to demands on us because the alternative is to be deemed 'not Nice'. The perpetual undercurrent of possible public shaming, trolling, and mean-girl behaviour that we might face if we step outside that 'Nice girls' line can, quite simply, feel like much to bear.

Chapter 3

I guess this is growing up: your family, your brain and other reasons you say yes

> Even for the most stalwart women, there comes a moment when our inner resolve fails us, and one of the simplest sounds in the English language (n-o) comes out as 'OK', 'sure', 'why not', 'all right', 'I suppose', 'if you really think so' – or just as a sigh of resignation.
>
> – Suzanne Gerber[1]

One of the great joys of being a journalist is getting to interview women at the top of their field. Week after week, I meet high-achieving women from a range of industries and walks of life. Often, their talents leave my head spinning.

It's easy to assume these women lead upbeat, entirely glamorous existences because, frankly, they're dazzling.

But perhaps I shouldn't be surprised that many of these brilliant women reveal a Yes Woman streak bubbling away just beneath the surface, if you just ask the right questions. They're experts at appearing perfectly at ease in their environments and looking like they have their shit together. By definition, Yes Women are chameleons.

Allow me to introduce you to four such women.[2]

Carissa Lee is one of Australia's best-known Indigenous actors. She's prolific on both screen and stage. She's also a writer and PhD candidate. In short, she's got it going on.

But Melbourne-based Carissa is a 'chronic people-pleaser', she tells me. Her people-pleasing comes partly from a rough childhood involving domestic violence and in which she was seen as a problem kid.[3] She has also experienced racial discrimination – assumptions that she's not as educated or intelligent as her white colleagues, for example – which has contributed to her feeling she doesn't belong and that she needs to work harder to 'fit in' than everyone else.

Then there's Arianna Huffington, founder and CEO of *The Huffington Post* and Thrive Global. She's hugely successful, by any measure – and she's also worked hard to overcome her perfectionist tendencies.[4]

When I reached out to her via email, Arianna Huffington responded – telling me she wished her younger self had known that 'perfectionism is a toxic ideal to inflict on ourselves'. She went on to say that she'd want her younger self to know: 'While perfectionism might masquerade as commitment to doing a good job, what it's really about is guilt, shame, fear of failure and a lack of self-acceptance, all of which she should cast aside as soon as possible.' Couldn't have said it better myself, Arianna (although I do give it a try in Chapter 4).

Then there's Larissa Waters, a senator for Queensland and a member of the Australian Greens. You might remember she made headlines for breastfeeding her baby in Parliament – a bold (and most excellent) move. But despite what you'd expect of an outspoken feminist politician, Waters tells me she's struggled with people-pleasing her whole life. 'I still find it difficult to say "no"; it's not something that is easily overcome – it takes practice,' she says.

Waters puts her people-pleasing tendencies down, in part, to gendered socialisation – the way girls are 'taught that speaking up for ourselves, putting our own needs first, or refusing a request is rude' (and, as a female senator, an extra challenge is that politics is a 'people-pleasing profession', she adds).

And then there's Alice Pung, an award-winning author, journalist and essayist based in Melbourne. She tells me her own perfectionism stems from being treated by beloved adults and well-intentioned teachers with 'benevolence and praise' whenever she achieved academically or 'succeeded'.

She also says growing up in a very low socio-economic working-class suburb played its part: 'those who didn't do so well had their expectations massively scaled back. They were told they were trouble-makers, would amount to nothing, would get on drugs, or would become teenage mothers,' she says. 'Maybe I grew up needing to escape these stereotypes of Southeast Asian refugees during the 1980s–90s, because we couldn't just be – we were either raging successes or "unwelcome" abject failures leeching off the grace and generosity of this nation.'

Carissa, Arianna, Larissa and Alice: four very different, very impressive women with unique backgrounds and career paths. Four women who, at different times of their lives, have fallen into the trap of trying to please others.

And then there's me.

The seeds of my own Yes Woman ways were planted when, at the end of primary school, I won a scholarship to a fancy private school. The leadership team at the new school insisted I skip a year level, too – so having just finished primary school, I bypassed year seven and was plonked directly into year eight.

It was a ridiculous and terrible plan. (Apparently the school's leadership team had missed the memo that 12-year-old girls are universally angsty creatures, and should not be fucked with in this way.)

So there I was, a tween in a teenage cohort that seemed preoccupied with grown-up concerns like dating, hair-dyeing and partying. I flailed about in my new year level, trying to maintain good marks while catching up on a lost year of school work. I'd caught on early that academic success was a way to continually gain praise and approval from teachers and my highly educated parents. And now that I'd been labelled 'the smart kid', I was desperate to prove to them all that I deserved the label.

So, I managed to excel academically – but socially, I was out of my depth.

In my new year eight classes, there was nobody to sit next to. The Queen Bees took against me on sight, taking my nerves for aloofness. Who the hell did this new girl think she was?

I was not in on the in-jokes. In class I'd duck my head, pretending to focus on my work. There I was, a perfectionist whose natural tendency was to do everything 'right', clearly failing at fitting in. It was agonising.

Hungry for approval, I kept my head down and tried to survive the best I could, learning along the way that agreeing to everything could help me stay safe. So instead of making waves, I just said 'yes' to whatever was asked of me.

Would I run the 400-metre sprint at athletics carnival, because the popular girls asked me to? Yes.

Would I take Latin, even though I had no interest in Latin, because that's what 'smart kids' were expected to do? Yes.

Would I let that arsehole jock put his hands in my bra at a party? Yes.

Would I embark on a radically restrictive diet because someone at school called me chubby? Yes.

The more I built a history of doing things 'right', the more I felt an overwhelming pressure to live up to my previous wins.

By the time I finished high school, I was on medication for anxiety. I'd ditched my old creative hobbies – art, amateur documentary-making, drama – in favour of a strict blow-drying routine every morning and a drastic diet that spiralled into an eating disorder. I'd come to automatically expect academic near-perfection in every task I completed; my overachiever status was so well-cemented that it seemed taken for granted.

But while I needed praise to sustain me, I didn't truly absorb any compliments lobbed my way. Instead I'd focus on any crumbs of negative feedback I could collect: the distinction that missed out on a high-distinction by half a mark; the cellulite I couldn't kick, regardless of my new intense exercise regimen; the professor who didn't seem to like me, no matter how hard I tried.

I was a classic perfectionist and people-pleaser. I'd followed a typical pattern described by psychologist Kimberley Norris. 'When they do that sort of people-pleasing behaviour they get praise, they get a certificate – and what happens then is we see this all the way through. So by the time they enter the workforce this is a very well-ingrained pattern of behaviour,' Norris says. 'It's like autopilot.'

The Yes Woman trap doesn't discriminate

I know, I know. Tiny violins aren't exactly playing in the background as you read this story of how I became a Yes Woman. It's a tale of great privilege. But I still ended up anxiously trying to please everyone, and desperately trying not to put a foot wrong. That's how powerful the forces that shape perfectionism and people-pleasing can be.

Not all Yes Women have it as easy as I did, of course. Some will have had childhoods that involved serious trauma, poverty or abuse – and in some such cases, that adversity can exacerbate those Yes Woman tendencies. Women from one or more marginalised groups who, as a result, experience overlapping forms of discrimination have also sometimes found that prejudice has shaped their desire for approval.

When you think of a perfectionist, you might perhaps call to mind a prim schoolgirl with an eating disorder and a prefect badge on her private-school blazer.

It's true that some Yes Women I talked to fit this mould – and one study has found that affluent girls do seem particularly vulnerable to perfectionism (as well as body dissatisfaction) compared to less affluent girls.[5] It's quite conceivable that the idea one 'must' be perfect can develop simply as a result of growing up in a social group where this kind of success is common and expected.

In middle-class society in particular, as journalist and writer Melissa Benn wrote, the thread of female obedience and deference to external norms still runs through the lives of modern women, involving '[l]ooking good which means looking thin; being clever, which means getting good exam results'. Benn adds: 'To achieve these "measures" is above all to be doing what one is told to do, conforming to an outer directed idea of who one should be.'[6]

But perfectionism isn't just a middle-class thing. It seems to be on the rise across the board – and we have neoliberalism and competitive individualism to thank for that, some researchers say. The emergence of these doctrines across the Western world has given us 'status anxiety', leaving us preoccupied with upward social comparison, and making us more likely to adopt materialism as a means of perfecting our lives in relation to others: according to UK researchers Thomas Curran and Andrew Hill, who conducted a meta-analysis of groups of people born from 1989 to 2016, perfectionism has increased over time.[7]

SIDE NOTE: Different types of perfectionism

You may have always considered perfectionism a positive. To be fair, there are a few different types of perfectionism, and researchers have described one type as 'adaptive', which is a healthy perfectionism: there's nothing wrong with setting high goals for yourself, if you don't beat yourself up for not always meeting them. (One woman responded in a survey for this book that perfectionism hadn't held her back at all: 'it's made me AWESOME', she wrote. Sing it, sister.)

The problem is, most Yes Women experience negative perfectionism – which means we're 'motivated to set high standards accompanied by, or as a result of, fear or negative evaluation or failure', as researchers put it.[8] As a Yes Woman, the chances are you're particularly prone to a negative type of perfectionism known as 'socially prescribed perfectionism' – where you believe that others expect you to be perfect, and will be critical if you fall short of those expectations.[9]

Bottom line: As a Yes Woman, you know, deep down, that there's just no way that you can do every single thing that's expected of you (or that we expect of ourselves, for that matter). But you keep pounding the treadmill of perfectionism, chasing that unattainable goal.

The rise of the doctrine of meritocracy has instilled in us a belief that '[t]he perfect life and lifestyle – encapsulated by achievement, wealth, and social status – are available to anyone provided you try hard enough,' Curran and Hill explain.[10] Young people, seizing on this idea, turn to perfectionism as 'a misguided attempt to procure others' approval and repair feelings of unworthiness and shame through displays of high achievement'.[11]

The experts I asked about this tended to agree that perfectionism isn't the domain of any particular class or socioeconomic group. Clinical and criminal justice psychologist Brenda Dolieslager, founder of Melbourne-based BMD Psychology Consulting, tells me she's worked with criminals from lower-income families, without much formal schooling, who suffer from perfectionism.

And Melbourne-based psychologist Krasi Kirova is adamant that perfectionism 'is absolutely not a class thing': 'I would argue that a lot of people don't even realise they're perfectionists, because they think perfectionism is about trying very hard to have a big career or become highly educated,' she told me in an interview. In reality, 'perfectionism really comes down to having very high, unrealistic expectations whether they're across the board or about particular things [and] being really hard on yourself when those expectations are not met,' Kirova explains.

For some women, perfectionism is most prominent in their professional lives or in graduate study. For others, it speaks to their sense of competence as partners or mothers, or it revolves around their creative calling; for others still, it comes up around their weight or appearance.

Ultimately, women from all walks of life can find themselves in the Yes Woman trap of trying to be everything to everyone, and to do it all perfectly. What they each have in common is that they've fallen victim to the twin Yes Woman traits of perfectionism and people-pleasing.

This chapter is about how our individual experiences and upbringings contribute to us becoming Yes Women, no matter how varied our backgrounds. Gender expectations are the first major cause of perfectionism and people-pleasing – they affect every Yes Woman. However, there are five other contributing factors which tend to apply to some Yes Women but not others. They include personality; upbringing; a predisposition to anxiety or other mental ill health; the feeling of being an outsider; and a rush to get things done before gendered expectations around caring responsibilities come into play.

Let's dive into each one in turn.

Your personality style plays a part

There are certain personality traits that can make you more susceptible to Yes Woman ways.

Psychologists like to talk about personality in terms of certain traits they call the 'Big Five': openness, extraversion, neuroticism, agreeableness and conscientiousness. Research shows that people who identify as perfectionists or people-pleasers often score highly on neuroticism, as do people with anxiety. (Yeah, I know. To be 'neurotic' doesn't sound great, but in psychologist terms, 'neuroticism' isn't loaded with judgement – it simply describes how likely you are to feel negative emotions, like anxiety, sadness, anger, envy and jealousy.)

Research also shows that those who score high on the traits of conscientiousness (attention to detail and a good work ethic) and agreeableness (warm, trusting and cooperative) are also more likely to be perfectionists and people-pleasers, respectively.[12] One research paper out of the US found that people who score highly on conscientiousness and agreeableness experience greater difficulty saying no.[13]

What's more, many Yes Women I spoke to described themselves as sensitive, or as empaths. Some said they were 'Highly Sensitive People', according to the definition outlined by Dr Elaine Aron – which involves having a rich and complex inner life, becoming easily overwhelmed by strong sensory stimuli and getting easily rattled by upsetting or overwhelming situations.[14]

Psychotherapist Imi Lo works specifically with what she calls 'emotionally sensitive and intense' clients – those who feel a wide spectrum of emotions in a more vivid and profound way than most people do. (This means, 'you are deeply empathic, sensitive, perceptive, and imaginative', she explains. 'It also means you are more prone to existential angst and depression.')[15]

When I came across Lo's work, I suspected there was a lot of crossover with my concept of the Yes Woman – so I reached out via email to ask whether she believed that emotionally sensitive and intense women (as opposed to non-sensitive and non-intense women) were often perfectionists and people-pleasers.

Lo wrote back and – bingo – told me that many of her emotionally sensitive and intense clients grapple with perfectionism and people-pleasing. 'The sensitive ones are extremely attuned to other people's feelings and often find it hard to not do anything about it when they pick up on others' needs,' she explained. Many emotionally intelligent people ended up slotting into the role of 'parent' when they were growing up – 'so their systems have been "trained" to be hyper-attuned to others' needs, to avoid conflicts, and to defuse any possibility of upset,' Lo added.

What's more, Yes Women have three more things in common with emotionally sensitive and intense clients: they were often smart or 'gifted' kids growing up; they often have always felt they were an 'old soul with a propensity to think and feel more deeply than their peers'. (There's a paucity of scientific research to back this up, but Lo also agreed with me that, anecdotally, there seems to be a personality-trait correlation between giftedness and perfectionism.)

Many Yes Women, as well as women who identify with Lo's description of emotional intensity, also feel that they have 'thin boundaries' as defined by psychiatrist Ernest Hartmann.[16] That means they take things personally and often take too much responsibility for what happens in a relationship; they may also have a fluid sense of identity, meaning they merge or lose themselves in their relations with others.

Your upbringing

It's time to take a deep breath and grab yourself a nice calming pot of tea, because this next section gets deep. We're about to dive into how your childhood environment might have contributed to the way you are now.

Part 1: Parents who valued achievements

Let's start somewhere simple: with high-achieving parents, or parents who emphasised achievements and external markers of success. We're not just talking about pushy stage mums who drill the idea into their ballerina daughters that failure is unacceptable (although I wouldn't be surprised to hear that this behaviour results in a prima ballerina with a severe case of Yes Womanitis). I'm referring, also, to the parents who subtly send a similar message by simply modelling perfectionistic ways of thinking and acting, and excessively praising achievements and accolades.

It's straightforward, really: children are wired to seek approval from their parents.[17] So when children are praised excessively for their achievements rather than their efforts or progress, the desire to please mum and dad can drive us to keep up those achievements – leading to Yes Women in the making.

But high-achieving parents don't always raise people-pleasers. '[I]f a child feels that they are loved regardless of how they perform, they are less likely to become people-pleasers,' says Austin-based therapist Ann Stoneson. 'However, if their parents' regard feels fragile, unpredictable or frequently contingent on the child's performance or some other factor not in the child's control, there is a strong likelihood that people-pleasing will result.'

Sahaj Kaur Kohli, a US-based therapist-in-training, founder of popular Instagram account *Brown Girl Therapy* and author of *But What Will People Say?*, has touched on how perfectionism can affect certain Black, Indigenous and people of colour (BIPOC) women, focusing on how children of immigrants can struggle with these tendencies. She writes that growing up with parents who only provided encouragement and verbal praise when the child reached a milestone or achieved something can foster perfectionist tendencies whereby 'anything less than perfect can feel like a failure'.[18]

This can make it hard to try something new even if you're good at it, accept criticism graciously, or go easy on yourself when you make a mistake in your work, explains Kohli. Addressing children of immigrants who were 'raised in an environment where social perception was emphasized', she says: 'you may have a hard time with being truthful in the workplace about your life, current problems, or mental health struggles out of fear that it will make you look bad'.[19]

Children of immigrants can also experience trouble with saying no at work when a superior asks them to do something, as a result of growing up 'in a household with a hierarchical order, where you're expected to respect and accommodate elders', Kohli adds.[20]

While Kohli's work focuses on children of immigrants, children from a range of cultures can experience perfectionism as a result of the way they were raised. Curran and Hill's 2017 research study – whose respondents skewed white – found that the number of young people who are perfectionists has increased substantially over the past three decades, and they blamed the now-widespread trend partly on 'increases in both anxious and controlling parenting'.

This anxious, controlling parenting style is driven by a societal idea that '[s]hould a young person be unable to navigate an increasingly competitive social milieu, then it is not just their failure, it is also the parents' failure too', the researchers argue. This drives many parents to spend far more time with their children on academic activities – and to adopt controlling parenting behaviours, combining high expectations with high criticism, which encourages children to 'strive for perfection, so [as] to avoid criticism and gain the approval of their parents'.[21]

So, even if your parents were loving and supportive, if they constantly praised you for being clever or talented or pretty ('I bet you'll get a high distinction!' … 'You're the prettiest girl in school!') you might have ended up believing you 'had to' keep demonstrating perfect scores, or winning the athletics prize, or being the best-looking girl in class, in order to maintain your worth. It's easy to see how that could contribute to perfectionism.

Part 2: A chaotic or unsafe childhood

Family environments can shape Yes Women tendencies in other ways, too. When I interviewed psychologist Kimberley Norris for this book, she explained that women who had a chaotic home life – a childhood where they didn't feel psychologically 'safe' – may be more likely to become people-pleasers.

To use technical terminology, your shitty childhood might have made you a Yes Woman.

Why? Because the messages we receive as children help us build our personal belief system – which is made up of beliefs that are centred around ideas of self-worth, achievement, acceptance and lovability, as London-based clinical psychologist Dr Jessamy Hibberd has written.[22] We often come to internalise these ideas, and they can follow us into adulthood, affecting the way we act in our friendships and romantic relationships.

If the messages you receive as a child are that you're only worthy of love if you suppress your own needs, deep down, you'll come to believe that in order to be loved or loveable, you need to put others' needs first. Your self-esteem will become dependent on pleasing other people.

Thus, women can become people-pleasers if they've been exposed to a background of trauma or domestic violence, as Norris explains: 'A lot of survivors will talk about "if you keep them happy [the violence will stop]."'

If you're a survivor of abuse – if your parents' discipline was unpredictable and unfair – you might also seek to avoid conflict or anger at all costs. The thought of saying no or disagreeing with a person's request might therefore be intolerable to you, so you might say yes when you really want to say no. You may have grown up with toxic stress caused by the difficult environment in which you grew up – and try to keep the peace by saying yes to authority figures.[23]

Psychologist Krasi Kirova says she sees perfectionism and people-pleasing in clients 'all the time because of complex trauma and childhood trauma'. She adds, 'When people have grown up in a chaotic environment … it can be a way to overcompensate or maintain control.'

Even if your childhood wasn't physically violent or unsafe – and in parts was very happy – your parents might have imposed rigid rules, or had dismissive or disappointed responses when you didn't do things 'right'. You might have learned to hold back emotions that weren't welcomed by your parents.

This was the case for Elsie, a writer who suspects her people-pleasing behaviour stems from messages her parents inadvertently taught her when she was little. 'I remember my parents having a dinner party and saying, "You can come down and say goodnight, but don't stick around and talk, because we care about what you have to say but others might not want to hear it",' Elsie recalls. 'So I grew up thinking you have to be really entertaining all the time or else people won't want to be around you … you're not worth their time.'

Elsie was raised to quiet her own voice and keep others happy as a way to receive approval – and she carried that people-pleasing tendency into adulthood.

SIDE NOTE: From parent-pleasing to people-pleasing – attachment theory in a nutshell

'Tell me about your childhood.'

If you've ever been to therapy, you might have noticed that this is one of the first questions your therapist asked you.

Here's why: she was probably examining your life story for clues, applying her knowledge of a widely accepted psychological theory known as 'attachment theory'.

If you're scratching your head thinking 'attachment what-now?' here's a quick primer: attachment theory describes how your relationship with your caregiver as a young child – your 'attachment style' – can impact the way you relate to lovers, friends, kids and others in later life. (Just like I said before: the personal belief systems we form young can follow us into adulthood.)

If you grew up with attentive and kind parents, you're more likely to have what's called a 'secure attachment' – an underlying assumption that your loved ones will be there for you if they're needed. As an adult, it's more likely that you will have trusting, long-term relationships; have high self-esteem; seek out social support; and feel comfortable sharing your feelings with other people.[24]

Secure attachment has been associated with healthy ('adaptive') perfectionism as an adult – the setting of high but achievable personal standards, a desire to excel, and self-satisfaction.[25]

On the other hand, if your caregivers parented unreliably and inconsistently – or your parents weren't attuned to your needs – you might have ended up with what's called an 'insecure attachment'. There are a few different types of insecure attachment, but people-pleasing is particularly linked with insecure anxious attachment, according to Ann Stoneson. (As the website for her business, Labyrinth Healing, states: 'People-pleasing behaviors evolve as a way to maintain connection and closeness with parents who are inconsistently available to their children.'[26])

So if you had a parent who was neglectful, emotionally

unavailable or even abusive, you might have learned that it wasn't safe to express your needs or feelings.

If you had parents who weren't consistently available because of drug or alcohol dependencies, or who often became emotionally overwhelmed because of mental health struggles, you might have come to believe that looking after your own needs is selfish; that you 'should' be comforting and looking after someone else first.

Your parents don't have to be out-and-out negligent or abusive for you to end up with an insecure attachment. If you were taught that part of being the 'perfect' little girl was always putting on a happy face and never expressing negative feelings, that might've kept you from feeling 'safe' to express your true needs, affecting your attachment with your caregivers.

So if you have an insecure attachment, where does this leave you?

Research shows that children who have an anxious attachment often grow up to be self-critical and insecure; while they seek approval and reassurance from others, when they get this reassurance, it doesn't actually relieve their self-doubt.[27] (All of which sounds very Yes Woman-esque.)

An insecure early attachment with caregivers is also associated with unhealthy ('maladaptive') perfectionism.[28] That's the type of perfectionism that gets Yes Women into trouble: it involves the setting of unrealistically high standards; compulsively doubting one's actions; trying to avoid negative consequences; and perceived large discrepancy between one's performance and personal standards.[29]

All of this is to say: for some Yes Women, their people-pleasing perfectionism stems from a rough childhood in which they felt loved only when they were conforming to the desires and needs of their parents. Feeling emotionally safe while growing up was about learning to keep their parents happy and – as Stoneson says – 'earning' love and approval.

So should you blame your Yes Woman tendencies on your parents?

Not so fast. Not all Yes Women have insecure attachment styles. In fact, you might've had the best parents in the world and still ended up a people-pleasing perfectionist because of a combination of factors including societal pressure, your underlying temperament, a predisposition to anxiety, and other factors that made life tough as you were growing up.

That said, if any of this chapter stirs up thoughts or memories about your own upbringing, I recommend you see a therapist and talk it through to discover if your parental attachment could be impacting your current behaviour – it's a lot to unpack on your own. You might benefit from what Stoneson calls co-dependency therapy, which is therapeutic work geared towards helping people identify their own desires and needs, and then to effectively assert their own boundaries. Basically, it helps people derive worth outside of being needed or caretaking all the time, Stoneson explains.

And if you do have an insecure attachment style? The good news is, you can transition to a secure attachment style.[30] It's never too late to learn a secure attachment style, the psychologists I interviewed for this book assured me.

The anxiety connection: mental ill health and the Yes Woman

Yes Women are often described as 'superwomen', but they're rarely described as 'chill'.

To be quite frank, Yes Women are often living with anxiety disorders. We're waking up at 4am to start pulling at the threads of worry about things we might've forgotten, ways we might've offended someone, or things that might go wrong. Typically, we've been this way since adolescence or childhood.

Alice Pung, author and self-described perfectionist, was once a university pastoral care advisor, and wrote about perfectionism in an article:

> [T]he High-Achiever is a person with severe anxiety problems. She will cry in the toilets if she gets an A instead of an A+. She will control her body in self-destructive ways, while the rampant fears in her mind are left unchecked. She may be the migrant who is studying at the library during lunchtimes because when she gets home she has to sew for her parents. Or she may be the middle-class model from Kew who coaches the debating team and runs a marathon. But often when she comes to see me, she is not a healthy person.[31]

Does this ring a bell? Pung might as well have been describing me – the middle-class Kew student with a rotating roster of extracurricular leadership activities. And just as Pung describes, I live with constant anxiety – which is a strong driver of my Yes Woman behaviour. Throughout this book, I focus on anxiety more than other conditions, both because of my own experience and because it's by far the most prevalent condition among the Yes Women I spoke to.

Research has also shown that people with Yes Woman traits are more likely to have an underlying predisposition to anxiety or a history of other mental health issues such as depression.[32] In fact, in one anonymous (and totally unscientific) online survey I conducted as part of my study for this book, a whopping two-thirds of respondents said they had a history of anxiety or depression; others said they lived with post-traumatic stress disorder, eating disorders, bipolar disorder, borderline personality disorder or other mental health conditions.

That's not to say that all perfectionistic people-pleasers struggle with mental ill health, but the two are often linked.[33] As psychologist Kimberley Norris told me, people-pleasers are particularly prone to a negative type of perfectionism known as 'socially prescribed perfectionism' – where they believe that others expect them to be perfect and will be critical of them if they fall short of those expectations, and so it's easy to see how this is strongly linked with people-pleasing tendencies. That type of perfectionism is most strongly associated with serious mental health issues, research shows.[34]

Anxiety in a Yes Woman can look like this: you promise yourself that you'll stand up to your pushy stepfather when he insists on you driving out of town for Christmas – but the thought of starting your family's own World War III brings on panic attacks, so you agree to your stepdad's unreasonable demands (and end up spending Christmas in Woop Woop to keep him happy again).

Or you feel sick with anxiety that your manager won't like you if you speak up at work, so you don't insist on that pay rise that was promised to you.

Or you agree to volunteer at your kid's school fete – even though the thought of manning a falafel stand all Sunday is your idea of hell – because you can't stand the thought of telling the head of the Parent–Teacher Association 'no'.

In these situations, people-pleasing is a way of managing our anxiety about coming into conflict with others. As Norris puts it, we think, 'If other people are happy with me, I'll be psychologically safe.'

Here's another way anxiety can drive your Yes Woman ways: it can cause you to seek to have control over plans and decisions – which can lead to you doing everything for everybody, and rarely letting other people help: 'It's easier to do it myself!'[35] (Sound familiar?)

I'm personally well acquainted with the I'll-do-it-all-myself syndrome: just ask my husband, who, ahead of our wedding, witnessed me scouring haberdashery stores all over Melbourne – then spending hours cutting vintage-style fabric into perfect squares – in order to hand-make 160 napkins for the big day.

On that (rather embarrassing) occasion, my anxious need to make sure I got the décor exactly right (quiet at the back please, no need to yell out 'control freak') stopped me outsourcing the task of procuring wedding napkins – which would've made my life so, so, so much easier.

(Oh, and not a single person noticed those bloody napkins at the wedding, of course.)

The feeling of being an outsider

Perhaps you have a clear bill of mental health. Perhaps your upbringing was pleasant and unremarkable. Perhaps your personality isn't even high in the neurotic or conscientious stakes – but you recognise yourself as a Yes Woman anyway.

Enter: the feeling of being an outsider. It's not a factor experienced by all Yes Women – but those who have experienced it tend to try to accommodate other people in a quest for validation and inclusion.

If any of this sounds familiar, your feeling of being an outsider may have contributed to your Yes Woman ways by driving you to work harder in order to please others and 'fit in'. In other words, your yes-ing and people-pleasing and perfectionistic tendencies may be you attempting to feel that you 'belong'.

Monique, 29, 'grew up below the poverty line' in western Sydney, but attended a prestigious girls' school on an academic scholarship.[36] The contrast between her home and school environments meant she often felt like 'the odd one out – both in my local neighbourhood, where they thought I was stuck up because I was always walking around in that school uniform', and at school, where she couldn't relate to her classmates' luxury lifestyles. 'It didn't help that I was highly sensitive and an introverted bookworm, either,' she adds. 'I tend to like deep psychological or philosophical conversations – and I have to make a real effort to make small talk about everyday things like the weather or gossip about people I know, which makes me feel like a weirdo in social situations.'

Monique got into the habit of trying to please others as a way of gaining approval young: 'At school, I would mimic the hair styles and language of the other girls so I would look the part, then I'd offer to help some of the more popular ones with their homework,' she says.

She even wrote down lists of conversational topics to use with classmates. 'And then after a social interaction I would internally review how that conversation went. Like a performance appraisal for myself, and I wanted always to get an A-plus.'

This feeling of being an outsider can amplify perfectionistic tendencies – causing some women to over-perform in an attempt to prove their worth or, sometimes, just be taken seriously.

This is exactly what writer and author Kai Harris notes about her experience as a Black woman. Growing up, it was drilled into her that she'd always have to work twice as hard for half as much; that she'd have to get highly educated, but even that wouldn't be enough to 'prove herself' to some people, as she describes in an article for *The Everygirl*.

Ultimately, she 'developed an intolerance for average. An insistence on exactness. A relentless pursuit for perfection'. It took some soul-searching – and therapy – she says, to realise that the urgency 'was coming from a sense of perfectionism that wasn't my own; it was a result of the world as seen and experienced by a Black woman for whom nothing came without a fight'.[37]

For Harris, these core beliefs eventually manifested in impostor syndrome, a psychological phenomenon whereby you doubt your own accomplishments, suspect you've only succeeded because of luck, and fear being exposed as a 'fraud'. The phenomenon goes hand-in-hand with perfectionism and people-pleasing – so it's super-common among Yes Women (one of my surveys showed 75 per cent of respondents agreed with the statement 'I have doubted my accomplishments and have a fear of being exposed as a fraud'.)

Impostor syndrome may be experienced more commonly by women from minority groups[38] because, as impostor-syndrome expert Valerie Young puts it: 'The more people who look or sound like you, the more confident you feel.'[39]

Actor and writer Carissa Lee, a Wemba-Wemba and Noongar woman, has been there. She tells me that racial prejudice and impostor syndrome has fuelled her people-pleasing behaviour. 'People-pleasing for me, has come [partly] from … previous jobs where I've been assumed to be uneducated or less educated than my white colleagues,' she says. 'It's so unfortunate just how much impostor syndrome can fuel the need to please people, as well as people making you feel like you don't belong.'

Some transgender women may also particularly identify with the experience of impostor syndrome. Melbourne-based psychotherapist Grace Lee told me she has grappled with 'uncertainty, self-doubt' and impostor feelings since coming out as a trans woman. 'Because I have come from a place of a conferred, assigned identity of male and masculine, I can often feel challenged about my feminine identity' when in the presence of cisgender men and women, she says. 'I have this sense of other people thinking, "You're really a man." And then that translates into, "How real am I?"'

At times, Grace has felt pressured to work harder to 'present' as a cisgender woman. Impostor fears have sometimes fuelled her to do 'all the work on myself – my hair, my makeup, all that superficiality' to 'demonstrate that I'd made the effort, so that people would say, "Oh, you do it so well,"' she recalls.

Many people who feel like impostors grew up in families that placed a big emphasis on achievement, according to US-based psychologist Dr Suzanne Imes, who, along with psychologist Pauline Rose Clance, first described the syndrome. It often occurs among high achievers who are unable to accept or internalise their successes.[40]

'Lots of women in leadership roles struggle with impostor syndrome,' Senator Larissa Waters tells me. 'If you're feeling like maybe you don't deserve your role, the need to validate yourself and "prove your worth" is constantly there ... Men don't experience that internal struggle in the same way.'

So if you feel like an impostor yourself, you're in good company. Actors Kate Winslet, Natalie Portman, Emma Watson, Jodie Foster and Meryl Streep are just some of the seriously impressive women out there who have alluded to feeling like impostors.[41] And legendary poet, memoirist, and civil rights activist Maya Angelou once wrote: 'I have written 11 books, but each time I think, "Uh oh, they're going to find out now. I've run a game on everybody and they're going to find me out."'

To learn more about impostor syndrome and what causes it, I spoke to Austin-based Ann Stoneson, whose work focuses on co-dependency therapy for the overworked and unappreciated. (She also offers feminist theory, so she approaches topics like impostor syndrome and people-pleasing through a feminist lens.)

'Impostor syndrome is basically a fancy label for shame,' Stoneson told me. 'Shame is, at core, a belief of not belonging or fitting in due to being inherently defective or worthless.'

And as you might recall, perfectionism and people-pleasing behaviours are both rooted in shame. (It's probably unsurprising, then, that in my surveys of Yes Women, the majority agreed with the statement, 'Just below the surface, I'm fairly certain that I'm not really worthy.') So these tendencies all fuel each other, in a vicious cycle of self-criticism: perfectionists set themselves unrealistically high goals, and then feel shame or disappointment when they fail. They then tend to fixate on any mistakes or flaws and take their failure as 'proof' that they're a fraud – or often work extra hard so nobody else can see how much of a faker they are. Eventually, 'Unconsciously, they think their successes must be due to that self-torture,' Imes says.[42]

Impostor syndrome also often causes feelings of stress, anxiety and depression rooted in feelings of inadequacy.[43,44] Even some women who are normally not anxious – including Monique, the scholarship student from western Sydney we met earlier – can experience anxiety in situations where they feel inadequate. Monique describes feeling 'never relaxed, often on alert, as if walking on eggshells and thinking "have they noticed yet that I'm not like them?"'

SIDE NOTE: When being an outsider instead builds 'immunity' to people-pleasing

Interestingly, for some women, the outsider experience actually pushes them to reject their Yes Woman tendencies. Yumi Stynes, speaking as host of the ABC's podcast *Ladies, We Need to Talk*, says that, as a child, she 'acquired a bit of an immunity to having to be liked at all times':

> Something that I learned very early in my life is that sometimes people didn't like me because of my race. And in a very unscientific survey I conducted of non-white friends, they agreed that one of the few benefits of being a woman of colour is that you've got some [practice] in having people hate you for no actual reason. So while approval seeking is still definitely a thing, self-respect is slightly less dependent on the opinions of strangers.[45]

There was a similar response from Allie, the Brisbane nurse who struggled with pressure to conform to heteronormative beauty standards prior to coming out as a lesbian. Now that she's out and proud, she no longer feels she has to work doubly hard to 'prove herself' as cute, nice and feminine – all those labels she tells me she feared she would lose by coming out. 'It's like the expectations and rules around heterofeminine beauty norms don't apply to me now, so I don't need to bother,' she says. 'And whatever – I'm cute as hell, anyway.' (Yes, girl!)

Rushing to do it all (before life gets in the way)

For some of us, the rushed, fast-lane style of living is more about racing to tick off our to-do list before life ties us down. Essentially, it's a form of FOMO – but we're driven by a specific fear that we'll regret not living up to our full potential, so we cram in as much as we can, while we can.

While this factor can affect women who are child-free, I noticed in interviews I conducted that it was mums – or women who planned to become mums – who experienced this phenomenon most keenly. Fearful that motherhood would stymie future opportunities for self-realisation, many of these Yes Women felt pressure to square away certain milestones or achievements ahead of having a baby. This tendency finds its form most clearly, perhaps, in the trend for some women to put together 'pre-baby bucket lists'.

Mollie, a 33-year-old financial services professional based in Singapore, put together one such list while pregnant.

'It was long and pretty ridiculous – especially looking back with my new pandemic-y perspective,' Mollie tells me. Her list focused on measurables that she felt she 'should' aspire to, 'like my job, my promotion, my body, my clothes, my homewares, my pics of travel on Instagram, my bloody Qantas frequent flyer status', she says. 'I believed kids were little ball-and-chains so I didn't think that the sort of things I used to aspire to do would be possible with them.'

Kaya, 32, also set herself a to-do list before getting pregnant with her first child in late 2020. When she turned 30, Kaya and her partner decided they'd 'have a year of fun before settling down and trying for kids', she says – so she proposed to her boyfriend, travelled Europe, partied like there was no tomorrow, then moved back to her home town and started her own business.

For some women, the 'pre-baby bucket list' includes a heavy focus on career and economic security – which makes sense, for those of us who've grown up reading headlines about how women with kids suffer a 'motherhood penalty' in the workplace.

Sydney-based Emily, 28, told me her main bucket-list item was to make it to the next 'big' promotion at work. ('Originally I thought "buy a house" should be on there too, but once I hit my mid-twenties it was clear that wasn't even vaguely on the horizon, so I dropped it off,' she adds.) The promotion was driven by practical concerns – she wanted job security before getting pregnant, and it 'would have been nice to be on a higher salary when I went on maternity leave', she adds. 'But at its heart I suspect it was a pride thing – sort of like once I'd achieved a certain level I would be "allowed" to step off the treadmill for a few years and take a break.'

For Kaya and Mollie, some list items were pure fun – but others were a reflection of societal expectations they felt they 'should' say yes to prior to entering the world of motherhood.

Kaya says her bucket list was fuelled by the societal script that says life ends at motherhood – that once we have a child, we should turn inwards to the child, while 'all of our sparkly, exciting, selfish faculties apparently shut down', as Kaya puts it.

'Since I was a teenager, I'd been fed a solid diet of, "get everything done before you have children",' the Brisbane-based Kaya tells me. 'The narrative was clear: once you fell pregnant, life stopped and became all about children. So there was always a ticking clock in my mind.' It's as if society tells us that 'those who aren't busy being mothers are meant to be busy preparing to be one', she adds.

Mollie, who says she 'absolutely' feels pressure to be perfect, was also well aware before having a kid that this pressure 'doesn't let up when you have a kid; it probably gets worse'.

Ding, ding, ding! If this is all ringing a very loud bell for you, there are good reasons.

The idea of having to work through a pre-baby bucket list can be explained in part, by a phenomenon described by British psychotherapist, psychoanalyst, writer and social critic Susie Orbach. In her seminal book *Fat is a Feminist Issue*, Orbach hypothesises that there's a certain type of intense energy and activity young women engage in that, from a feminist viewpoint, is about attempting 'to be involved in as many activities as possible as a protection against the exclusion she anticipates on entering womanhood because, in projecting into her future, she sees that the world is made up of men who are rewarded for being out in the world and women who are either excluded from activity in the world or, even more devious, included but not rewarded'.

In a young woman's frantic activities and involvements, Orbach writes, 'it would appear that she is trying to give herself a broader definition than her social role allows. She is striving to make an impact in a world hostile to her sex'.

Orbach's book is actually about body image (and she makes the connection that women with anorexia frequently feel a sense of hyperactivity that is similar to what I think of as the Yes Woman experience: 'a compulsion to do well in school, excel at sports, and keep on the go at all costs').[46]

But even if we take body image out of the equation, this hyperactivity and busy-ness that starts in early adulthood, for myself and many other Yes Women, feels like an attempt to do as much as we can before we become working mothers – and societal barriers thump heavily into place.

Addicted to approval

Did you recognise yourself in the last two chapters? Some readers might have related to two or three of the circumstances explored. Or maybe you nodded along throughout this entire chapter – in which case, I should give you a trophy (Lord knows, we Yes Women like a trophy!). Whatever unique combination formed your own personal flavour of perfectionistic people-pleasing, if you're a Yes Woman, I'm betting you and I have one thing in common: at some stage, we both got hooked on approval.

That's how Yes Women find themselves feeling trapped on the treadmill of being everything to everyone: early on in our lives, we become dependent on our need to please others, or our need to do everything perfectly. We then develop a fear of anger and confrontation; we worry that if we say no, we'll offend somebody or become exposed to conflict, shaming or violence.

Fast-forward to early adulthood, and people-pleasing behaviours are second nature.

Once these Yes Woman tendencies take root, they can spiral fairly easily. We can even take the 'need' to please others so literally that we actually can't see the alternatives – believing that we have to please others and do what is asked of us in order to feel loved and valued.[47]

Remember Taylor Swift's mantra, growing up – 'do the right thing, do the good thing'? If that's been your experience, too, you might also feel you've been 'trained to be happy when you get a lot of praise', as the singer once put it.

You might have developed a compulsion to do everything right, to put you beyond reproach. Or as Tay-Tay describes it: 'I was so obsessed with not getting in trouble, that I was like, I'm just not going to do anything that anyone could say anything about.'[48] (I never realised I had so much in common with a country-pop singer till I wrote this book, truly.)

So many of us – even today, in the 21st century – continue this conflict-avoiding, people-pleasing, never-put-a-foot-wrong behaviour.

So we say yes to cleaning the kitchen; yes to remembering to buy family birthday presents; yes to keeping tabs on the kids' after-school activities. We say yes to helping colleagues at work without taking the credit; yes to the first salary we're offered, without negotiating; and yes to taking on a side project that won't actually progress our careers.

From little girls raised to believe that standing up for our own needs is best avoided, we grow into Yes Women who suppress our own desires in our quest to make life comfortable for others. We agree to obligations or expectations we truly don't have time or energy for. We straitjacket ourselves with Niceness.

And we pay one hell of a price.

Chapter 4

Being Nice has a price

When a man gives his opinion, he's a man. When a woman gives her opinion, she's a bitch.

– Bette Davis[1]

Writing a book isn't easy, but it's particularly challenging for a recovering perfectionist who's spent her life trying to avoid criticism.

The thing is, perfection is impossible when you're churning out 90,000 words to a deadline. Especially when you're wrangling detailed research and dozens of interviews with women around the world – and throwing in a personal account of a brief stay in a psych ward. Mix that in with five government-mandated lockdowns during the coronavirus pandemic in Melbourne, and add a side of screaming toddler in the background. Shake with a part-time job. Garnish with a generous sprinkle of fear about Twitter deciding to cancel me – and serve.

The point is, writing this book has been a process of routinely second-guessing myself – and coming smack-bang up against some of my own tendencies to try to be everything to everyone (and do it perfectly).

At times, I've avoided starting a new chapter for days lest I write a mediocre first line. I've procrastinated in new and imaginative ways rather than starting a new paragraph that might not hit all the right notes.

Then it's hello, 3am.

I've lain awake contemplating the reality that there's no way – literally zero chance – that everyone who reads this book will like it.

That's not how books work (especially when they dare to be feminist). It's almost guaranteed someone will shout at me on Twitter for not liking my tone, for 'leaving men out', for doing feminism wrong.

I'm sharing all this to make the point that perfectionism, people-pleasing and a default response setting switched to 'yes', as it turns out, are all very good at derailing our goals. And keeping us quiet. And distracting us from the things we actually want to do.

In fact, Yes Women tendencies undermine us in a whole slew of ways – which we'll dig into now.

Paralysed by a fear of failure, we procrastinate

When I surveyed women from Australia, the UK, and the US about the ways perfectionism and people-pleasing held them back, many of the comments could have been copy-and-pasted from my own experiences writing this book.

'I hardly ever try new things, even if it's something I really want to – like taking a ceramics class,' Allegra, a 25-year-old perfectionist living in Nashville, Tennessee, tells me.

'It's because unless I am immediately great at everything, I get upset with myself and feel like I've wasted time that could otherwise have been spent productively.'

Farrah, a 28-year-old postgraduate student living in Cambridge in the UK, tells me she regularly encounters the 'blank screen of terror' because her perfectionism makes it hard to start her uni work. 'I'm always tempted to put off projects in favour of more ideal working conditions, and in the end, there's never really a "perfect" time so I put it off and have to rush through it,' she says.

Kezia, a 35-year-old journalist living in Hong Kong, is held back by her perfectionistic tendencies in her dating life. 'A typical example is telling myself I'll start dating again but only after I lose 10 pounds,' she says.

And Malka, a 43-year-old travel-industry IT specialist from Los Angeles, tells me she wastes time and spins her wheels trying to get things started because she doesn't know the 'right' way to start. 'I think endlessly rather than doing. True for small seemingly meaningless tasks, not just larger important ones,' she says.

It's one of the most unifying experiences of Yes Women: we get caught in the trap of not trying something at all, because we might get it wrong. And while many of us eventually push past our procrastination and do get shit done, we've wasted a hell of a lot of time fretting and putting off our hard work first.

So what's this all about? Well, on the one hand, research shows that women, in general, tend to have a more pronounced fear of failure than men.[2] Yes Women – bless their perfectionistic socks – feel this fear particularly keenly because we're obsessed with doing things right.

Often, this is a rational response to the misogynist system in which we live, which penalises women for mistakes more harshly than their male counterparts. Hence, Sudanese-Australian writer and media presenter Yassmin Abdel-Magied, who had an early career as a mechanical engineer, says in an interview that she worked 'super, super hard' in her engineering career, wanting 'to make sure that no one can ever say you weren't committed enough', adding, 'It's that concept of, women haven't yet earned the right to be mediocre.'[3]

But other times, women procrastinate because they're scared. Put simply, they fear putting their work into the world until it (and they) are completely beyond criticism. As American journalist and author Elizabeth Gilbert writes in her book *Big Magic*, this form of perfectionism is 'just a high-end, haute couture version of fear':

> [P]erfectionism is just fear in fancy shoes and a mink coat, pretending to be elegant when actually it's just terrified. Because underneath that shiny veneer, perfectionism is nothing more than a deep existential angst that says, again and again, 'I am not good enough and I will never be good enough.'[4]

♣

So what exactly is wrong with procrastination?

Those of us who expect every tiny detail of work we do to be perfect tend to waste time on the smaller things. We can feel we need to know every scrap of information before we start a project, and we constantly look for new certifications to improve our skills.[5] We endlessly polish and re-write our reports. We overcomplicate our projects. We decide to study for a degree rather than just launching ourselves into a new career. Yes Women tend to overprepare, overperfect, and overestimate the amount of experience we need to get a job.

The irony is, the Yes Woman is often an intelligent, capable, creative person. But without trying new things, her pursuits can be constrained. The best artists, entrepreneurs and professional risk-takers I know aren't perfectionists – they're the people who think, 'Screw it! Why not try?'

The procrastination that can stem from this desire to do everything right is also a serious liability when it comes to our careers and savings accounts. Research has linked it with poorer results at works, lower salaries, and even a greater likelihood of being unemployed or under employed rather than working full-time.[6]

That's why you need to introduce the maxim 'done is better than perfect' into your life, stat. (Get ready, because we'll work on this in the next chapter.)

An antidote to perfectionist procrastination

Shameless podcast co-hosts Zara McDonald and Michelle Andrews mentor a number of young women who want to get into podcasting. They tell me many of these mentees fall into the same old trap of striving for perfection before taking their first leap.

'So many women say, "I'm going to start a website or I'm going to start a blog," and then they spend months figuring out what the name of the thing is, and what colour codes to use, and what the artwork is going to be,' says Michelle. 'And Zara and I are, like, pulling out our hair! [Y]our first episode is probably not going to be good. But if you don't start now, you're wasting valuable days!'

One antidote that Zara likes to sermonise is the approach: 'close your eyes and go'.

That's precisely what they did when they decided to launch the *Shameless* podcast – despite having never edited audio before, and having to rely on YouTube tutorials to work it out. They set a date and told themselves they were launching in six weeks. 'That was so great for us because we just did it,' Michelle says.

This just-dig-in approach has paid off: the podcast had been downloaded more than four million times as of August 2019, and has now been written about in publications including *The New York Times*, *The Guardian*, *The Age* and *Marie Claire*.

SIDE NOTE: Technology takes Yes Woman tendencies to the next level

Many of the negative consequences of Yes Woman tendencies are exacerbated by technology – and specifically, our addictions to our smartphones and social media.

Now, I promise this is not another call for us all to burn our iPhones and start charting our travel routes using a compass. But we do need to acknowledge that for Yes Women trying to make conscious choices, smartphones are a danger zone.

It's not an accident that our phones are distracting. Platforms like Instagram, Facebook and Twitter – some of the most popular smartphone apps – are manipulative by design. They make billions of dollars from grabbing our attention and getting us to interact, which in turn, attracts yet more users. It's great for them, and terrible for our own ability to determine what we actually want to do.

Social media tech companies actively create these apps to make checking notifications addictive: when you check your Facebook notifications or messages and are paused, waiting for the numbers to come up, dopamine – which makes us feel excited – is released.[7]

So, like rats who press a lever to get a treat, we learn to associate checking notifications with rewards – and we do it over and over again to get that dopamine hit.

Over time, our brain releases dopamine any time it's reminded of our phones – and we start to crave it, as science journalist Catherine Price explains in her illuminating book *How to Break Up with Your Phone*.[8]

US computer scientist Tristan Harris has knowledge of this world firsthand: he spent time at Stanford University's Persuasive Technology Lab before heading to Google, where he worked as a design ethicist. Speaking on Netflix documentary *The Social Dilemma*, Harris argues powerfully that social media tech companies colonise users' attention for nefarious purposes – wielding a 'totally new species of power and influence' over us. These social media tech giants use sophisticated data and advanced artificial intelligence (AI) technology to work out what you like, and what your next move is likely to be.

As Harris puts it, there are:

> 1000 engineers on the other side of the screen using notifications, using your friends, using AI to predict what's going to perfectly addict you or hook you or manipulate you, or allow advertisers to test 60,000 variations of text or colours to figure out what's the perfect manipulation of your mind.[9]

There's also evidence that using social media on our phones is terrible for our mental health. As Price points out, multiple studies have associated the heavy use of smartphones – especially when used for social media – with negative effects on neuroticism, self-esteem, and with sleep problems, anxiety, stress and depression.[10]

Some of these effects have also been described by psychologist Dr Larry Rosen, who came up with the term 'iDisorder' to describe a modern affliction where our brains struggle to keep up with excessive use of technology. Some of the problems Rosen said he was seeing, particularly among young people who used smartphones more heavily, include diminished attention spans, impaired learning, and sleep problems.[11]

Sounds eerily familiar, doesn't it?

This is all a long way of saying that many of the ill-effects of Yes Woman behaviour you experience are made a squillion times worse by technology that leaves us distracted, torn in too many directions at once, anxious, and desperate for social approval.

We stymie our own growth

I have a guy friend who's refreshingly open about the things he doesn't understand. He'll often stop me mid-sentence to ask for a definition or explanation ('bell hooks? Who's that?').

I'm not saying his willingness to admit ignorance is a male trait – there are many blokes who don't do this. But I've noticed that many Yes Women aren't comfortable fessing up when a conversation's going straight over their heads.

Stuck in a dinner party conversation with someone quoting an obscure concept, a Yes Woman is unlikely to interject and ask what the hell 'Übermensch' means so she can follow the conversation. Instead, she'll nod and play along – awkwardly trying to conceal her knowledge gap, all while stifling a yawn. (Never mind that, more often than not, the guy droning on about Nietzsche would far rather you ask – and give him the opportunity to explain the concept.)

This isn't just my own observation. When I interviewed Hobart-based psychologist and researcher Dr Kimberley Norris for this book, one of her first observations was that women with people-pleasing and perfectionistic tendencies often tend to hide their shortcomings in this way.

By concealing their true selves in the attempt to be perfect, women lose the opportunity for self-development, mentorship and true intimacy, explains Norris, who is an associate professor with the School of Psychological Sciences at The University of Tasmania.

'If you are constantly in a pattern or state of behaviour that's about hiding your deficits, then those areas of development are hidden from those with the resources to assist you in developing that skill set,' Norris says.

In other words, for high-achieving Yes Women who strive to be smart and well-read, this fear of trying new things can hold them back from asking questions that will help them grow. Someone tell Alanis Morissette, because that is ironic.[12]

SIDE NOTE: The 'good schoolgirl' effect

You were probably a good student. And, sorry, but I don't mean that as a compliment.

The thing is, lots of Yes Women I talked to for this book used to be good at school. They aced their English classes, brought home big red A+ marks on their maths tests, and joined the debating team. Maybe their school even deemed them 'gifted and talented' and gave them extension classes when they were still in primary school.

Most of these former smart kids used to love the work when they were small. But something changed along the way: pushed too hard by overzealous teachers and parents, many of these former gifted kids lost their internal motivation.[13] As teenagers, they sometimes began to ask themselves, who am I doing this for?[14] Or the alternative: they learned to pin their sense of self-worth, and even their happiness, on whether others were pleased with them – and whether they were living up to some 'perfect' ideal others expected of them.

Why don't all formerly gifted children go on to maximise their potential in the real world? I believe it's because they're frightened to try new things. The skills they honed in school – writing an essay the right way, getting the spelling right, working out a complex equation – has a right answer that can be marked and quantified.

They're moulded into good little girls awaiting a gold star on their homework.

As Stefanie Preissner recalls in her book *Can I Say No?*:

> I came out of my education so institutionalised I couldn't put a value on myself. Without teachers around to grade me, praise me, or tell me where I could improve, I had no sense of how I was doing in the world. Was I adulting properly? Was I correct? Was I doing the dance moves right?[15]

Ultimately, as San Francisco-based career coach, speaker and author of *Playing Big* Tara Mohr has written, the 'core ability students gain in doing that is the ability to rapidly perceive, interpret, and meet the expectations of authority figures'.[16] This skill serves us in certain parts of our careers – but if we want to be leaders and influencers, we need to be (and influence) authority figures, rather than just pleasing them.

In the real world, actual success demands more than just preparing for the tests and diligently doing things 'right' – putting our head down and meeting our work targets, hoping someone will notice us and give us a promotion. We have to strategise, innovate, think on our feet, speak out (even against authority) at the right moments and promote ourselves to get ahead. All of this can feel scary to Yes Women – which is understandable, because it clashes head-on with a lifetime of training to be quiet and agreeable.

We drive ourselves mad (and sad) with stress

Saying 'yes' all the time also, quite simply, makes us unhappy.

When writing this book, most women I spoke to identified all too closely with my own experiences of feeling overcommitted, overwhelmed and just plain over saying yes to invites and favours that drained me. Like me, they found that, despite all the work they'd put into creating a life of their choosing – building a career, perhaps raising children, nurturing their relationships, keeping their appearance in check – they were left feeling harassed and tired rather than satisfied.

More than a few Yes Women also admitted that their daily schedules were so busy that even minor inconveniences could tip the day into chaos. (Ever found yourself near-murderous because your housemate forgot to buy milk?)

There's no way to totally avoid stress. In fact, a certain amount of it can be fine. Stress can even motivate us. But too much stress can make us physically and mentally unwell.

And too much stress is exactly what many of us are experiencing, chronically. Research has found that, as a society, our stress levels jumped by about a third during the decade prior to 2017[17] – with stress levels among women being 50 per cent higher than among men, according to one UK study.[18]

SIDE NOTE: The pandemic has amplified our stress levels

The COVID-19 pandemic has driven up stress levels for everyone, but particularly women.

Women – who tend to earn less, who lost jobs in greater numbers during the first year of the pandemic, who have typically juggled caring responsibilities amid school and day care closures,[19] and who are more likely to hold insecure and informal jobs – have borne the brunt of the social and economic consequences of the pandemic across the world.[20]

That holds true in Australia, too. In mid-2020, as I was writing this book, a Monash University study on mental health found that women in particular were experiencing higher levels of depression, anxiety and stress in response to the pandemic.[21] The Monash findings showed that 27 per cent of women reported 'moderate to severe' levels of stress. (By comparison just 10 per cent of males said they were experiencing those stress levels. Go figure.)

♣

As well as being overwhelmed, many Yes Women experience what psychologists call 'stress contagion' – when we feel the stress of our partners, colleagues, bosses or kids rubbing off on us. As women, we're culturally deemed the providers of caregiving – so people unload on us, ask us for advice, and vent without asking if we have the time to listen.

It's easy to become overwhelmed and frustrated by not being able to make things better for everyone.[22]

Add all this stress – and stress contagion – together, and what've you got?

You end up dissatisfied, resentful, and feeling like you've got 'nothing left in the tank', says Norris.

Excessive and prolonged stress can cause burnout – a state of emotional, physical, and mental exhaustion, or 'compassion fatigue' – where you're so burned out from doing things for other people that you end up with a diminished ability to empathise with others.

Burnout and compassion fatigue are huge risk factors for depressive disorders like depression or anxiety, Norris tells me. No surprise, then, that one meta-analysis examining decades of data found that perfectionists had strong links to higher levels of burnout, anxiety, stress, workaholism, and depression.[23]

And that, my friends, is how you end up in a psych ward.

Our bodies suffer

I've met a lot of women whose bodies wear the signs of constant 'yes-ing'. But perhaps the most dramatic example is Ellie, who – of the hundreds of women who agreed to help me with my research for this book – was one of the very first to tell me about her Yes Woman tendencies.

'I knew my people-pleasing behaviour had gone too far when I found myself scrubbing my property clean days after major surgery,'

Ellie told me over the phone in an interview.

I could tell Ellie was a bona fide Yes Woman even before we started our phone interview. She agreed to the first time I suggested – and only later mentioned that she was travelling in the UK at the time, which meant she'd be taking my call in the middle of the night. Saying 'yes' to the interview would lose her half a night's sleep – but she wouldn't dream of inconveniencing me!

When we did connect, Ellie shared the story of how, in order to keep others happy, she risked having her surgical wounds become infected. It went like this:

After a diagnosis of breast cancer, Ellie underwent a mastectomy. She was under medical advice to rest – but there was a hiccup. Ellie runs an artists' retreat in regional Victoria with her girlfriend – and at the time of Ellie's mastectomy, the retreat kitchen needed some minor emergency repair work.

Ellie arranged for some handy-people to do the job, then asked her employee Alex to move some boxes off the kitchen benches in readiness for the workers' arrival.

Alex refused: 'That sounds like cleaning, and it's not in my job description.' (It was.)

Ellie explained that she couldn't lift the boxes herself, but Alex wasn't budging. So rather than inconvenience Alex, the tradies or the artists-in-residence who needed to use the kitchen, Ellie swallowed her pain pills, winced through the agony and lifted those boxes. Then, for good measure, she scrubbed down the kitchen, in case the tradies needed to make themselves a cup of tea during their workday.

By the time the tradies arrived, Ellie was exhausted and her incisions were throbbing. She was quietly seething at Alex, who was contentedly tapping away at the keyboard of the office computer while Ellie did the physical work.

Recounting the incident to me on the phone, Ellie described the incident as the 'crunch moment', where she realised her Yes Woman habits had spiralled out of control. 'It was good to realise how bad I was. I knew I was a people person, but I'd always convinced myself it wasn't a bad thing,' Ellie told me. 'I kind of got sucked into being the person who has to make everyone happy. When I realised I was letting that dominate, that's when I realised I had to make changes.'

♣

Ellie's 'crunch moment' highlights one extreme example of how perfectionistic people-pleasing can carry a high physical price. But even for those of us who haven't found ourselves scrubbing the kitchen days after surgery, there are other, subtler, physical ramifications of Yes Woman behaviour.

In the short-term, trying to be everything to everyone can cause physical symptoms of stress: headaches or backaches, sleep problems, a tight chest or other chest pains, nausea, or dizziness. Longer-term, you may suffer the physical tolls of living in a state of chronic stress, which can cause immune, hormonal and digestive dysfunction, and a spate of afflictions including ulcers, colitis, and heart disease.[24,25]

Yes Women can suffer from what stress specialist Barbara Brown calls 'states of unwellness' – those in-between states in which one is not sick enough to have a real diagnosis, but where stress incubates and stress illnesses breed.[26]

These afflictions arise because, as neuroendocrinology researcher and author Robert M Sapolsky writes in his book *Why Zebras Don't Get Ulcers*, when humans experience stress, our body turns on the same physiological responses that an animal's does.[27] It's as if we've seen a lion in the wild, and our body's 'fight or flight' response kicks into gear. The problem is, modern-day humans don't resolve conflict through fighting or fleeing, like animals do. Instead, we keep subjecting ourselves to the same stresses, day in, day out: in the case of Yes Women, we stay in the busy job while trying to keep our families nourished and loved ones pleased with us. We live in a constant state of physiological arousal; we're always on. Over time, this chronically activated stress response makes us literally sick.[28]

There's also a strong link between stress and substance abuse. Research shows that women are more likely than men to misuse prescription opioids to self-treat for anxiety or tension,[29] and women are generally more likely to drink to regulate negative affect and stress reactivity.[30]

This is no small problem: while drinking to cope with the stress of modern life has fuelled more than a few light-hearted memes (often shared with hashtags like #mumlife), in reality it can have deadly consequences.[31]

We lose out by faking it

Then there's the fact that it's difficult to be friends with a phony.

If you've spent your life trying to desperately conceal your flaws and put your best foot forward – even to your mates – you're probably holding them at arm's length.

If that sounds like you, I don't blame you. I get it. Girls often begin to conceal their 'real selves' around adolescence when, as psychologist Mary Pipher has written, we enter a sort of 'social and developmental Bermuda Triangle' for girls' self-esteem: 'Just as planes and ships disappear mysteriously into the Bermuda Triangle, so do the selves of girls go down in droves,' she writes. 'Their voices have gone underground – their speech is more tentative and less articulate.'[32]

Immersed in a sexualised and media-saturated culture, teen girls feel immense pressure to split into true and false selves, Pipher writes. So we smooth over the daggy, weird, complex parts of ourselves. We ditch the hobbies we used to enjoy; our fondness for 90s rock; our hard moments and weaknesses; our bad but enthusiastic dancing. (In my case, I also ditched my DIY bright-red dye job – which was probably a good thing.)

While it often sets in around adolescence, this kind of concealment of our 'real selves' can last well into adulthood. It's common among grown-up women who struggle with assertiveness: 'In an attempt to preserve an important relationship, you may hide or withhold parts of yourself that you fear might not be accepted by the other person; you don't want to create distance with your baggage and emotional idiosyncrasies,' psychotherapist Julie de Azevedo Hanks wrote in her book about assertiveness in women.[33]

This act of withholding can paradoxically damage the relationship, as the person doesn't get to know the real you.[34] In other words, we cannot be genuine when we're desperately trying to manage how others perceive us.[35]

Working hard to conceal the 'real you' is also, frankly, exhausting. It takes up a lot of time and energy. And as Brené Brown has written, when we're busy trying to create the appearance of perfection, '[w]hat has to give is everything behind the scenes: everything we hold dear to ourselves'.[36]

So, as we pour our efforts into polishing our facade, we begin to bury or neglect the things that make our hearts truly sing. We try to be agreeable, to be Nice – but Niceness is one-dimensional, and doesn't allow much room for us to be complex, imperfect, messy human beings.

We try to please, but end up disappointing

As a lifelong people-pleaser, you might expect me to be an attentive friend. But here's a guilty secret: I forgot one of my very best friend's birthdays last year.

Worst. Friend. Ever.

I blame it on my Yes Woman ways. Because that's another deep irony about the desire to please everyone: all too often, those efforts cause you to end up disappointing them.

You know what it's like – you commit to seeing three family groups on Christmas Day, only to end up doing fly-by visits that are spent glancing at your watch and planning your next route. You spread your time and money among too many friends and commitments throughout the week, so by Friday night you're too exhausted to bring your A-game to your friend's party. And in my case, I crammed so much into a particular week in October that I forgot to look at the calendar – and completely missed my plans to surprise my mate with a birthday picnic lunch. (She was very lovely about it and we had a make-up picnic lunch the following week. Thanks, Vic, for putting up with my frazzled ways.)

This pattern is all too familiar to many Yes Women – among them, a well-known author and journalist I'll refer to as Maggie. When I placed a call-out on social media asking for women to tell me about their people-pleasing ways, she put up her hand straightaway (which did, to be fair, please me.)

'I'm riddled with this anxiety about saying no to things: if a friend asks me to do something and I can't do it, because I'm literally double-booked, I'll say yes and promise myself I'll sort it out later,' Maggie told me when I interviewed her over the phone. 'So I grew up, with friends, having this weird anxiety about letting them down. If I can't make something, I'll leave it until the really last minute until it's too late to actually let them down, and then I'll let them down even more.'

So, just like me, Maggie's plans to keep everyone happy backfired – leaving her friends in the lurch, and leaving her feeling guilty and anxious. For a people-pleaser, that's a lot of people left feeling unpleased.

There's another side-effect of saying 'yes' to keep your mates happy, too. When I interviewed psychologist Cass Dunn about people-pleasing traits in women, she pointed out that people-pleasers often end up bitter and twisted (my words, not hers.)

'Too much people-pleasing behaviour – which happens when people … want to be liked and want to be seen as a good person or a Nice person – can result in this underlying resentment,' Dunn explains. 'And then that festers and that undermines the very relationships that they say are important to them.'

Repeat after me: manoeuvring to make the other person happy all the time isn't a recipe for a healthy friendship. And if your loved ones pick up that your 'yes, let's do that plan' acceptance of an obligation is through gritted teeth, it's not going to make them feel closer to you.

We're distracted from our true priorities

'The difference between successful people and very successful people is that very successful people say "no" to almost everything.'[37]

If you haven't heard that phrase before, I hope you'll go back and read it again. Then go back and read it one more time. It should be your new mantra.

The thing is, if you're spending your time, energy and money on the things other people demand from you, you'll have nothing left to spend on the things you actually give a damn about.

It's liberating as all get-out to realise this. (And there will be more on this in Chapter 7, when we drill down into working out what you actually want.)

It keeps us quiet

When American actor Jennifer Lawrence learned that she'd earned millions of dollars less than her male co-stars for her starring role in the film *American Hustle*, she didn't put up much of a fight. Why?

Partly, she wanted to remain likeable. She wanted to remain Nice.

'I would be lying if I didn't say there was an element of wanting to be liked that influenced my decision to close the deal without a real fight. I didn't want to seem "difficult" or "spoiled",' Lawrence wrote in an essay for *Lenny*.[38] It's a gender thing, she added: 'I don't think I've ever worked for a man in charge who spent time contemplating what angle he should use to have his voice heard.'

Not many of us have to joust with our male peers over multi-million-dollar Hollywood movie deals – but the underlying thrust of J-Law's dilemma still resonates. Because, in these brief sentences, the megastar touched on one of the most troubling implications of Yes Woman behaviour: it can silence women's voices.

⁂

So far, this chapter has looked at how perfectionistic people-pleasing – and saying yes all the time – makes us mentally and physically unwell and can damage our relationships. The consequences are serious and detrimental on a personal level, yes – but it's far greater than that. Keeping ourselves censored has political ramifications, too.

So let's go there, shall we?

Women's struggle to say no – held in place as it is by societal expectations that women be everything to everyone, and do it all perfectly – quiets our voices and undermines our agency. Our people-pleasing ways can stop us from 'making a fuss' over our wants and needs. Coaxed into being 'Nice girls' and fearful of the ramifications, we bite our tongues.

We say yes instead of, 'That's not fair.' We say yes instead of, 'I've earned that promotion.' We say yes instead of, 'You know what? I don't want to watch another Michael Bay film.' (Ha.)

But there's a price we pay for keeping quiet. As the saying goes: if you don't speak for yourself, somebody else will speak for you. That saying is amplified for women, as author, journalist and former model Tara Moss has pointed out, because we have long been denied a part in any decisions about our own public or private lives.[39] This goes twofold for Black women and women of colour – who have been oppressed not just on the basis of their gender, but by white men and women alike.

It's no accident that women were historically assigned this quieter, more subservient cultural role. Female silence allows men to continue making the rules, as feminists have long claimed: traditionally, male-dominated institutions have upheld that status quo by denying women a public voice – that is, not allowing women to vote or run for office – and punishing or ridiculing them for speaking up.

Thus, in classical times, society smiled upon 'modest women' who kept quiet; scarcity in speech was seen to be intimately related to sexual restraint.[40]

(It's worth noting here that 'modesty' and its sister qualities – silence and restraint – have historically had classist overtones. When suffragettes Christabel Pankhurst and Annie Kenney were arrested in 1905, for instance, the court report observed that 'the defendants' behaviour was such as one was accustomed to attribute to women from the slums'. The spectre of working-class women was invoked, as Helen Lewis comments in her book *Difficult Women*, in order to socialise young middle- and upper-class girls to be docile – not to be difficult.[41])

In ancient times, as British classicist Mary Beard has explained: 'public speech was a, if not the, defining attribute of maleness' and so 'women who claim a public voice were treated as freakish androgynes'.[42] More recently, in the 17th century, women with 'unruly tongues' could be legally punished as a 'scold' – with scolds sometimes publicly humiliated on a 'cucking stool' (or with a painful muzzle-like device called a 'scold's bridle'. Yeuch.)

Today, women in much of the world are ostensibly encouraged to take part in speech-making, debate and public comment. And there are quotas. Women's restrooms in parliament. Laws against assaulting your wife. If aliens flew to Australia in the 2020s and saw the great-sounding gender-equality laws we have in place, they'd be forgiven for thinking we'd solved sexism once and for all.

But despite modern-day rhetoric about the importance of outspoken women leaders, the subtle silencing of women's voices continues to pervade our culture – and it borrows directly from the historical themes of women who speak being deemed manly, difficult, and 'not Nice'.

In today's culture, we are not actually silenced – but we pay a very high price to have our voices heard, as Mary Beard argues.[43] Shock jocks and conservative politicians criticise women for 'vocal fry' or 'creaky voice', for whinging or whining, for sounding too hesitant, too childish, too strident, too 'hysterical'. (The complaints about female 'upspeak' and vocal fry ignore the fact that men also engage in these habits, as Stanford linguistics professor Penny Eckert points out.[44]) These tactics strip the authority from what women have to say and trivialise their concerns.

The relentless online abuse, the misogynistic slurs by politicians and the dismissive shut-downs by male colleagues in the boardroom can be seen as just another way of socially enforcing the old, culturally-sanctioned model of female 'Niceness' and virtue.[45]

Some misogynists, including Twitter trolls, actively engage in voice-policing as a concerted tactic because they want you out of the conversation, according to novelist, critic and feminist Van Badham. 'This isn't a conspiracy theory, this is just standard political strategy,' she argues. 'If your opponents are organising and you can disrupt their organising model, you do it.'[46]

♣

Remaining silent is one of many ways in which Yes Women behaviour can strip women of their power. But in some ways, it's the most important – as it has implications that extend far beyond each of our individual lives.

If we choose not to speak up, we help maintain patriarchal norms around women's 'Niceness' and subservience. If we choose not to speak up, we're legitimising our opponents – voting with our feet (and closed mouths) to say that whoever's the loudest or most threatening deserves more power, as Van Badham says.[47]

What does the alternative look like? If we spoke our minds and voiced our fears – if we said no to demands that drain our time and energy – we'd become walking, talking refutations of this status quo.[48] That would particularly be the case if we actually – and here's a radical thought – expressed frustration or anger at the fact we've been silenced for so long. As Soraya Chemaly explains: 'Anger remains the emotion that is least acceptable for girls and women because it is the first line of defence against injustice. Believing that you have the right to use your anger with power reflects multiple, overlapping social entitlements.'[49]

♣

All this is not to say you're a 'bad feminist' for being a Yes Woman – as we've explored, there are many forces at work that make us this way. And for those women who risk violence, estrangement from family or cultural groups, or other serious consequences, speaking up might pose a very real risk to our health and wellbeing.

But for women who now have the option of sitting at the table and being part of those conversations? Let's do so – for the benefit of ourselves and for other women who can't.

Let's 'raise really good hell for people who cannot', as American writer, sociologist, and professor Dr Tressie McMillan Cottom puts it.[50] Let's pipe up. Let's take up that space. Let's tell our stories (this book is my attempt to do just that) and let's encourage other women to share their perspectives.

Let's commit ourselves to saying no to all those garbage expectations that drain you of your time, energy and power.

And let's remember: well-behaved women seldom make history.[51]

Chapter 5

Busy is best, and other myths we've swallowed

Caring for myself is not self-indulgence, it is self-preservation, and that is an act of political warfare.

– Audre Lorde[1]

Hair up, bra off, trackies on. I was in my early 20s, we'd just finished dinner in my share house, and I was all settled in with my bestie for a movie night.

As the credits started rolling, I noticed my dodgy manicure needed a fix, so I ducked to the bathroom and grabbed my nail kit. The first scene started, and I remembered a text I had to fire back to a friend. Five minutes later, I was paying bills on my phone while peering at the film between nail polish strokes – and my best friend turned to me and said, 'Do you know how to just *relax*?'

I opened my mouth to protest that I *was* relaxing (while also taking the opportunity to finalise a few odd jobs), before realising how unhinged that sounded. Was I seriously trying to multitask my chill-out time? Had I *forgotten how to relax?*

It was the first time I really noticed my tendency to operate in a state of constant, almost automatic busyness – a state based on a deep (and totally bogus) belief that to be efficient and productive at all times is best. It's the same busyness that drove me to burn out soon after I had my daughter – so, clearly, it took me a long time to learn the lesson. But in the last year, I've been actively calling myself out when I notice myself buying into the old busy-is-best mentality, and I've noticed that the ways I feel and act have changed as a result.

Hi, my name is Grace, and it's been 12 months since my last multitasking 'relaxation' session.

That's progress.

♣

This chapter is all about the kind of self-calling-out I just described. Because knowing we want to stop saying yes to everything isn't enough to *fix* the problem. For your Yes Woman ways to really *change*, you'll have to unlearn some lessons you've held close for your entire life (and sometimes, the lessons many generations of women have passed on, too). You'll have to challenge the mental roadblocks that are stopping you from saying no when you really want to (in later chapters, you'll do the same with behavioural roadblocks).

How are we going to do all this? By borrowing from the principles of cognitive behaviour therapy, a type of psychotherapy that aims to help change unhelpful or unhealthy ways of thinking, feeling and behaving by identifying and challenging certain thoughts.

Think of it as a deprogramming – and reprogramming – process. We'll recognise that we all have blueprints for the way we think and behave, we'll identify some of the problematic blueprints you might have, and then we'll challenge and modify that belief system. That, according to psychologist Brenda Dolieslager, is the beginning of change.

This chapter explores some of the core beliefs Yes Women tend to hold. Remember, the point of challenging them isn't to stop ever having any of these thoughts again – they will still surface from time to time – but rather, it's so that you can live with that little voice of self-doubt without being defined by it. *You're not the boss of me, bitchy little inner voice!*

Myth 1: Busy is best

I moved to New York in my mid-20s, hoping to absorb the city's wacky, creative buzz by osmosis. The energy would get into my bones and elevate my work to a new level. I'd ride high on waves of creative zeal and success, leaving me giddily happy and successful. Or so I figured.

But what I didn't count on was that too much busyness can crush a hungry young person.

What I learned over my two years there is that New York City reeks of ambition and anxiety. Jammed with people who moved interstate or overseas with one big dream or another, it's a city of perfectionists and high achievers. On the crammed sidewalks, young upstarts take their meetings on the go, Bluetooth headsets permanently switched on. Some New Yorkers make a habit of listening to podcasts with the speed doubled, such is their rush to cram as much knowledge-acquisition into their morning commute as possible. Locals make no bones about their hurry to be somewhere: the 'Hey, lady, I'm walkin' here!' cliché is a real thing. I once witnessed a tourist stopping a local for directions, only to be told, 'You have 15 seconds, then I gotta keep walking.'

It's not just the pace on the street that's fast: long work hours are not only *de rigueur*, but a status symbol. When I was living in New York, there was a trend for meal replacement drinks called Soylent, which allowed people to totally skip their lunch break. The subways were lined with ads for startups offering time-saving services. Those who could afford it almost invariably had food and laundry delivered direct to their apartments. Locals could even buy their pot through dealers who would come direct to their apartment with a briefcase of 'goods' to choose from.

Those who can't afford these time-saving conveniences in New York are, nevertheless, also in a rush. Crushing rent prices, a privatised healthcare system, insufficient social welfare and a lack of government-paid maternity leave contribute to wealth inequality, driving many to work multiple jobs. While the rich maximise their time by outsourcing menial tasks, ordinary New Yorkers share an attitude of 'Don't try to steal a minute of my time, because I can sell that time to rich people in the form of services such as bartending or personal training,' as I once saw it explained.[2]

New York is the epitome of the culture of busyness revered by the 21st-century Western world. It exemplifies the capitalist mindset that being busy and productive is intrinsically good and important, and gives worth to our lives – a mindset that's addictive and toxic to Yes Women.

While living in New York, I became swept up in the pace, and downtime went out the window. At one point I went through a stage of trying to do my 'mindful meditation' while legging it to the subway and squeezing into a seat on the train. (There was no time in my morning to sit down and meditate for ten minutes – I was TOO BUSY.)

We don't all take busyness to the unhinged extent I did in New York, but all Yes Women, to some extent, deprioritise rest and quiet time in favour of being busy, busy, busy. And the belief that 'busy is best' is a harmful myth that undermines us. It makes us feel like crap: worried about endless to-do lists; bored and disoriented if we find ourselves unoccupied for a second; guilty or ashamed or even disgusted at ourselves when we do occasionally slow down; or indignant when something interferes with all that multitasking. ('Why is there no phone reception in this train tunnel, dammit?')

The 'busy is best' myth also fuels frantic Yes Woman behaviour like overcommitting ourselves, rushing from one thing to the next, being forever connected to phones and technology, saying yes to invitations when we're already overbooked, obsessively seeking overachievement (often at the expense of our wellbeing), and attempting to multitask (by, *ahem*, fixing our nail polish and sorting out our finances while watching a movie).

As a Yes Woman, you really, really need to kick the belief that busy is best. Try reframing that thought: in reality, busyness is a societal pressure that drains us, rather than making us more effective.

In her book *How to Do Nothing*, California-based writer and artist Jenny Odell says that millennials, as a generation, are currently fighting a battle for our time – 'a colonisation of the self by capitalist ideas of productivity and efficiency'. She fears that the contemplative, fertile parts of our mind and spirit, where creative ideas blossom, are under attack. As she puts it: 'The parks and libraries of the self are always about to be turned into condos.'[3]

It's time for Yes Women to recognise that, as Odell puts it, 'much of what gives one's life meaning stems from accidents, interruptions, and serendipitous encounters: the "off time" that a mechanistic view of experience seeks to eliminate'.[4]

Busyness crowds out spontaneity. It leads to chronic stress, with all the attendant physical and mental effects noted earlier. The 'productivity-as-importance' mindset also sidelines people who can't, and don't, take part in the 'working-hard economy' – those with chronic health conditions or disabilities or life circumstances (such as caring responsibilities). And it undervalues the arts, except solely those arts events that contribute to the bottom line.

♣

If you're stuck in the trap of thinking busy is better, it can help to envisage emotional and mental capacity like a bucket of water: a full bucket means you're emotionally overloaded and have no bandwidth to deal with any further stress or strain. If you're a Yes Woman, your default state is probably to have a bucket almost full to the brim. You can get by if everything runs smoothly – if your car doesn't break down, if you don't catch a cold, if your kid doesn't have a tantrum that completely derails your morning. Your bucket can just about hold all your demanding obligations on a good day.

But if it rains – you get hit by an unexpected bill, a friend asks you to arrange her hen's party on short notice, your boss hits you with an extra project due on Monday – your bucket quickly overflows. There's no buffer to contain the unexpected twists and turns of life.

As a Yes Woman, you'll need to learn to avoid being so busy that you have no room to accommodate the rain. You'll need to start actively noticing, and calling yourself out, mentally, when you get caught in 'busy is best' thinking.

You'll need to remind yourself that (and isn't this a radical thought?) *your worth isn't based on your productivity.* Your value as a person is a given, not defined by how much you tick off your to-do list, how much money you make, or how busy you are.

Myth 2: Boundaries are selfish

'*You selfish bitch.*'

Before I started paying attention to my Yes Woman ways, if you really wanted to push my buttons, those three words would do the trick.

Nobody wants to be called selfish, especially women – in a culture that demands female sacrifice, the word is a particularly loaded slur. But Yes Women tend to take their aversion to selfishness to the next level. They're not only scared of feeling 'mean' and terrified of provoking conflict by declining a request, they also feel guilty, embarrassed or self-critical when they do put their own needs first, and they sometimes also fear being abandoned or rejected if they do lay down their boundaries. So they struggle to draw a line around their own time and resources, letting askers and takers (and sometimes even users) drain their energy. They neglect their own basic needs to make sure their family members, their friends and their workmates are happy.

They're the ones running themselves ragged to put the finishing touches on a group university assignment; making nutritious meals for their family but skipping lunch because they're too busy; dipping into their savings accounts to buy a farewell gift for a colleague because nobody else has arranged it. Yes Women are excellent at caring for others, but often forget to care for themselves.

♣

Setting boundaries – knowing and making clear your limits, and making clear what is you and what is not you – is a vital part of looking after yourself. Without boundaries, we allow others to encroach on us, we take on other people's issues, and we open ourselves to manipulation or disrespect. And that's not Nice. It's unhealthy.

Now, here's where it gets tricky for Yes Women. Many of the women I surveyed during my research expressed feelings of guilt or uncertainty when drawing a line around their own self-care.

For Aimee, a 34-year-old entrepreneur from Melbourne, this tension came to the fore in August 2020 during Melbourne's coronavirus restrictions, when visitors to the home were prohibited by law. 'My in-laws came to visit during lockdown in Melbourne, and I kept thinking, they *should not* be here,' Aimee tells me. 'I felt sick and full of anxiety because I just wanted them out of the house and I was worried about getting sick, but I couldn't just say that. I managed to get out, "I feel really uncomfortable that you're here and I hate that I feel like this."'

Aimee's in-laws soon left, and she felt better that they were gone. But she spent the rest of the week mentally wringing her hands over whether she'd offended them. 'I'm not used to saying, "This is what I need or what's good for my wellbeing, and it might not be what you want,"' Aimee reflects.

Let's be real. There are times where the only right thing to do is to help others and meet their needs: perhaps you have to support a loved one at a funeral, or you have dependents who need food on the table. But if it's the norm, rather than the exception, that you set your own needs aside to take care of others, chances are your beliefs and behaviours are perpetuating this pattern. In that case, it's time to challenge those beliefs.

Start by learning the difference between self-care and selfishness.

Self-care is about replenishing your resources and setting boundaries. It doesn't mean you have the right to do anything you want all the time because you deserve it. It's also more than endless 'me time'. Remind yourself that self-care benefits everyone around you because it rejuvenates you, enabling you to give of yourself when it's actually needed. It's that oft-repeated self-helpy adage, 'You can't pour from an empty cup.' It's like putting your own oxygen mask on first before helping others in an air travel emergency.

Whichever metaphor you prefer, it's time to promise yourself you'll take care of your own needs.

SIDE NOTE: The politics behind 'self-care'

I sometimes cringe at the term 'self-care' because it's now so commercialised and clichéd (companies use the term to sell aromatherapy and vaginal steaming, for Chrissake). It's also an appropriation of a term that, when Audre Lorde used it, had a deeply political meaning: Lorde was writing as a Black, lesbian woman in a society that placed her on the bottom rung of the societal ladder. Self-care, for Lorde, was about preserving herself in a world that was hostile to her identity and community.[5]

Though I'm not using the term here in quite the same politically meaningful way Lorde used it, if you are someone who wants to challenge societal boundaries – even in seemingly small ways, such as challenging your racist uncle over the dinner table, or speaking out against pregnancy discrimination at work – taking time to calm and preserve yourself and build your energy for the fight is crucial.[6]

♣

One easy 'trick' that can help when prioritising self-care is to consider the things you do for others, and consider whether you're acting in the same caring way towards yourself. Or even think about whether you find it relatively easy to say no on behalf of others, and then make a point of doing the same for yourself.

'I'm bad at saying no, but I say no on my partner's behalf constantly,' says Newcastle-based Maya, a 33-year-old communications specialist whose partner works for a large tech organisation. 'People are always asking via me for his tech abilities – even extremely Google-able things, or things completely unrelated to his work like their remote not working. I absorb the frustration and the awkwardness of saying no on his behalf.'

Maya's currently learning to channel her 'no' abilities towards protecting her own time and energy, too.

As for me, I'll often prepare several healthy, easy-to-reheat meals for my young daughter on a Sunday so I know I have ready-to-go food for her during the week – but I sometimes have to remind myself to have nutritious, grown-up food in the house for myself.

Look, I know I'm an adult and I don't need to snack every few hours like a toddler (although that sounds rather nice), but you get my point: it's as important to look out for your basic needs as those of your loved ones.

SIDE NOTE: Another perspective on selfishness

Maybe, just *maybe*, it's not such a terrible thing for women to be selfish, in any case?

Melbourne-based feminist warrior, author and podcaster Clementine Ford powerfully argues in her book *Fight Like a Girl* that 'selfishness in women isn't the great crime that people like to pretend it is'. She goes on:

> Why is everyone so pathologically terrified of selfish women? The word is thrown around like an insult, as if the worst thing a woman could possibly do (aside from being fat, having sex with whomever she pleases and whenever, swearing, having an abortion, drinking alcohol, standing up for herself and being a working mother) is to decide that her life matters.[7]

So perhaps it's time to accept that although taking care of your needs doesn't have to be selfish, it's actually *okay for women to be selfish*, anyway. It shouldn't be considered a privilege to be able to express what we need, to be able to set our own priorities, and to seek to live a life according to our own values.

Myth 3: Good isn't good enough

If Yes Women had a motto, 'go hard or go home' would be a strong contender.

Perfectionistic people-pleasers tend to think in black-and-white terms: either 'I was a total boss in that meeting' or 'I completely put my foot in it.' Either 'My dinner party was a roaring success' or 'It was a goddamn embarrassment that we shall never speak of again.'

While these tendencies affect people of all genders, I wonder if women are particularly prone to this all-or-nothing mindset. They can think, 'If I can't do it perfectly, I won't throw my hat in the ring.' Consider, for example, that women apply for a promotion only when they believe they meet 100 per cent of the qualifications; meanwhile, men apply when they meet 60 per cent.[8]

So we see that, before starting a new project or pursuing a passion, Yes Women often diligently try to get all their ducks in a row before taking the first step:

I'll definitely write that book – but first I have to do three professional writing courses, find a mentor and save up for a fancy new laptop to write it on.

I'll definitely start trying for a baby – but first I want to lose 5 kilos, move into a bigger house and read a dozen self-help books.

They also constantly refine (and sometimes overwork) their projects in the pursuit of perfection; regularly hone in on mistakes or imperfections; refuse to celebrate or acknowledge outcomes that fall short of perfection; and tend to focus on the end result while disregarding the journey or process.

Sometimes, it's motivated by competitiveness: a drive to get all that lovely credit. But more often, I find, these behaviours are tied to feelings of shame about one's failures being on display; to the fear of disapproval or being thought of as 'lazy'; to feelings of sadness, annoyance or devastation when one doesn't achieve one's goal; and to feelings of self-judgement and inadequacy. (After all, as Maria Shriver once said, 'Perfectionism doesn't make you feel perfect; it makes you feel inadequate.')

Now, I acknowledge that sometimes a certain amount of prep work is necessary to give a new project the best chance of success. And historically, as Tara Mohr writes, it has often been necessary for women to prove their (over)qualifications:

> The 20th century saw women break into professional life – but only if they had the right training, the right accreditations. These qualifications were our ticket in, our way of proving we could do the job. We weren't part of an old boys club in which we'd get the benefit of the doubt. As a result we may overestimate the importance of our formal training and qualifications, and underutilise advocacy and networking.[9]

But in today's world, this focus on getting all the conditions perfect can prevent us from diving in. I suspect it's a fancy form of procrastination, stemming from fear and a lack of confidence.

To move past your Yes Woman ways, you're going to have to challenge this all-or-nothing mindset. Part of this is accepting that failure and vulnerabilities are sometimes part of life. Sometimes, aiming for perfection stops you from doing anything good (or anything at all), to paraphrase Voltaire.[10]

To reprogram yourself, you're going to have to be a little more accepting of your foibles, your imperfections, your vulnerabilities and, yes, even the prospect of screwing things up. You're going to have to make a jump and wait for the net to appear. You'll have to get a little bit comfortable with things being *just good enough* – at least some of the time.

Ever heard the phrase 'carry yourself with the confidence of a mediocre white man'? That's your new aim.[11]

Myth 4: You're responsible for solving other people's problems

Smoothing over a family crisis. Finding a plumber to fix your boyfriend's bathroom. Volunteering to help your sister move house.

Yes Women often lump these tasks onto their to-do list because they feel it's up to them to fix their loved ones' problems. Partly, this is because Yes Women struggle to delegate. As psychologist Brenda Dolieslager tells me, people-pleasers often think things like, 'I can't say no to this because if I don't do it, it won't happen, or it won't be done properly.' But it's also because many Yes Women feel guilty when they don't take action to alleviate the other person's problems – and they may also struggle with a fear of rejection or abandonment or of no longer being needed, which leaves them hungry for the approval of others.

If you fall into this trap, it can help to remind yourself that it's not on you to solve other people's problems, or to manage their feelings. In fact, every time you take on someone else's problem, you're effectively sacrificing your own time, interests and resources. In doing so, you're placing a lower value on your own time – which, I bet, isn't doing much for your self-esteem. It will just make you exhausted.

That's not to say you should never be of help to a loved one, or that you should act with no regard for other people's feelings. A favour here and there can be part of a healthy two-way relationship. But if you're constantly feeling the pressure to fix other people's problems, and to absorb their emotions, chances are you're undervaluing your own time and needs.

If your 'it's up to me to fix things' mentality is due to feeling anxious about delegating in case it all goes wrong, it can be useful to 'examine the evidence for and against the belief', says Dolieslager.

So what if your 12-year-old son forgets to pack his apple for recess? In reality, the whole day won't fall apart. Maybe he or your partner will learn to check his lunchbox before setting out for school. And so what if your needy cousin has to look up the number for a house-moving service? It's probably good for her to learn a bit of self-sufficiency.

You get the idea.

Myth 5: A polished, picture-perfect life is possible

We're smart women. We know real life doesn't look like Instagram. We know everyone has days where the kitchen bench is grubby, the jeans feel a bit tight, and the cat gets sick on our best rug. (*What have you been eating that's so green, Tigger?*)

But even though our logical brain knows it's all smoke and mirrors, part of us buys into the myth that a polished, Instagram-worthy life is possible. We buy into the media messaging that our toddlers 'should' have clean noses and matching socks, that our beach snaps 'should' look like a Byron Bay influencer's account, that our skin 'should' be unlined.

Against all logic, we cling onto this myth that a flawless, picture-perfect life is possible – and it makes us feel inadequate, anxious that we're not keeping up and scared of getting it wrong. We find ourselves preoccupied with what others think and freaked out at the prospect of somebody seeing our less-than-perfect bits.

Many of us also fear becoming ordinary: in a culture that measures the value of people's contributions by their level of public recognition, to be mediocre is now seen, by many of us, as shameful. To borrow the words of shame researcher Brené Brown, 'In many instances, we equate ordinary with boring, or even more dangerous, ordinary has become synonymous with meaningless.'[12]

We fear putting a foot wrong and being exposed as imperfect, so we try to curate our own image. We carefully choose the way our likeness is posted on social media (one recent study claimed 68 per cent of adults apply some kind of photo editing before they share any photo online or with a friend).[13] We take photos of our food. We go big on proposals, kids' birthdays and engagement parties, hiring photographers to get 'the perfect shot' where it would have been unheard of generations ago.

Our quest to curate a picture-perfect lifestyle extends to our leisure activities and luxury possessions, too. Research shows that young people born in the late 1980s really want to be rich – more than their parents did. Social psychologist Thomas Curran has claimed this generation borrows more money and spends more than any before them on status possessions for lifestyle displays on social media.[14]

In the professional sphere, we seek to publish the sleekest professional profile on our LinkedIn; to strike the right tone in our Facebook posts about current affairs; to impress the right clients with our website; to tweet our support for the most of-the-moment causes.

The instantaneous feedback available online is a match to the flame of our people-pleasing, perfectionistic tendencies. We check and refresh our social media feeds to see how close we've come to our definition of perfect.

Ultimately, social media has created an overarching 'culture of polishing', psychologist Cass Dunn told me when I interviewed her about what causes perfectionism.

'It's like, "I can polish and perfect everything and edit out the uncomfortable bits, and therefore [in real life] if I can't do that, I become even more consumed with not making a mistake,"' she says.

SIDE NOTE: Obsessing over your 'likes' is bad for you

Humans have evolved to care about whether other people in our tribe approve of us or not, because being part of a cohesive group protects us.

But, as Tristan Harris notes in Netflix documentary *The Social Dilemma*, we didn't evolve to be aware of what one thousand (or more) people thought of us.

'We were not evolved to have social approval being dosed to us every five minutes. That is not at all what we were built to experience,' he says.

'We curate our lives around this perceived sense of perfection, because we get rewarded in these short-term signals – hearts, likes, thumbs up – and we conflate that with value and we conflate it with truth,' adds Chamath Palihapitiya, former VP of growth at Facebook, in the same documentary.

'And instead what it really is is fake, brittle popularity that's short-term,' he says.

'It forces you into this vicious cycle where you're like, "what's the next thing I need to do, because I need it back?" Think about that compounded by two billion people, and then think about how people react to the perception of others. It's really, really bad.'

The health ramifications of constantly scrolling through social media on our smartphones are startling.[15] Professor of Psychology Jean Twenge, of San Diego University, in her book *iGen*, points out that rates of teen depression and suicide in the US have skyrocketed since 2011–2012 – the years that most Americans started to own mobile phones.[16] And in 2017, when a US study examined whether social media caused unhappiness (as opposed to simply appealing to people who were already unhappy), it found there does appear to be a causal relationship: 'We found consistently that both liking others' content and clicking links significantly predicted a subsequent reduction in self-reported physical health, mental health, and life satisfaction,' as the researchers wrote in *The Harvard Business Review*.[17]

In other words, one big challenge in tackling your Yes Woman tendencies might be in disconnecting from the devices designed to play on them.

The belief that perfection is attainable is the Yes Woman's Achilles heel – we know it's stressing us out, but it's just so hard to let go.

That's partly because it can feel so good when we do (however briefly) get a sense of achievement that we're pleasing others and doing things 'right,' even if that sense of achievement is hollow because we don't actually get a chance to enjoy it.

Your idea of 'perfect' is a composite image

For things to change, you'll also have to realise that achieving the picture-perfect life you crave isn't actually attainable. In fact, it's particularly *un*attainable in today's world, where there are more overlapping visions of what it means to be 'perfect' and 'successful' than ever before – and the Yes Woman is usually trying to tick the boxes tied to several of those visions simultaneously.

Take a moment to imagine your idea of your best, most perfect self. A version of you that you'd love your obituary to one day describe. What would she look like? What kind of illustrious job titles would feature on her CV? Would her home and social life look fun, yet somehow simultaneously blissful?

The thing is, you probably have in your mind a composite of a range of different successful women. As Brené Brown has written: 'When we're aiming for perfection, we're basically saying "we want to edit together all the best clips of what we see to form our lives".'[18] The problem, of course, is that if we internalise a belief that we 'should' be like three or four whole other high-achieving people – combined – our resources are inevitably stretched.[19]

(Personally, I'd like to order some kind of worthy career like Amal Clooney; a fluent grasp of politics like Julia Gillard; and legs like Jessica Simpson's in *The Dukes of Hazzard*. Plus a PhD while having three kids, like my mum. What could go wrong?)

By comparing our reality with some fantasy version of ourselves, Yes Women are on a hiding to nothing.

The tendency for our image of perfection to be an amalgamation of different role models is stronger in women than in men, according to psychologist Dr Harriet Braiker, whose area of expertise includes people-pleasing.[20] That's because men have traditionally confined their achievement criteria to work and money: 'Women, on the other hand, apply a literal double standard,' Braiker writes.

So, to be 'successful' as a contemporary woman means not only achievement by objective standards in the workplace, but achievement in the personal arena of life as well.[21]

Don't get me wrong – clearly, it's fantastic that women have the choice to focus on their career, or their creative pursuits, or their family – or all these things. I certainly don't want to rewind the clock back to the 1950s, when there were few role models for women of colour, for LGBTQI women, curvy women, or women who wanted to do anything other than raise a family and keep a pretty home.

But the downside of seeing all these role models in all facets of life is that, today, our vision of 'perfection' is broader than ever before, and involves checking off several more boxes than it once did. Yes Women, rather than choosing just one version of success to pursue, fervently try to pull them all off simultaneously – and we beat ourselves up if we don't.

The problem is, since success for achievement-oriented women means acing both the career and personal realms, the only way to play the game and try to win is to say yes to everyone and everybody. As I learned the hard way, it's a recipe for exhaustion and sets you up to feel like a failure.[22] So, ultimately, you have to realise that you simply *can't* be everything to everybody. You can't please everyone. And perfection is, quite literally, impossible.

Myth 6: You really *should* be doing that thing

Yes Women tend to live their lives according to a list of 'shoulds'.

I should tick off every item on my to-do list today.

I should pay a visit to my uncle.

I should get my hair fixed.

The word 'should' cropped up innumerable times in my interviews with Yes Women. (You might even be reading this book thinking, 'I really SHOULD kick my Yes Woman habit.' Ah, the irony.)

But 'should' is the language of obligation and guilt. The belief that we 'should' do this or that leaves us groaning under the burden of our responsibilities, squeezing out the everyday moments of lightness and joy. We end up preoccupied with what others think, exhausted –

and partaking in classic Yes Woman behaviours like overcommitting, rushing, and burning the candle at both ends.

Eliminating the s-word from your vocabulary is a crucial step in saying yes to things you want to do, rather than things you feel obligated to do.

So, from this moment forward, I encourage you to banish 'should' from your vocabulary and reframe the things you're hoping to achieve. Instead of 'I should call my mum every day', how about, 'I'd like to feel close to my mum by calling her more often'? This acknowledges your desires, but leaves wiggle room to not have to make it happen immediately, or to the extent you consider ideal.

Myth 7: Someone doesn't like you. You must be a bad person!

I first met Zara McDonald, co-host of the popular *Shameless* podcast, when I was a senior editor at *Mamamia*, and she was one capable intern. She's now zoomed past me into podcasting stardom, along with co-host Michelle Andrews, another uber talented *Mamamia* alumna. They've also published a book and founded a Sydney-based podcasting company, Shameless Media. Not bad for a couple of 26-year-olds, hey?

You might assume that Zara is a fearless, gives-no-fucks, hear-me-roar kind of media personality. After all, she talks about some heavy and complex stuff on her podcast: health problems, ill family members, sex. In reality, though, Zara has always cared deeply about pleasing other people – and she's done a lot of work to unlearn her beliefs around criticism and self-worth.

'One of the greatest flaws of my personality forever has been this deep care about what people think, and it's probably why I was such a fucking goody-two-shoes as a kid,' she once said on the podcast.[23] 'I always conflated people liking you with you being a good person, and I thought if people don't like me that must mean that I'm not putting good into the world.'

It was only once Zara took a job in the public spotlight that she came to realise that nobody can please everybody. 'You have to rewire your brain to get your head around the fact that just because somebody doesn't like you, it doesn't mean you're a bad person,' she says.

Do you recognise yourself in Zara's words? I do.

Yes Women all too often take criticism as an objective truth about their worth, or talent, or ideas. (If a Facebook commenter tells me I'm looking fat or tired, I'll probably believe him; if a boss tells me my work's taken a nosedive, I'll take that right to heart.) They may even be their own worst critic, transforming any whiff of disapproval into an attack of self-criticism, and even dwelling on feelings of guilt about having done 'wrong' by whoever did the disapproving.

Placing this amount of stock in the opinions of others, Yes Women will often seek feedback from a wide range of parties before making a decision. They end up living their lives according to what will please the greatest number of people. They'll ring their friends, their mum, their sister to make life decisions that only really impact them: should I apply for this job? Should I cut my hair? Should I go on a third date with this person I'm not really vibing with?

But this approach can dilute your power. You can end up toning down your opinions, pursuing areas that don't truly spark passion, or holding back brilliant ideas.

And the truth is, you're *never* going to be liked by everyone. People can take against you for all sorts of reasons: you remind them of a friend who slighted them in school, or you have an offbeat sense of humour and they prefer quoting *The Simpsons*, or they envy your work ethic.

The cure to equating criticism with your self-worth is to remind yourself that even if someone doesn't love you or what you're doing, you're still a valuable, worthy person. And if you're in a situation where someone has disapproved of something you've done, it's also crucial to check any guilt. Ask yourself if you're *actually* guilty, or if the other person is simply guilt-tripping you (these are very different things). Then repeat after me: just because someone clucks their tongue and makes a passive-aggressive comment about you skipping the primary-school bake sale, it doesn't mean you've actually done anything wrong.

It can help to restrict your feedback-seeking to two or three trusted confidants or mentors, too, rather than seeking input from multiple sources.

Zara takes a similar approach. 'I have a certain amount of people around me who will pull me up if I'm not doing something right' – and if that trusted circle is supporting her, she figures she's doing okay.

If your trusted circle doesn't approve of your ideas or decisions sometimes, it's even okay to ignore their feedback. Untangle that criticism from your sense of self-worth, and filter through it to find the guidance that's most useful in achieving your goals.

Trying to bust these myths? You'll need to ruffle some feathers

Rejecting these deeply ingrained myths and finally saying no certainly doesn't have to mean confrontation and conflict. But the truth is, a certain type of person might prefer you be subservient and quiet. Here's a hard truth: some people won't like you asserting boundaries, so you're going to have to come to terms with not being liked.

On top of that, if you're ever going to innovate, or express a bold vision – be it a business idea that rubs competitors the wrong way, a controversial opinion, or a creative work that's different to everything else out there – you'll need to accept that some people won't get it, and some people won't appreciate it.

'Women who play big get criticised. Period,' as Tara Mohr puts it. 'One of the most important mental shifts a woman can make to support her playing big is to stop thinking of criticism as a signal of a problem and to start thinking of criticism as part and parcel of doing important work.'[24] Or as Helen Lewis writes in her book *Difficult*

Women, 'making progress means making enemies. There is no way to do feminism that will please everybody.'[25]

When it comes to getting over your fear of being criticised for pushing back or speaking out, it can help to realise the problem is rooted in larger issues – so when you say no, to paraphrase Maya Angelou, you're taking a stand for other women who are also in your situation. This doesn't mean being nasty or shouty (unless you have to be); the 'Difficult Woman', in Lewis's conception, 'is not rude, petty or mean, she is simply willing to be awkward, if the situation demands it; demanding, if the occasion requires it; and obstinate, if someone tries to fob her off'.[26]

And the beauty of unlearning the Yes Woman myths and asserting boundaries is that anyone who has a problem with that isn't worth your time, anyway. As Chimamanda Ngozi Adichie puts it, 'Of course I am not worried about intimidating men. The type of man who will be intimidated by me is exactly the type of man I have no interest in.'[27]

Chapter 6

Work out what you want (what you really, really want)

Unlearn the things that this world has thrust upon you, and your body, and your identity, and your voice, and your experience.

– Janet Mock[1]

I could write a whole book about the things I've spent time on that I didn't really want to do.

Working a corporate job in a law firm. Wearing high heels. Celebrating New Year's Eve. Paying bills, cutting carbs, and watching the *Lord of the Rings* (or any other film that takes more than two hours).

Some stuff – like death and taxes – is just part of life. But some things I could have chosen to say no to, I just didn't feel like I should.

What's more, it's taken me decades to figure out that I really *don't like* high heels, New Year's Eve, cutting carbs or ultra-long movies. Because here's the thing: sometimes, Yes Women have pushed aside their own needs for so long, they have trouble identifying what they actually want or need. We grapple with a sense of not recognising ourselves – and it's often after a major life transition. A career sabbatical, a relationship breakup, having a baby, moving out of the family home for the first time, retirement: these can leave us scrabbling around for threads of identity (hence the haircut-after-a-breakup cliché.)

But Yes Women can face this dilemma even in the absence of a major life transition. Sometimes, having lived their lives for two or three or four decades on a well-worn path of 'shoulds', they reach a certain age and ask – do I even like doing what I'm doing? What is it I really enjoy?

This is a challenge described particularly adeptly by Irish writer and actor Stefanie Preissner (a woman after my own heart), who wrote a whole book on her own struggle to say no. In *Can I Say No?* Preissner recounts that her lifelong struggle to 'get things right and fit in' meant that, as an adult, she realised she 'wasn't able to figure out who [she] was or what [she] actually liked or disliked'.[2] By the time she reached adulthood, she'd become 'so skilled at replacing [her] true feelings with more appropriate ones that eventually, years, later, [she] came to realise that [she] didn't know [her] true feelings any more'. She recounts: 'Like those children who stop crying because they know no one is listening, my feelings stopped making themselves known because what was the point?'

After decades of struggling to say no to expectations and requests, Preissner had lost her sense of self. As she puts it: 'The endless yes-es, compliance and people-pleasing wore me down until I was like the stump of my blue crayon.'[3]

Cultural expectations can play a part

Yes Women from all backgrounds and walks of life can struggle to differentiate their own needs from those of their family and community. But this can especially be the case if you've come from a family, or culture, that expresses very clearly the path you 'should' be taking through life, and what that 'should' look like at each step.

Imi Lo, the UK-based psychotherapist, art therapist and founder of Eggshell Therapy and Coaching, describes how in collectivistic cultures, women can face intense social pressures to conform: to look a certain way, study in specific fields, and marry a particular type of person by a certain age.[4]

In reality, of course, many women in these cultures don't want to follow those paths: 'Not all Asian women want to be a lawyer, a doctor, or an accountant. Not all Asian women want to bleach their skin white or to stay stick-thin. Not all Asian women want to be married by 30. Not all Asian women are quiet and submissive,' Lo writes. Thus, some Asian women are torn between two voices as they move through life – the family-pleasing, society-conforming self that asks 'What do *they* want?' and the true self, that asks 'What makes my heart sing?'[5]

It is not only women of Asian heritage who hear these competing voices, of course: in essence, each Yes Woman suffers from the conflict between pressure about what they 'should' do and what they truly want to do.

In my own secular, Anglo, middle-class, inner-city Melbourne circle, many young people I knew aspired to follow what's known as 'the golden path': a legal career consisting of clerk, then solicitor, then barrister, then hopefully silk, and perhaps judge. (It's no surprise I ended up working in the law myself, for a while.) Women following this path were expected to rack up university degrees, before having kids in their early-to-mid 30s, and then springing back into their high-ranking legal career without missing a beat. Owning one's own home and marrying a fellow professional were also part of this picture of 'shoulds'.

The path I've just described is the stuff of great privilege, and I'm certainly not complaining about having access to those opportunities. But most cultures and social circles have their own version of what a woman's life path 'should' look like – and often, Yes Women internalise these expectations and take years to realise that these 'shoulds' don't really resonate with our interests and values.

It can be daunting to admit that we don't want to live a life of 'shoulds' anymore. What's more, even if we know the path of 'shoulds' isn't right for us, it can be difficult to identify what we want to do instead.

Choice can be daunting

Meet Thea, a 39-year-old physiotherapist who recently left her 15-year marriage.[6]

Thea's husband was always the decision-maker in their relationship. He'd decide on the family dinner most days of the week, 'and it was pork ribs pretty much every Sunday', says Thea, who lives in Sydney's western suburbs. When Thea left the relationship, she felt a sense of freedom but was also confronted with a feeling that she didn't know who she was anymore, or what she wanted to do with the rest of her life.

She'd grown up in a family in which the men were breadwinners, and the women were 'the backbone of the home – they'd have the kids, do the dinners, keep the family strong', as she puts it. Those traditional gender roles were encouraged within the church her family attended – and their social circles, which revolved around church, left her with no doubt about what was expected of her as a woman. Divorce was taboo in her family and community, so when her relationship broke down, there was simply no script for her to follow.

'I was at the supermarket and I was like, what's my favourite thing to eat? I don't know. I guess I'll buy pork ribs,' she says.

It wasn't just choosing dinner that became daunting, either. 'I went through almost a small identity crisis,' Thea says. 'I did the cliché divorcee thing – I took a bunch of courses, pottery, calligraphy. I signed up for a volunteer program. I was like, am I a sporty outdoorsy type? Am I secretly arty? The choices were almost overwhelming.'

Thea is describing the tension between the narrow expectations imposed by her family, religion and marriage and the seemingly endless choices available to her as a Western woman in 2020.

This dilemma is not as contradictory as it sounds. It's possible for women to – on the one hand – want to break free of narrow gendered expectations of what they should do, and celebrate hard-won opportunities to go to university, join the workforce, and control their reproductive systems, and – on the other hand – feel daunted by the weight of choices now on our shoulders. It's like arriving in a restaurant and seeing a four-page menu: you can spend an age staring at the menu and still have no idea whether you want the toastie, the noodles or the salad.

We're now making about 35,000 conscious decisions each day.[7] That's a hell of a lot of deciding whether to say yes or no.

Rashida Dungarwalla, a Sydney-based psychologist, tells me these choices are even more overwhelming now that globalisation and technology have opened up a new world of options to us. Not only can you choose to work or have a family or study, or do all three – you can do them in the city you were born in, or you can apply for jobs overseas, or you can meet someone online and get married in a different country, Dungarwalla points out.

The options are, seemingly, endless.

Ultimately, having so many choices can be stressful and paralysing.[8] (Psychologists even have a term for this phenomenon: 'decision fatigue'.) We can also panic and make the wrong choice. (When people are given too much choice, psychologists say, they're more likely to choose things that make them less satisfied.)

What makes choosing all the more stressful, in our Western neoliberal society, is the societal attitude that 'people must choose for themselves, sometimes sticking to their guns, regardless of what other people want or recommend. It's called "being true to yourself",' as Sheena Iyengar, an expert on the psychology of choice, says in her TED Talk, 'The Art of Choosing'.[9] This attitude demands 'that everyone treat choice as a private and self-defining act', she says.

In other words, choices are now positioned as a necessary expression of personal freedom, an act of consciously defining who we are and what our values are. A t-shirt isn't just a t-shirt: it can signal our alignment with a particular ideology or social group. A haircut isn't just a haircut: it can indicate that we're a 'Karen', or that we're into punk music, or are aligned with the alt-right. The idea of choice-as-identity is also pushed by brands: are you an Apple or PC person? Do you drive a Ford or a Holden?

This capitalist-driven obsession with choice places constant low-level pressure on each of us to define ourselves through our choices:

where we live; what music we listen to; even what names we give our babies – which, as I once reported for *ABC Everyday*, are becoming increasingly 'unique' because of modern-day society's focus on individuality and self-expression.[10]

Technology can make it harder to know what we want

High on the list of things I've spent time on that I didn't really want to: staring at my phone.

You know the feeling: you've just settled down with that novel you really want to finish – and your phone buzzes. So you put down the book and check a text message. Then a Facebook notification pops up, so you have a read. Another buzz. Just one more swipe, one more tap … Until, 30 minutes later, you're still scrolling. Your brain's overloaded, your eyes are tired, and you can't even remember why you grabbed the phone in the first place.

The average millennial checks their mobile 150 times a day.[11] While some of these interactions are very helpful (how would I live without Google Maps!?), many others are mindless and automatic. It can feel as if our smartphones are sucking our time and energy – as if our phones are the boss of us, and not the other way around.

For Yes Women wanting to get clear on what they want, it can be helpful to set some boundaries around phone use. We'll be better placed to freely determine our priorities without those dozens of apps sucking up all our energy and attention – and without being at the beck and call of anyone who has our phone number (telemarketers included).

And if you're trying to prioritise deep thought, whether it's for study or doing your best at work, there's another reason to set some boundaries with your phone: scientific evidence suggests that phone use is damaging our abilities to focus and think deeply – it's literally rewiring our brains, as Catherine Price explains in her book *How to Break Up with Your Phone*.[12]

SIDE NOTE: Want to say nope to your phone?

Ready to take some simple steps to wrestle your phone addiction back into submission (rather than whittling your time away on Candy Crush and Instagram meme accounts)?

Try these:

Consciously introduce alternatives

One sneaky and effective way to reduce phone usage is to think about the key functions you really need your phone for – and delete everything else.

For example, in *How to Break Up with Your Phone*, Catherine Price suggests buying an alarm clock so you're not sucked into the rabbit hole of phone notifications the moment your eyes ping open in the morning.[13]

While you're at it, give some serious consideration to deleting at least one of your social media apps. I've deleted my Facebook messenger app – and while I still check and reply to those messages when I'm back at the computer, it's cut my engagement down from two dozen times a day to just a handful.

Put your phone in prison

In social settings, phone use is contagious: if one person gets their phone out at dinner, the rest of the family does, too.

So if you feel you want to spend more time on quality relationships and family time, consider setting some ground rules about phones in the house: banning their use at dinner time, while watching TV with others, or in the bedroom, for example. Even better, designate a specific place in your home as the 'phone prison' – the place where phones are locked up during those times.

You can even buy a time-locking kitchen safe for this purpose – or a tiny phone bed (outside your bedroom) to ceremoniously retire your phone to at night – if you're feeling cashed-up.

Say nope to work use in your personal time

As a journalist, it's *de rigueur* for me to engage with Twitter trends, sniff out story ideas on Facebook and contact sources on LinkedIn. As a result, the boundary between work and life can be awkwardly thin.

Many women in a range of industries are in different variations of the same boat: you might be expected to promote your business on Facebook, or have a schmick-looking LinkedIn profile, or post gorgeous product photos on Instagram – and above all, engage with conversations and responses, often after hours.[14]

There's no perfect solution to setting boundaries with work-related social media obligations. If your job allows you to shut off social media after-hours, do it – ideally, have the platforms or apps only on your work phone, and switch it off at 5.30pm or whatever. If after-hours social media promotion is a required aspect to your job, consider using a scheduling tool to create automated posts, so they will be published without you needing to log on after dinner. You can also try adopting a 'bare minimum' approach to social media for work: unless you're an actual 'influencer' (or work in a particularly visual field such as photography or floral design), your client base probably doesn't depend on whether you're crafting witty, compelling Instagram posts thrice a day. So make sure you have a simple website, limit yourself to an occasional Facebook post, and call it a day.

Make 'phone-check times'

As I write this, my phone's imprisoned in another room to minimise distraction – and I've set an alarm to tell me when I can finish writing and check my texts.

It's depressing that I need to contain myself in this way – but, hey, it works.

Consider designating certain times throughout the day where going online or checking your socials is alright – say, once in the morning, once at lunchtime, and once after work.

You might want to reply to messages only at set times, too – during one or two of your designated 'online times'.

Carve out phone-free moments

If you're a hardened phone addict, it's probably unrealistic to only check your phone three times a day. But you can still set small rules that deal with the worst of your distracted, obsessive phone-checking behaviour. You could vow to yourself never to use your phone when walking; to always keep your phone out of sight when you're catching up with a friend, or to never look at your phone when your partner's talking to you.

(Also – safety first, friends – vow not to text while driving, okay?)

These rules are particularly important if you're feeling frazzled, overwhelmed and strung out. As writer, activist and public speaker Anne Lamott once said: 'almost everything will work again if you unplug it for a few minutes, including you'.

So, how do you figure out what you want in life?

It's tricky. In a world of 'shoulds', and with endless choices and distractions, how do you work out what you truly want to do?

You can take the trial-and-error approach: give a few different hobbies and life paths a whirl, like Thea, and see what sticks. This approach is similar to the one Preissner describes in *Can I Say No?*:

> In an effort to find out who I was, and what I wanted in life, I had to reassess every aspect of myself to see if it was truly me or something someone had decided for me … From politics to brands of teabag, I had to test the fedora against the beret.[15]

You might want to also try some or all of these little tricks:

Ask yourself what you'll regret later

What will you regret when you're lying on your deathbed?

It's a morbid question, but an important one. So important, in fact, that Australian woman Bronnie Ware – a former palliative care worker – decided to put the question to dying patients and wrote a book about what she heard.

The number one regret of dying patients was: 'I wish I'd had the courage to live a life true to myself, not the life others expected of me,' Ware writes in her book, *The Top Five Regrets of the Dying*.[16] Of all the regrets and lessons shared with Ware as she sat beside their beds, this was also 'the one that caused the most frustration, as the client's realisation came too late', she writes.[17]

It might not surprise you to learn that Ware is a big proponent of learning to say no – no to things you don't have room for, in order to have room for the things you most want to say yes to.[18] 'We owe it to ourselves to honour our own needs and joy,' she adds.[19]

So, take a critical look at the expectations you're fulfilling – as well as the requests and invitations – that you might just regret at the end of your life. You might find some helpful clues about what you don't actually care about – and what you do. (I'm telling you, it's been years since I watched a three-hour movie, and I haven't looked back.)

Try a values-clarification exercise

Values are core beliefs and attitudes that direct your decision-making and behaviour and guide the way you look at the world. So it's worth reflecting on which key values define you – and to distinguish between activities and 'asks' that align with these values, and those that don't.

Values clarification exercises – a common method in cognitive behavioural therapy – generally involve choosing and writing down the three or five values that most strongly resonate with you.[20] (For example: adventure, collaboration, growth, security, versatility, wealth or loyalty.)

Not sure which values to choose? Imi Lo suggests teasing out the answer by searching online for a 'values list', and then studying one of these lists while asking yourself questions such as:

What makes me angry or passionate?
What brings me joy?
What have the 'highlight' moments in my life been?

Who do I most look up to and what qualities do they embody?
What would my seven- or seventy-year-old self want me to do?

Once you've narrowed your key values down to a list of three or five, try to list some specific goals and behaviours you want to start doing in line with those values. If one of the values you wrote down is 'adventure', you might set a goal of exploring more of your hometown. The new behaviours you adopt might be: walking a different way home once a week; planning a camping mini-break with a friend; or trying a new restaurant in your city once a month.

It might also be helpful to write down a list of the things you'll have to say no to in order to make those goals happen. For example, if you want to work on your creativity on the weekend, you'd better limit your big Friday nights out to special occasions.

What do you want to be known for?

Writing down a sentence or two about what you're best known for, and what you want to be known for, can help clarify what's really important to you.

In her oldie-but-goodie book *Nice Girls Don't Get the Corner Office*, California-based executive coach Dr Lois Frankel urges readers to finish this sentence: 'There goes a woman who …'[21]

Personally, I found it useful to adapt this slightly. Instead I suggest that, in 30 words or less, you finish a sentence starting with:

'In an ideal world, I am proudest of myself for …'
(Phrasing it this way takes away the focus on the perceptions of others.)

It can help to jot down a list of behaviours required to make that statement a reality.[22] So, if eating a family dinner together at least once a week means sitting out that dull 5pm meeting that you don't really need to be there for, do it.

Draw a pie chart

Visualising what parts of life dominate your mind and your time can similarly help you figure out where your priorities lie.

In her book *The Mother of All Jobs*, Christine Armstrong suggests drawing a pie chart of your life and allocating sections according to what takes up brain space: work, partner, exercise, social media, friends, home life, kids, grooming and dieting, hobbies, and so on.[23]

It worked for me: my own pie chart showed a shocking amount of social media time, and not as much time with my husband as I would've liked. It was an eye-opener, and it prompted me to get strict with my smartphone.

So get charting.

You might also then want to draw a second pie chart, showing what you wish to spend your time and focus on – perhaps reflecting the values you worked out above; comparing the two charts should give you an idea of what you'll need to stop doing to make space for your real priorities.

What makes you angry?

Anger gets a bad rap. As girls, we're taught that to be angry is to be unruly, unlikeable, un-Nice – so, as adults, Yes Women tend to be scared of their own anger.

But anger isn't always an unhelpful emotion. It's normal to feel anger in response to injustice, and anger can provide a clue that you're being treated unacceptably – by yourself, or by others.[24]

Anger is also a powerful tool that can drive change – for example, through protest. In fact, as Soraya Chemaly argues powerfully in her book *Rage Becomes Her*, contrary to the popular self-help rhetoric about anger management, 'the reality is that our rage is the most important resource we have as women, a force for creation rather than destruction, our sharpest tool against both personal and political oppression'.[25]

Anger can be a useful tool for Yes Women to gauge whether they're feeling mistreated by saying yes to others and no to their own needs – and to work out how they want to be treated instead.

So if you feel angry, tune into why that is. There might be a very good reason for your anger: you're feeling pressured into saying yes to something that doesn't suit you, for example.

Feeling anger that is justified doesn't mean you have to express your anger in a shouty way. You're more likely to get your way by being assertive, not aggressive (we'll discuss the difference between the two in the next chapter).

Some questions to ask yourself before you say yes

Still struggling to differentiate the 'shoulds' from the things you *really* want to do? If you're feeling uncertain, you can try to find out the reasoning behind your urge to say yes by asking these questions:

Am I doing this because I expect the other person to give something back?

If you want to give something to or do something for another person, do it because your head and your heart say it's a good idea – not because you expect something back.

If you're going to be resentful if you don't get something back – don't do it.

Am I doing this out of guilt?

This is another fast-track to resentment. Abort mission.

Am I doing it because I'm worried about what the other person will think?

The truth is, whatever you do in life, people will have their opinions – and there's nothing you can do to change that.

If you say no, somebody might be irritated or even think you're rude, sure. But if you say yes to everything – if you do everything 'right' – others equally might think you're a pushover (or a wee bit boring. Personally, I like a few quirks and a rebellious streak in a person).

The point is, regardless of whether you say yes or no, you can't win over everyone. So why waste energy focusing on it?

I'm not usually one to quote random, unattributed Pinterest memes, but this one's a goodie: 'What other people think of you is not your business. If you start to make that business your business, you will be offended for the rest of your life.'

Are my body and brain up to this?

Sometimes it's not other people demanding that you juggle 18 tasks to perfection while maintaining flawless winged eyeliner and well-groomed children. Sometimes it's your own inner voice insisting you have to do things a certain way – or just the fact that you're an extrovert with FOMO who loves trying all of the things, all of the time – that has you saying yes on autopilot.

Emma, a 29-year-old nurse from Townsville, told me she finally learned to set limits with herself due to the chronic pain she experiences from several conditions, including endometriosis and fibromyalgia:

> After I was diagnosed with endometriosis during surgery in my early 20s, the recovery was a lot harder than I'd anticipated and I was still in the mindset of, 'I should be going out multiple times a weekend.' I was really stuck in this mindset of what someone my age 'should' be doing.

She adds, 'I was very much still trying to pretend like everything was fine. I was smashing these two competing things together and, shock horror, it didn't work out.'

Emma's pain often caused her to cancel plans, and if she pushed herself to her physical limits, her pain often got worse. So she's re-learned what her body is capable of. Today, she blocks out time to rest. She's actively worked to untether her self-worth from the 'busy is best' mentality.

'Because we are so output-driven as a society, whether we as people want to be or not, we're constantly having to fight against this overarching process of how society works, which is that we spend the vast majority of our lives working and generating output, whatever that may be,' she says. But she's now accepted that 'if I am generating output at the same rate as everyone else, there are going to be significant sacrifices in my life for that to happen. Or if I want to make some vague attempt at a well-rounded life, my output will be significantly reduced compared to other people.'

She goes on: 'I've had to accept that there are things I want to do – but sometimes my body's the one saying no.'

Whether you live with a chronic illness, chronic pain or physical or mental ill-health, all Yes Women need to become comfortable with saying no to themselves sometimes.

If you haven't been looking after yourself recently – sleeping, exercising, eating healthy foods, resting your brain – that's a sign you might have to say no to your urge to make plans, and focus on your wellbeing for a bit. Nothing massive: you can start small, with a 20-minute bath or walk, if 'me-time' seems hard to come by.

Before saying yes to plans, also ask yourself: are you exceeding your limits? What is your body going to allow? How will saying yes make you feel later – exhausted, mentally drained, in pain?

Am I saying yes because I'll beat myself up otherwise?

Saying no to yourself can also involve putting your foot down with yourself, mentally, when your self-critical inner voice pipes up. If that voice starts telling you that busy is best, that slowing down is lazy, that your own needs are worth less than others – you'll need to tell that voice *enough is enough*.

You can think of this as setting boundaries, says Melbourne psychologist Krasi Kirova – except this time, it's an internal boundary you're setting (with yourself), rather than those external boundaries we set with others.

Setting internal boundaries feels a bit like standing up for yourself … against yourself.

'If someone rages at you, you'll set an external boundary and say, "that's not acceptable" and walk out of that room,' Kirova explains. In her clinical practice, she sees women feeling some rage or guilt towards themselves – and finding it hard to tell themselves to cut it out.

What can help them is to set limits – internal boundaries – with themselves, Kirova says: 'They might say, "You know what? I'm not going to do that. I'm not going to speak to myself in that way."'

Recognising cultural pressures vs. taking responsibility for your choices

If you're a Yes Woman, it's not your fault that you find it hard to say no. There are powerful social and cultural pressures teaching you to say yes.

At the same time, you've hopefully now identified which yes-es are deserved, and which aren't – and have started to unpack some of the key beliefs underpinning your 'yes training' – and so will have some control over what you do next.

'Part of learning to say no is to take responsibility for your choices, rather than dis-owning your choices and trying to lay the responsibility elsewhere,' says Krasi Kirova.[26]

'How often do we say, "I had to" or "She/he made me" when explaining why we did or didn't do something?' asks Kirova, adding, 'We need to take responsibility for our choices.'

As a Yes Woman, your challenge is to shake off the 'shoulds', step through the stress associated with endless choosing, and remind yourself that you're allowed to enjoy your life – to run it the way you like.

It's not your fault you were taught to always say yes – but you can take control back.

Trust me: living a life that's aligned to your values will feel a heck of a lot more rewarding than living a life crammed with things you did because you felt you 'should'.

Chapter 7

Getting to no

Me: 'Say no. Just say no. Try it: No. No no no. Got it? N-O.'
Me: 'Yes.'

– Anna Spargo-Ryan[1]

Just ask for a pay rise. Just tell your colleague to rack off. Tell your cousin you couldn't think of anything worse than attending her Tupperware party.

You've probably read articles, or heard self-help coaches, telling you it's that simple: 'Just say no,' or 'Just set limits,' or 'Just stand up for yourself.'

And if you're anything like me, you've thought: '*Oh, no worries!* I'd never thought of that before. I'll simply overcome my staggering anxiety about letting people down, even though I've struggled with it my entire life. DONE.'

It'd be hunky-dory if we could click our fingers and overcome our bad habits, wouldn't it? But – whether those habits are drinking, smoking, or saying no – it's simply not that easy.

That's why this entire chapter is dedicated to tackling the practical, behavioural aspects of saying no and laying down boundaries. We'll look at ways of saying no that are productive, comfortable, and – if you're desperately scared of violating the 'Nice girl' stereotype – that won't leave you feeling like an enormous b-word.

Repeat after me: 'no' doesn't have to be nasty

Let me assure you: saying no doesn't have to be rude, confronting, or aggressive.

The key is to say your no in an *assertive* way. That can be tricky for some of us, because many of us mistake speaking assertively for speaking aggressively – and as a result, we struggle to assert ourselves.

Being assertive is an essential part of setting boundaries – limits we set that identify reasonable ways for other people to behave towards us. Strong boundaries tell people, in the nicest way possible, what is you and what is *not* you, and what you'll accept and what you won't accept.

Being assertive isn't aggressive

Let's get clear on the difference between passive communication, assertiveness and aggression.

Being passive involves not expressing your opinions or feelings, and yielding to others' needs, ignoring your own rights or allowing others to do so. It's classic Yes Woman mode. (I bet you have a few of these emails in your outbox: 'Sure, yep, definitely happy to take on that project, and do you actually want it a day early? No worries, would love to! ☺ ☺ ☺')

Being aggressive, on the other hand, is behaving in a forceful, hostile or confrontational way. It's making your point in a way that seems angry, or disrespectful. (Can you make the 9am meeting? '*Hell no.*') Unsurprisingly, aggressive speech tends to put people on the back foot.

Being assertive sits somewhere in the middle of the spectrum – smack-bang in-between being passive and aggressive. Being assertive is about showing confidence and standing up for your personal rights in a calm, direct and honest way – without becoming upset or belligerent. (Can you make the 9am meeting? 'Unfortunately, my schedule's packed; I'm going to pass.') It means being able to express your point of view in a way that's clear, direct and also respectful.

Your tone, as well as your words, plays a part in determining whether your communication is assertive or aggressive. Consider the words 'thanks a lot' delivered in the following ways:

- With a sneery, sarcastic tone and a frown: scary, mean; likely to send Yes Women into a frenzy of self-doubt and stress about potential conflict
- With a brief smile and firm handshake at the end of a meeting: assertive and professional vibes; everything's fine here
- With an abundance of smiley-face emojis and a 'Definitely, whatever suits you!' thrown in at the end: passive communication, projecting some serious eager-to-please energy

If you're assertive, you say what you mean and you mean what you say. You're self-assured, confident, firm, and determined. You're respectful of yourself and others. You're able to ask for what you want, without twisting yourself up in knots about whether it will offend other people.

How good does that sound?

I'm quite into vegetable gardening, so I like to think of boundaries like crushed eggshells I sprinkle around my garden beds to keep out the slugs. If there's a gap in the eggshells, the slugs slither among my beautiful strawberries – my rights and wellbeing, in this analogy – and munch them up.

If you're a Yes Woman, the slugs in your life are the time-sucks, the favour-askers, the takers, and the others making demands you frankly don't have the time, energy and resources for. Without a strong eggshell boundary, you're open to being taken advantage of by those slugs – and you'll end up exhausted and resentful.

Learning to say an assertive – not aggressive – no is your way of lovingly sprinkling eggshells around yourself. *Slugs, begone.*

SIDE NOTE: A quick word of warning

A common stumbling block for recovering Yes Women is to go hard on the 'no' early on – perhaps harder than they even mean to.

When I was learning to say no, in my eagerness to assert myself I sometimes got the tone a bit too forceful, stubbornly doubled down on things that didn't matter all that much, and lost perspective. The art of saying no involves picking your battles – and sometimes, spending some time adjusting your tone so it falls on the right side of assertive (not aggressive).

Easing into it

A psychologist and feminist counsellor in Edmonton, Canada, Nicole Perry's work focuses on shame resilience and setting boundaries. I asked for her top tips on setting boundaries with family, and she kindly obliged – giving me a response that I found useful for saying no more generally. 'The biggest advice I can give is to only do it when you're ready,' she told me:

> One of the hardest parts about boundary setting is finding our resolve when we receive pushback. It often happens that people set sweeping boundaries early before they're ready to act on them – because a well-meaning friend or therapist has told them it's time, or because they're really hoping that by doing so, their family member will finally make the change they've been waiting for.

Unfortunately, if you set a boundary that you're really not ready for, and then the other person doesn't react in the way that you were hoping, it's easy to slide back into an old pattern of people-pleasing, Perry explains.

Keep in mind that in some families and cultures, the 'shoulds' are so strong that it can take longer to work up to setting even small boundaries. As Sahaj Kaur Kohli, founder of the popular *Brown Girl Therapy* Instagram, puts it: 'Boundaries aren't a one size fits all. They're shaped by our family/community dynamics and our cultures. For children of immigrants, setting boundaries can be the hardest thing. Sometimes it takes years to build up to making one that is too small for others to even notice.'[2]

And even if it takes years to build these little boundaries, Kohli writes, 'these are wins nonetheless. The one "no" after the 500th "yes". We have to start small. Setting boundaries with the expectation that they'll be respected is a privilege not everyone is accustomed to.'[3]

So take your time, and do what you've gotta do.

Then, when you're ready, here are some techniques that'll help you evolve from Yes Woman to expert boundary-setter.

Buy yourself some time

'No' is a complete sentence, or so the saying by writer and activist Anne Lamott goes. But for a Yes Woman, responding with a simple no feels preposterous.

If giving a flat-out no sounds too scary, you can always buy yourself some time before giving an answer. Try this one: 'Let me get back to you.' When you're put on the spot, you're not in a carefully considered position to say yes. So always reply with 'I'll get back to you' and then come back with the carefully considered response later.

This trick has worked wonders for Ramona, a Yes Woman I surveyed, who is often asked by her sister to dog-sit over the holidays.

In the past, she would desperately want to say no – but usually gave in after her sister 'hassled and guilted' her, Ramona tells me.

As she's grown older, Ramona has learned strategies to buy time before agreeing to a favour. 'I now say I would have to get back to her or double check if I was free, instead of immediately saying yes,' she tells me. 'This gave me more time to back out and set dog-sitting on my terms.'

When you don't want to give a hard no

If you're not totally against an invitation or 'ask' but the setting or level of commitment is too much for you, you can soften your 'no' by suggesting an alternative.

Say you're invited to an old friend's baby shower, but you've been trying to conceive for a year and you know all those pregnancy-related games are a recipe for misery. You can decline the invite with a sentence like this: 'I can't make it to your baby shower, but I'd love to see you next week if you have time for a walk?'

Or if an old colleague wants to grab a coffee and 'pick your brain' about job applications? You might respond, 'I'm flat-out and don't have time for a coffee, but is there a specific question or two you have in mind? I can email you back some thoughts when I get a moment this week.'

Or if you've decided to cut back on booze and a friend invites you to her cocktail night, go ahead and tell her: 'I'm not drinking during the week anymore and I'm steering clear of bars for a while, but I'd love to see you next week. How about brunch?'

This also works when you actually *do* want to see someone or do something, but are having a busy month. Say a friend's been keen to catch up, but you're up to your eyeballs in work. Try: 'This month's not good for me, but I'd love to see you once this big deadline passes. Can I give you a buzz when my schedule clears up and we'll make a plan?'

The art of the 'gracious no'

One golden rule of saying an assertive no is to keep it gracious. Remember, there's no aggression involved – so even a Yes Woman with the greatest fear of confrontation should be able to handle this approach.

The Tanya Plibersek 'no'

I sent out dozens of interview requests to busy, high-profile women as I was writing this book. From politicians to musicians, I aimed high with my pitch emails, half-expecting to never hear back from most of them. So I was pleasantly surprised to receive an email response from the office of Tanya Plibersek, member of parliament for Sydney and former deputy leader of the Labor Party.

When I opened the email, I saw Plibersek had declined my

request for an interview. But the thing is, she gave such a gracious and thoughtfully worded 'no' that her response taught me more than any interview could have done. Here's what she wrote:

> Dear Grace,
> Thank you very much for your kind invitation to contribute to your book. It sounds like an excellent project and with your experience writing for the Financial Times Group and *Mamamia* I'm sure it will be a success.
>
> I have very much enjoyed *ABC Life* and the stories you and your colleagues have covered so sensitively and thoughtfully there. [Here, she takes a few lines to detail articles she particularly enjoyed and mention what she actually liked about them.]
>
> While your book sounds great, I'm afraid I am not able to contribute to it at this time. The sheer volume of requests I get makes it impossible for me to do justice to your project.
>
> I look forward to seeing it in publication, and I wish you all the very best with it.
> Yours sincerely,
> Tanya Plibersek MP

There's a certain format to a gracious, professional written rejection – and it's personified by the above response letter, so I like to call it 'The Tanya Plibersek "no"'.

The Tanya Plibersek 'no' is best used for work requests or other formal modes of correspondence. It contains these ingredients:

- **Gracious thanks.** ('I appreciate this opportunity, and it sounds like an exciting project.') Give thanks for the opportunity and, if you like the idea or think it sounds like the project will be a success, let them know.
- **A brief explanation of your predicament.** ('I've had a range of commitments recently that have made it impossible to accept

them all.') By suggesting your rejection is down to circumstance or other commitments, it makes it clear your 'no' isn't personal.

- **Gracious declination.** ('Unfortunately, I'm unable to contribute right now, but I wish you all the best.') Note that we're not apologising – we're just declining the offer and sending goodwill.

There you have it. In just five or six lines, you've ducked out of that professional request – no hard feelings.

Everyday phrases to memorise

Not all requests require a formal rejection email, of course. Your cousin's request for babysitting help; your colleague's invitation to after-work drinks; an old friend asking you to look over her job application for her: all these requests can be knocked back in just a few words.

I strongly recommend memorising these four phrases:

'Sadly, I'm flat out right now. You know how it is.'
'I can't right now.'
'Not this time.'
'That won't be possible.'

If this feels scary, try starting with a few friendly words to soften your response – you can thank them for thinking of you, or tell them you admire the work they're doing. So the exchange might look like this:

They ask: 'Do you want to come to karaoke with some of the girls from the office?'

You say: 'Thanks for thinking of me, but I can't do it this time.'

They ask: 'Will you proofread my job application for me?'

You say: 'I admire how organised you are, but sadly I'm flat out right now – you know how it is!'

Make it a policy

It can also help to make certain rules or personal 'policies' about what you say no to. That way, when you turn something down, it's clear the rejection is nothing personal.[4] (An added bonus of this approach: it saves brainpower, as you don't have to mull over a decision if your policy has already made it for you.)

This kind of 'no' looks like this:

They ask: 'Do you want to come to this gig? The headliner comes on at 11pm.'

You say: 'I try to always hit the sack around midnight so I'll pass – but have fun.'

They ask: 'Should we get the kids together at one of those huge indoor play centres?'

You say: 'Not for me, thanks – I swore off play centres last time my kid threw up in the ball pit.'

They ask: 'Can you take a call from my neighbour to give her some free career advice?'

You say: 'Alas, I can't give career advice anymore because I barely have time to get my own paid work done, but I hope she finds what she needs.'

No apologies, no excuses

One thing you might've noticed about the examples above: they rarely apologise, and they don't spend time waffling on or giving detailed excuses.

Yes Women feel compelled to say 'sorry' a lot and give reasons when they decline an invitation or request. But to apologise makes it feel – to the other person, and to yourself – that you've done something wrong by saying no. And to launch into your reasons for saying no can invite a negotiation or seem like an invitation to the other person to push harder; in reality, often the asker won't challenge your 'no' – but they'll challenge the excuse you've given.

Another good tactic to keep the apologetic tone out of your 'no'?

Take a leaf out of American speaker and author Byron Katie's book, and try replacing the word 'but' with the word 'and':

'It sounds exciting, and I'm not able to make it this time. I'll look forward to hearing about it!'[5]

If you can't face the thought of not apologising (and I get it – it does feel uncomfortable for me even after a year of trying to kick the habit), feel free to just say sorry once and move on. Or end your 'no' with another friendly phrase: how about 'best of luck', 'enjoy' or 'wish I could be of more help'?

Withdrawing a 'yes' (because, yes, that's a thing)

We've all been there: Monday rolls around, and you realise you've completely overbooked yourself for the week.

You've had a bad night's sleep, you've got a headache, and the mountain of commitments before you is completely daunting: you've got life admin you've promised your partner you'll deal with; two coffee dates; an appointment with the accountant; four work deadlines; a meeting with your mentee; a gym class with your buddy; some sort of book-week creation you're meant to make for your older kid; and a playdate for your toddler. And that's only before Thursday.

The beautiful fact is: you can withdraw your previous yes-es!

It took me a long time to realise that a 'yes' isn't a blood contract. Things change, shit happens, and people are often more flexible than you realise. Try these:

- 'I've had a look at my to-do list and there's no way I'll be able to fit this in. All the best with it.'
- 'When I agreed to this, I thought I had the bandwidth to do a great job. I've now realised I need to step down from this commitment.'
- 'Unfortunately, I've looked more closely at my schedule and realised I can't fit another project in.'
- 'I don't have time to take meetings outside my paid work at the moment. Thanks for understanding, and best of luck with it.'

- 'On reflection, I don't think I'm the right person for this task. It's an exciting project, and with my packed schedule, I can't do it justice.'

We're going on a guilt trip: learning to flex your 'no' muscle

It might take some time getting used to the discomfort we can feel by not apologising or explaining our 'no'.

Just sit with it. And remind yourself that despite what your Yes Woman training has taught you, you're not doing anything wrong by saying no or setting a boundary. You don't have to give in to the guilt. With time and practice, you'll become more assertive, and saying no will become easier. You'll find that friends, relatives, co-workers and maybe even your kids will become more respectful of your time and your right to say no.

It can sound easier said than done, but the key message is: *hold your ground.*

Once you've said no to something, you might get pains of discomfort and guilt. You might start stressing that you've come off as pedantic, selfish or as an enormous bitch. But it's just like dealing with a toddler-tantrum: if you give in when the toddler makes a fuss, you're not teaching her limits – you're teaching her she'll get what she wants if she just pushes you harder.

So instead of capitulating, here are a few phrases to keep up your sleeve and fire back if someone pushes you on your 'no':

- 'I'd just rather not, but thank you so much for thinking of me.'
- 'I appreciate you getting in touch but I'm not doing [whatever it is] at the moment – good luck.'

And if you still really struggle to say no, get practising. Yes, *literally*. Write down the phrases you're going to use and have a few trial runs in the privacy of your own home before you start using them IRL.[6]

And go easy on yourself if it takes a while to get it right.

The first few times, saying no might make you feel uncomfortable. You may have to say the word dozens of times before it loses its hold on you.

Practice makes – well, not perfect. We're done with perfection – but better.

Chapter 8

A friend in need

> If we treated ourselves the way we treated our best friend, can you imagine how much better off we would be?
>
> – Meghan Markle[1]

Women's friendships are a powerful force.

Our friends aggressively support us, send us excellent memes, and think we're great despite (or perhaps because of) our awkward habits.

They know us well enough to give insights we might've missed. They defend us and reassure us. They believe we deserve the world. They are, as Jane Fonda once put it, 'a renewable source of power'.

For good reason, female friendships are celebrated widely in pop culture. There are countless TV shows about the bond between women – from *Sex and the City* and *Girls*, to *PEN15, Broad City,* and *Grace and Frankie*. And, of course, *Friends*. There are songs about getting by with help from our friends, leaning on friends, counting on friends, and being able to tell when you're going to be friends. There are quotes about friends being the family you choose, and friends being as rare and valuable as diamonds, and friends being the ones who reply to your frenzied texts at 4am.

And because friendships are – for the most part, rightly – so revered and celebrated, it can feel mean-spirited and uptight and, well, not very *friendly* to tell a friend no.

This chapter looks at saying no to friends in a few contexts – from declining favours from much-loved mates, to brushing off acquaintances when you just don't have the time for a coffee catch-up.

But let's start with a Yes Woman's number one friendship issue:

the *toxic* friend. Toxic friends tend to stick their thumbs right into our Yes Woman pressure points – they overstep our boundaries, make unreasonable demands, and guilt-trip us when we try to say no.

Identifying and dealing with a toxic friendship can feel tricky – but for a Yes Woman, learning to stand up to a toxic friend can feel incredibly freeing when done right.

You're toxic, I'm slippin' under ...

At first, Stella's friendship with Essie was intense and exhilarating. The two hit it off in dental school, spent two or three nights a week hanging out at Essie's place, and posted countless cute Instagram photos documenting their adventures together.

But when Stella got a part-time job, she didn't have the time to catch public transport to Essie's every time, so she suggested they start meeting somewhere in the middle – and Essie reacted with hurt and anger.

'She was kind of like a jealous boyfriend; she got quite cold, and she was like, "I just don't think you're making the same effort in our friendship as you used to,"' Stella recalls.

Months later, Stella came out as bisexual and started dating a woman.

'When I told Essie about my girlfriend, she was one of the first people I told. And she just hated any discussion of it,' Stella tells me:

> Then she started to get really shitty that I didn't do the stuff I was 'meant' to do. In her eyes, we were meant to be doing the things at the same time: we were going to dental school together, we'd go on and get jobs at the clinic next to each other, we'd have these boyfriends, and we'd end up getting married at the same time. And every time I would start deviating from that, she'd get angry.

The friendship limped along, but Stella felt like she was walking on eggshells. If she was unwell and had to cancel plans, Essie sulked. If she didn't post on Instagram about a fun activity they'd done together, Essie would say she felt underappreciated.

'It's like she was keeping receipts: "Look at all this stuff I do for you and you never do back to me," is what I got told over and over again,' says Stella.

The tension came to a head when Essie began planning her wedding and Stella couldn't keep up with all her demands.

'She wanted us to buy these $500 dresses, and wanted everyone to get these professional spray tans done on the same date, and wanted everyone to get these manicures done on the other side of town,' recalls Stella. 'Then she asked me to make the invitations and all the stationery and she gave me three days' notice to make the wedding programs, and I'd already helped her organise her wedding cake.'

But it wasn't enough for Essie, who sulked and sent messages saying: 'I feel like you've been a bit distant, and you haven't been liking my photos online,' Stella recalls.

When she cancelled Stella's maid-of-honour speech the day before the wedding, Stella knew she had to end the friendship.

♣

Stella's describing a classic toxic friendship – characterised by a friend who guzzles up your time, money and energy, according to Dr Hannah Korrel, a Sydney-based clinical neuropsychologist, registered psychologist, and author of *How to Break Up with Friends*.

Bad friends, Korrel wrote in an article for *Sunday Life*, are 'the ones that make you feel like you are walking on eggshells, never reciprocate, put no effort in, are passive aggressive or just plain aggressive aggressive. Ultimately, they leave you feeling exhausted, used and emotionally battered.'[2]

These toxic friends can also be what author Mark Manson has described as 'emotional vampires', so called because they tend to drain the emotional energy out of everyone they come in contact with. 'They're exhausting. They need constant attention. They always have some crisis or major life event. They're experts at eliciting emotional reactions out of others and then feeding off those emotions, regardless of whether they're positive emotions or negative emotions,' he writes.[3] 'Emotional vampires also believe that little to nothing that occurs is their fault – and lack the self-awareness to recognise their self-defeating patterns,' he adds.

Korrel says, 'The first thing I've been saying is, go with the feeling. If you feel worse after the interaction then that's a pretty good sign' that it's not a good friendship. If you're maintaining contact with this person because they need a shoulder to cry on and you feel bad, that's not enough to hold a friendship together.

'There is no such thing as an altruistic friendship,' Korrel explains. A true friendship is about give and take.

Ending a toxic friendship

We can end up holding onto friendships that aren't good for us because we've been taught true friendship means loving someone enough to give without expectation of getting something back. Or because we're not sure if they're really being unreasonable. Or because we do want to keep these people in our lives, even if we don't want to give quite as much of ourselves as they're asking. Or because it's hard to make new friends in your 20s and beyond – and, well, we don't want to be lonely.

But none of those excuses is a legit reason for staying in a toxic friendship. And as much as I hate to break it to you – a relationship like the one described above isn't actually a friendship at all, it's a one-sided martyrdom, says Korrel.

So how do you actually end a toxic friendship?

One golden rule is to not break up with your friend in the heat of the moment.

'Don't do it quickly. It's a planned and measured approach,' Korrel says. It's also best to avoid a mud-slinging match, where you go into the nitty-gritty detail of every little thing they've done wrong, she adds: 'All that's going to do is open the floodgates and give the toxic friend an opening to argue with your reasons.'

Your aim, instead, is to approach the breakup with honesty, focusing on your own feelings and needs – specifically, the fact that you're no longer able to invest in the relationship. Avoid the temptation to ghost your friend or abruptly block their number like some kind of petty teenager – it's important to act with maturity and honesty here.

'A breakup actually is about you and what you're choosing to do with your time and your energy and your money from now on,' Korrel says. 'You are saying, "I'm no longer able to put the time and the energy and the money into this relationship."'

Keep it clean: make it clear your decision has been made, wish them the best, and resist further attempts to re-engage.

Not breaking up, but pulling back: the friend who wants more than you can give

What if your friend's not controlling or nasty, but is simply trying to force a closer relationship than you're interested in pursuing?

Perhaps you appreciate this friend as a person, and are genuinely pleased when you grab coffee with them every couple of months – but you're constantly feeling bad about batting off her requests to go away on girly weekends together, and can't seem to keep up with her daily voice messages.

This is a step down from a toxic friendship, where 'there's nothing wrong with them, but we can't commit the kind of time they're seeking in a relationship, and [there's] guilt associated with that', says Korrel.

Often, these situations occur when your friendship stable is already full – say, you have five or fifteen close-ish friends already, and feel you just might not have enough yes-es to go around. If that sounds harsh, rest assured it's a theory held by many researchers, who say humans are only built to handle five very, very close relationships; fifteen good friends; and fifty friends overall. (We can also handle

150 meaningful contacts – known as 'Dunbar's number' after British anthropologist Robin Dunbar – as well as 500 acquaintances and 1500 people you can recognise.)[4]

'It's actually really normal for you to have friends who fluctuate in and out of these levels,' says Korrel. It's also normal for an individual to fluctuate in terms of how much time and energy she's able to commit to each of those friends, she says.

So how do you handle it if a friend or acquaintance is trying to edge into your inner circle, and you just can't find the time or mental energy?

It can be tempting to 'pussyfoot around it [by] telling white lies', says Korrel. ('I'd love to join your book club, but I'm busy this month!') But the most effective – and arguably, most respectful – way to proceed is just owning where you're at and saying: '[A]t this point of my life, I know I'm letting you down, but I can't put in as much time and effort as I know you want from me', Korrel says.

Rather than spreading yourselves thin over dozens of distant friends and acquaintances, this tactic can help free up time and mental energy – and your 'yes-es' – for a distinct few close relationships.

Saying no to your good friends (even though you love them to bits)

All this is not to say that you can never say no to your besties. It's absolutely possible to graciously say no to even your 'magic circle' of five, ten or fifteen good friends – whether it's because you're too busy, your mental health requires you have a good lie down, you're not comfortable with the request because it edges into financial or business territory, or you simply have zero interest in the singles party they're trying to rope you into.

Kate Leaver, London-based journalist and author whose books include *The Friendship Cure*, is a firm believer in saying no to mates 'when you need to, and to be honest, even when you [just] *want* to'.

'There is no school of thought I would endorse that says that friendship means you say "yes" all the time, no matter what someone asks you,' Leaver tells me. 'I think friendship requires commitments and the investment of energy and love and dedication to another person, but I don't think that is unconditional.'

There's no question it can be much harder to say no to good friends than it is to unpaid work or random acquaintances: '[W]hen it's someone you love, your instinct can be, I'll do anything you want, to the moon and back,' as Leaver puts it.

And sometimes, it's completely healthy and fine to say yes to an event or favour you're not crazy about – not because you're feeling pressured or trying desperately to gain your friend's approval, but as an act of love. (Leaver once asked her friend to attend a gig of an artist her friend wasn't a fan of – and the friend accepted. 'I did consider her attendance at that event as a gesture of friendship,' she says.)

But being comfortable enough to say no is a sign that you're in a healthy, loving, compassionate relationship, Leaver says.

SIDE NOTE: Not sure what to say? I wrote you some scripts

Wondering what exact words to use when rejecting a good friend's favour, request or invitation? Try these:

When your mental or physical health makes the request difficult

Feel free to say something like: 'I'm sorry, my mental health is not in a place right now where I can do that' – or adapt your response depending on your closeness to your friend and your comfort levels.

'I think you can tailor your response depending on how comfortable you feel to tell the truth,' says Leaver. 'Our dearest friends can make us feel safe if we say, "I'm too scared to leave the house," or "I'm having a flare-up of my fibromyalgia,"' she says. It's up to you exactly how much detail you want to go into, and it doesn't have to be a full-blown life story or a really exposing moment, Leaver says.

Ultimately, while you don't owe the details of your health issue or disability to anyone, being upfront about any mental health issues or invisible illness you live with can help build understanding and compassion; reassure your friends that your 'no' is nothing personal; and make friendships closer and more manageable long-term.

When your friend asks a money- or work-related favour
Your best bet: explain you have a policy against mixing business with pleasure, or loaning money to friends, if applicable. Try: 'I'm excited to hear you're starting your own business, but I promised myself a long time ago I wouldn't invest in business ventures of anyone I'm close to – I'm just not good at mixing friendships and money. It sounds like a great idea and I'm sure it will be a big success.'

When you're just not into whatever your friend's suggesting
It's fine to admit that something's not your thing and suggest another option (or make an additional catch-up time) instead: 'You know, I'm not crazy about costumes, so I'll let you go to that Halloween do with the rest of the girls this year. But I'd love to see you for dinner if you're free next week?'

Two golden rules when accepting social commitments

Hands up if you've ever enthusiastically accepted three or four separate plans for the weekend, only to dread your jam-packed schedule the moment Friday night rolls around.

Keep your hands up if you've ever felt a powerful rush of relief when a friend cancels on you, because you were feeling overbooked.

Yeah, me too. On both fronts.

As a people-loving extrovert, I'm guilty of signing myself up for way too much – often leaping between coffee with one friend, an exhibition with another, and drinks with the girls. If I'm feeling bad about neglecting a friend for a month or two, I'll try to wedge in some plans on a Sunday morning. If I miss my old workmate from a past job, I might throw in a walking date with her, as well.

Before I know it, it's Sunday night and I'm completely exhausted from all the social commitments I've ploughed through – cursing past-me for signing up for wall-to-ceiling engagements. What was meant to be some enjoyable, leisurely friend-time has become an obligation, and I'm sometimes not relaxed enough to enjoy these catch-ups as much as I'd hoped.

There are two brilliant rules I've recently learned to apply when I feel myself giving in to this tendency to say yes to too many social engagements.

Ask: would you do it tomorrow?

The first is a trick taught to me by Zara McDonald and Michelle Andrews (it's actually a trick Michelle learned from her dad – *thanks, Mr Andrews!*).

This strategy involves asking yourself: would I agree to do this thing tomorrow?

The idea is to 'only say yes if you would push everything off your plate to do it tomorrow or right now', says Michelle, 'because it's easy to say yes to things in the future'.

If a plan sounds like a drag that you wouldn't sign up to tomorrow, don't agree to it at all. As Zara explains: 'If you're really not going to want to go to that thing tomorrow, you're not going to want to do it in a month – and then it's just going to be more awkward to cancel at the last minute.'

Would your tired, most introverted self say yes?

Another trick I learned is to consider what I'd be up for doing on my most tired, introverted day. It's a tactic described by Stefanie Preissner in her book *Can I Say No?*:

> When I'm in my extroverted phases I need to be really careful. I always want to say, 'Yes!' to offers made to me on those days. But

I've learned to say, 'Can you leave that with me?' so I don't throw introvert Stefanie under the bus or let people down. I call up my most introverted day and think, would I be able to do what is being asked of me on that day? If it's a yes, I'll generally say yes.[5]

SIDE NOTE: When to say yes to a friend (a quick and dirty checklist)

- I want to do this thing
- I have the time, energy and resources to do it
- We both give and take in this relationship, and this favour is something they'd do for me
- It's a big event, and it feels important to show up to the friendship
- My mental and physical health will allow for me to do this thing
- I'd say yes to this event/invitation if it were tonight or tomorrow
- I'd probably say yes to this thing even if I was having a tired and introverted day
- I'm not doing it because I feel it's the only way to gain their love or affection, or because I'm scared they'll get angry or guilt-trip me if I say no

Chapter 9

Fam, damn

> 'No worries if not,' I cry cheerfully to my sobbing family as they sit around my death bed. 'No worries if not!' my final breath expelled. 'No worries if not!' stands my epitaph.
> But reader, there were worries.
>
> – Milly Thomas[1]

What is it about family that makes the word 'no' feel impossible?

We tend to view our parents as 'Those Who Must Be Obeyed', as Brooklyn-based editor, writer and self-described recovering perfectionist Sarah Knight has written, and that's a sentiment that resonates with Yes Women the world over.[2]

Countless women have told me, during interviews for this book, that they've struggled to knock back requests from parents or other relatives – be it an invitation to lunch with that weird uncle, or a request for babysitting help from a cousin. Real-life examples I came across in my surveys include:

- Robin, in her early 30s, attended a family reunion with her dreadful relatives to support her mother. 'I felt physically uncomfortable and anxious but I felt obligated to attend because of a perceived debt to my mother for past assistance given to me,' Robin told me. 'I hoped she would tell me I didn't have to go.'
- Rachelle, in her late 20s, agreed to see her father, who had been abusive to her and her mother throughout her life. 'I felt obligated to do it after he begged,' she tells me. 'What sort of person would I be if I said no?'

- Tatiana is in her 60s and recently agreed to host a whole-family gathering because her mother demanded it. 'I felt I had no option but to oblige her,' Tatiana tells me. 'I cleaned and rearranged the whole house to accommodate the crowd and to make things look as good as they could when I had no money to spend,' she adds. On the day, she was so anxious and upset that she suffered debilitating tummy troubles.

It doesn't matter how grown-up we are, the age we left home, whether we've moved far from our home town or whether we have kids of our own – telling our family no can make us feel naughty, rebellious, and sick with guilt (or in Tatiana's case, give us a dodgy tummy) even when the alternative – saying yes – is also making us stressed out, sick or miserable.

It's a lot. That's why saying no to fam requires a chapter all to itself.

Why is it so damn hard to say no to our family?

At some level, most of us feel we owe our parents. In most cases, they literally *made* us. Their approval has always motivated and encouraged us: they were there to cheer us on when we took our first steps, learned how to eat real food, and stepped through the school gates for the first time. We also spent the most formative years of our life learning that they're the boss, and they know best.

Most of us also really love our families. We often also *like* them. So it makes sense that rejecting their requests or disregarding their wishes feels uncomfortable – and can make us anxiously anticipate a conflict over even small knock-backs.

Depending on your cultural background, there may be different expectations and obligations that further ingrain the value of respecting your parents, and make it even more difficult to say no. Psychologist Rashida Dungarwalla puts it this way: 'Sometimes collective cultures require you to believe that you have to put other people before yourself – and if you're not doing that, you're not feeling like you are a good member of that community.'

Of course, regardless of your cultural background, most of us have ongoing relationships with at least some of our family members – meaning the repercussions of brushing off their demands can feel longer-lasting (and thus, more daunting) than saying no to a telemarketer, colleague or acquaintance. As a result, we often feel that pushing back on familial demands just isn't worth the conflict, guilt-trip or other headaches we fear will come from saying no.

When to say no: finding the balance, and working out where your limits lie

This chapter isn't about to argue that we should all callously break up with our relatives whenever we find their invitations vaguely irritating ('No, I'm not free for a family Christmas photo shoot. TAKE THAT!')

As with all relationships, family ties do generally involve some give and take – and sometimes it's worth saying yes to obligations that aren't our first preference. If you want a loving, reciprocal relationship with your brother, for example, you'll want to occasionally accept his invitations to a birthday lunch even though he's two hours away (urgh). And if your cousin asks you to be a bridesmaid and you value that relationship, it's maybe worth agreeing enthusiastically, even if you privately hate the thought of posing all day in a fuchsia satin dress.

But it's also important to draw healthy limits around your own privacy and autonomy – whether it's saying nope to relatives who offer repeated, unsolicited opinions on your parenting decisions, or setting expectations with an overzealous mother-in-law who regularly drops by unannounced.

There are other boundaries Yes Women can absolutely benefit from drawing with families for the sake of your own health or wellbeing. You absolutely don't have to 'grin and bear' your family's toxic guilt-tripping or rigid expectations that you'll follow a particular life path, and you don't have to put up with cruelly critical remarks, such as body-shaming and name calling.

It sounds obvious, but setting boundaries starts with getting clear, with yourself, on what those boundaries are – and what your values are as an individual.

Say your mum disapproves of your decision to pursue a freelance creative career and tends to make snide remarks about how you could have made a great doctor. Getting really clear on the fact that you value your creativity and freedom in your work – and that you need to set a limit with your mum and let her know you're not keen on her unsolicited advice – can embolden you to actually go ahead. (On the other hand, if you actually value a high income and a stable career, her words may resonate with you and cause you to rethink your job.)

When it comes to balancing individual values with those of the family, particular tensions can arise here for children of immigrant parents or 'third culture kids' – particularly when their parents are from a collectivistic culture, which emphasises the goals of a group as a whole over the needs and desires of each individual.

'You are being asked to follow values or ways of living according to one cultural community, but then [outside of your family] you are living in this different culture – potentially in a society that values being an individual,' says Dungarwalla. 'I think it's a fine line between how do we keep our agency and autonomy, and at the same time recognising you don't want to completely ostracise your cultural community,' she adds.

This tension can arise, for example, 'if you're getting asked to come to all of these different cultural events or days – and you feel like you're constantly saying yes and going to them all without having capacity,' and feeling overwhelmed and put-upon as a result, says Dungarwalla.

Working out your own values – and where you need and are able to set boundaries – can take time. You may also need some space to figure out who you are without being told who you're supposed to be.[3]

You may find that your values and goals are so different to those expected of you by your family, culture or wider society that you need to strike out boldly on your own and work hard at setting boundaries. Alternatively, you may be surprised to find that your values and goals are actually rather aligned with those of your family or culture – but you want to be able to choose them of your own volition.

Once you are able to pick your own values and set your own limits, you might find the pressure eases, Dungarwalla says. (If you quit your freelance creative career and decide to become a doctor, after all, you'll be doing it out of knowledge of your own values and having set your own limits.)

'A sense of relief can come, maybe later in life, if the pressure is slightly removed from the family or the community, and then you are picking and deciding what you do or don't want to be involved in,' explains Dungarwalla. 'Then you're feeling you have a sense of autonomy and then you feel you actually have made the choice.'

The two commandments of family boundaries

Regardless of whether you're dealing with some of the more challenging and meaty issues I've just mentioned – or whether you just want to push back on the occasional family reunion – it's crucial to accept two simple principles I've come across in my research.

Firstly, as an adult, **you have the right to enjoy your own life**, *even if that means disappointing your parents or other relatives.* Accepting this truth involves giving yourself permission to make choices your family may not agree with – rather than externally seeking that permission.[4]

A second, related principle for all Yes Women to adopt is: **you don't have to feel guilty about prioritising your happiness and wellbeing, or refusing to take on your family's issues as your own.**[5] In other words, taking care of yourself and becoming healthy and happy doesn't mean you don't love your family, or are not being loyal to them.[6] And, as Sahaj Kaur Kohli puts it, prioritising your mental health does not mean you are rejecting your parents, culture, or community.[7]

Start gently; escalate as needed

If you're feeling daunted at the idea of setting limits with your family, take a breath: setting boundaries doesn't have to be callous.

You don't even have to go in hard with the 'no-es' straight away, according to Canadian psychologist Nicole Perry.

'The thing I find is that people can often equate boundaries with saying no to other people and asserting ourselves,' Perry tells me. 'That's part of it, but setting boundaries, in my view, is so much more than just saying no. And honestly, saying no to other people may not be the best or even easiest place to begin.'

She urges readers to start small – because making huge changes all at once can be overwhelming for our nervous systems, and it more often results in us going back to where we started, she says.

> We can get so excited about the prospect of setting boundaries (because we're DONE with letting other people walk all over us! And tired of feeling tired all the time!) that sometimes we swing from one end of the pendulum to the other. And then it doesn't take much – a bit of guilt maybe – to swing back to the other side again.

So – take it easy. It's best to only start saying no when you feel ready to deal with potential pushback. As Nicole Perry says, this might mean gathering your strength, and working with a therapist so you feel more resourced to handle what happens in the aftermath.

Another way of gently easing into setting boundaries with family is to start by setting small boundaries in ways that don't involve the word 'no': 'It can come in really small steps – even just taking extra long in the shower for yourself throughout the day, and if you build up these small habits then you have more time for yourself,' says Dungarwalla.

Go ahead, make your boundaries clear

Once you've eased yourself into the idea of setting boundaries with family – and if you feel you haven't quite been heard – it may be time to set your limits. Your best bet is to be gentle, calm and kind – but very clear – when telling your family what you need and what your boundary is.[8]

If you're dealing with a relative who tends to take the word 'no' as a rejection or a sign you don't love them, it can help to make it clear you're coming from a place of love ('You know I love you, but I'm going to make my own decisions about who to date.')

Gentle, clear boundary-setting looks like this:

- 'Uncle Joe, I love you, but it's too stressful to drive between three different events on Christmas Day, so that's not going to work for us. I'd love to see you on Christmas Eve if you're free?'
- 'I know you're trying to give advice to help me, but I don't need you to parent anymore; I'd love for you to just listen and support me on this one.'
- 'I know going to Mass means a lot to you and *yiayia*, but it's not for me, and I'm not going to join you this week.'
- 'Thanks for thinking of me, but I can't make the family reunion this year.'

What next?

Sometimes you calmly and directly set your boundary – and your parent or relative walks all over it. What then?

Try these:

Set consequences

Psychologist Krasi Kirova says, 'If the person isn't picking up on what you're trying to tell them, you move to being assertive, and then if that's not working you can move down the continuum and that's where you need to set some consequences.' She suggests thinking of setting boundaries 'on a continuum, so at one end of the spectrum you start off with these brief suggestions, even body language.'

So if your mother-in-law comments about your low-cut top, even raising an eyebrow can be a good way of expressing your dislike without actually saying no. If she keeps making those comments, at a later point you can escalate slightly to calling the comment out in a light-hearted way.

If you don't yet feel comfortable saying a flat out, 'No, I don't like that,' Kirova suggests 'you might first of all say it jokingly: "Thanks, I didn't realise I was asking for opinions on my clothes" – it's still in a light way.'

If she keeps going, you can set some consequences. (My suggestion: if your mother-in-law relentlessly criticises your clothing, stop inviting her over so much, so she doesn't have the opportunity.)

In other scenarios, consequences might look like this:

- Your little brother Dave constantly bums money for rent and never pays you back – but he's happy to splurge on boozy nights out with friends. You've told him you expect to be repaid within the fortnight, but there's no money in sight. The solution? Lay down the law, and stick to it: it's as simple as repeating the line, 'I can't lend you money anymore.' *Sorry-not-sorry, Dave-o.*
- Your mum insists on disciplining your kids with a smack whenever you visit her – and while you're super uncomfortable with corporal punishment, your mother won't relent ('My house, my rules!'). The consequence: you explain to your mum that you won't be bringing the kids for visits anymore. She can come to yours – and play by *your* rules.

Remember, you can't 'fix' others

What if the other person keeps walking over your boundaries, ignores the consequences you're laying down, and just won't respect your limits?

I'm reminded here of an episode of the advice podcast *The Struggle Bus*, which dealt with the question from a listener: 'How do I set boundaries for my mum when it comes to our wedding and our whole marriage?' The listener was planning a radical feminist, atheist, Marxist wedding between two women – and was trying to dance around the disapproval of her own evangelical Christian mother, who didn't seem to understand, or approve of, the relationship.

The listener asked: 'How can my fiancée and I reflect our values and who we are without my mother thinking we will go to Hell? How can I set boundaries while helping my mum feel loved and included?'

The hosts, Katharine Heller and Sally Tamarkin, made a great point: 'You can be kind and you can be empathetic, but if you're trying to prevent her from being upset, that's not possible.' The best they could do is try to 'turn the page and say, this is how we're going to do things now' – and let the mum choose whether to come along for the ride, they concluded.

Ultimately, it's crucial to remind yourself that focusing on fixing others doesn't work, says psychologist Nicole Perry. 'We can get caught in thinking that the work of boundaries rests in dealing with other people. Really, a large majority of the work rests within us. Remember, boundaries are about honouring our body wisdom and living in line with our values, not changing other people.'

Krasi Kirova takes a similar view. 'Don't be so concerned with the other person's reactions,' she says. 'You may have no impact on them, but it's really about your own self-respect.'

In other words, your family may have different values or political views – and while that can feel disappointing or hurtful, you can't necessarily change them.

Or, to return to our earlier example: your mother-in-law might keep making judgey comments about your outfits. You may not be able to stop her – but by gently asserting your boundary each time, at least you'll be honouring your own values.

When to cut ties

When you begin setting boundaries and taking care of yourself, family members will often attempt to pull you back into the old system and roles. You don't have to comply. Their refusal to respect your boundary is their own issue.[9]

There are some family situations that just aren't healthy or sustainable long-term. If your parents or relatives are critical or dismissive of who you are and what you do with your life – ridiculing or criticising your sexuality or religion, for example – it can be vitally important for your sense of self-worth and confidence that you draw limits and perhaps even walk away, if the relationship is toxic.

Perry says some things you might want to look for in helping you decide if you're ready to step back from a relationship include:

- It's hurting you
- There has been trauma or abuse that hasn't been repaired
- You no longer want to be in it
- You've outgrown the relationship
- It's causing feelings of resentment or bitterness
- The other person isn't willing or able to change
- The other person shows a lack of accountability for the hurts that have been caused
- You've been pouring a lot of energy in, and don't feel you're gaining anything back

If any of these sound familiar, you may wish to take a step backward with the relationship. This can – but doesn't need to – involve cutting ties permanently, says Perry.

'We think that when it comes to relationships, we need to be either all in or all out. As it turns out, we can create boundaries within relationships, if we choose. We can take a step backward while staying in connection with people,' she says.

For example, rather than walking away from a relationship permanently, you could reduce your contact or change the type of connection you engage in with them: rather than endless face-to-face support sessions, you could try side-by-side activities, suggests Perry.

♣

Ultimately, setting boundaries with families or family members can feel tricky. 'It's okay to take your time. Boundary setting is a process, and as healing as it is, it's not easy,' Perry says:

> So, breathe easy. As you learn about boundaries and consider making changes, know that you don't need to jump into action. You don't need to do anything differently just yet. To be honest, when we push ourselves too hard, too quickly, it can end up taking longer to get where we're aiming to go.

Allowing yourself that time and space, and moving at your own pace, will support your growth.

Chapter 10

Meet me halfway: give and take in dating and relationships

When someone shows you who they are, believe them the first time.

– Maya Angelou[1]

I once went on a date that I regretted almost immediately.[2]

The bloke was 20 minutes late. He ordered for me. He didn't ask me a question about myself until dessert. He talked incessantly about making silly money – knowing full-well I was an unpaid intern at the time – and didn't offer to fork out for more than his half of the bill (even though he'd chosen the priciest restaurant on the block).

And then at the end of the night when – shock! – I didn't want to come home with him, he kicked back in his chair with his hands behind his head and drawled, 'C'mon, we're both adults here,' as if being legally underage was the only reason a lady might not wish to dive into bed with him. At that point, I briefly fantasised about dramatically tossing my shiraz onto his bespoke suit.

But here's the thing: even after the world's shittiest first date, I actually agreed to see the guy again.

When I was living in a new city a couple of years later, Mr Bespoke Suit (or Mr BS, as he shall be known) popped up in my inbox saying he was in town. He wanted to have a drink.

I was lonely at the time. I contemplated his undeniably nice-to-look-at profile picture. I told myself maybe he wasn't the absolute douche-canoe I remembered.

And then I texted back – wait for it – 'yes'.

In an outcome that will surprise nobody, date two was a dud. In a bar crowded with drunk bankers, Mr BS spent the evening ordering himself vodka-sodas without the ice: 'Because you get more bang for your buck when the ice isn't taking up half the glass,' he proudly announced more than once.

I made my excuses after about an hour and ducked his kiss on the way out. And looking back, I wonder: why do so many of us say yes to dates with such d-bags?

If you've said yes to a shitty dating life, you're not alone

I'm not the only Yes Woman who's done this. A number of the women I spoke to while researching for this book had said yes to requests in relationships or while dating, even though they didn't want to – or didn't have the time or resources.

Mila, 26, from Melbourne, said yes to a non-monogamous relationship because of an ultimatum. 'An ex-girlfriend once informed me that we had to be in a poly/open relationship (after two years of monogamy), or I was a bigot. It wasn't even like I refused and then she called me a bigot, it was within the sentence – "I want to be in an open relationship and if you refuse you're a bigot,"' says Mila. 'I'm all for open communication and not oppressing my partner's sexuality, but I think it's only reasonable to discuss these things, not demand them.'

Kellie, 35, from Birmingham in the UK, told me she agreed to move in with her then-boyfriend despite having second thoughts. 'I mentioned to him that maybe we weren't ready and he told me that if we didn't move in together, we were done,' Kellie says. 'We moved in, fought for two long years before it was finally over. I wanted to leave so many times and I was trapped in this lease.'

Looking back, she can see he was manipulative: 'I should have trusted my gut that day when it was saying I wasn't ready to live with him.'

Tina, 34, repeatedly agreed to reconcile with a needy on-again-off-again partner, despite a heavy toll on her mental health. 'I took on a lot of emotional baggage and care for him – midnight phone calls when he was in a low place, constant worry and stress that sent me into two breakdowns within six months,' says the Auckland-based Tina. 'It ended, of course, badly, with him cheating and ending it quite brutally, and two years later I still feel the effects.'

Then there's the more run-of-the-mill stuff we agree to spend our time and money on because we want to make our partners happy. Meet Adelaide-based artist Ari, 46, who for a decade changed up her whole look depending on her partner at the time.[3]

'I'd go to these gigs – punk gigs! And wear my hair all short, because my live-in partner then was in a punk band. I even got a face piercing because he liked them,' says Ari.

Then she broke up with him, and met a woman: 'The new girlfriend liked soft rock, and guess what I spent our free time doing? Going to Grinspoon gigs because it's what she wanted,' says Ari. 'My favourite musician is Sarah McLachlan, by the way.'

Finally, there's 34-year-old Mariana, who used to tag along on camping holidays with her former partner – even though she's 'better suited to five-star hotels than pit toilets', as she puts it. 'I definitely went along with trying to please him by pretending to be excited about sleeping outdoors when it is most definitely not my thing,' says Mariana, a Melbourne-based doctor. 'We even did an intense five-day bike touring holiday. I always found myself miserable and cold as camping is most decidedly un-fun when it rains.'

Looking back, she wishes she'd been more honest. 'I think now I would say, "It's not my thing, but I'm happy to do it every now and again because it's something you love." But I wouldn't pretend that it's going to be the best thing in the world for me.'

When to say no to your partner (whether they're brand spankin' new or long-term)

Saying yes in a relationship doesn't always make you a pushover. Relationships are about give and take, and sometimes you'll have to grin and say 'sure, honey' when your partner asks something of you. Airport pickups at an ungodly hour, having dinner with their dull workmates, or grin-and-bearing it when they take up a space-sucking new hobby in the backyard – all can be part and parcel of the compromise that comes with coupling up.

But there's a big difference between healthy give and take and endlessly putting up with requests or expectations that are making you miserable. Setting those healthy boundaries – and saying no to things that are too much of an ask – can be the difference between a great relationship and a dysfunctional, draining one.

As a general rule, the four following scenarios suggest it's time to learn the word 'no' when it comes to your love life.

It's their way or the highway

If you're the only one doing the aforementioned airport pickups – and your partner prefers to let you catch an Uber home while he or she has a lie-in – you may be dealing with a selfish partner.

Same goes if he or she expects you to be committed but wants to date other people; won't make the effort to meet your friends; or he says he 'isn't into' oral sex – giving it, that is; he's more than happy to receive it (I use the male pronoun here because heterosexual men have a pretty terrible track record with selfish sex: research from the US shows that fewer than two-thirds of heterosexual women in monogamous relationships are regularly satisfied in the bedroom compared with 88 per cent in lesbian relationships).[4]

Yes Women – who are more commonly 'givers' – can be magnets for these types of 'takers'. And that combination is a recipe for resentment, US-based relationship counsellor and dating coach Samantha Burns tells me.

In a healthy relationship, 'both need to be a giver', says Burns, who specialises in millennials' love lives and runs the popular Instagram account *LoveSuccessfully*. 'It's about equal effort. There might be times where one partner needs more, but in general it should balance out.'

So when is it time to pack your bags?

You can try working through your problems with a couples therapist – but if you're keeping score and feeling resentful, and nothing's changing, Burns says it might be time to call it quits.

'[I]f things don't improve it's always an option to end the relationship rather than investing years with a selfish partner who brings you down, doesn't support you, takes advantage of your kindness, and doesn't make you feel adored and loved,' she says. 'Remember you are worthy of those things.'

You're always there for your partner. But vice versa? Not so much

Perhaps you spend a lot of time and energy supporting your partner because he or she is struggling. Maybe your girlfriend drinks too much. Or your fiancé is in a self-destructive struggle with body image. Or your partner is flat all the time and you suspect he's depressed.

These situations are tricky – because, on the one hand, all relationships involve caring for our loved ones and being there for them ('in sickness and in health', if you've taken those vows). But if the situation is an endless one-way street – you're taking on all their issues and finding no space at all for you to have your own problems or emotions – the dynamic may not be healthy, nor sustainable. And propping up your partner may also be doing more harm than good for them.

Women tend to fall into this pattern of taking on all their loved one's problems, because we're socialised to manage the emotions of people around us, as journalist Yumi Stynes notes on an illuminating *Ladies, We Need to Talk* podcast episode on this issue.[5] More than men, women often let our boundaries fall when somebody needs us, adds psychotherapist and clinical psychologist Dr Jacqui Winship, speaking to Stynes on the same episode.

'Propping up [your partner] can also mean that you're somehow working too hard, that you're actually doing too much, and I think that's a pitfall that women in particular need to watch out for, just because we're socialised to be self-sacrificers and put our own needs second,' Winship says.

The risk of doing too much is that you and your partner will become totally enmeshed – which deprives your partner of having their own self-identity as well.

So when is it time to draw the line?

If you find that you're the one doing all the 'fixing' and your partner is knocking back your suggestions, it may be time to step back and say nope to being the only fixer in the relationship.

If you're feeling angry or resentful, or like you can't find room for your own self-care, that's another sign you're doing too much.

It may be useful to see a couples therapist, as well as seeing a psychologist individually to work on strategies to care for yourself while also loving your partner. The aim is to find a healthy balance. 'It's okay to try to help, and particularly to help them to help themselves,' says Winship. But the key is to avoid being the one to make all the positive actions happen, while dragging your partner along in your wake, she adds.

SIDE NOTE: Abuse and sexual assault

This isn't a book about domestic abuse or sexual assault. They're hugely prevalent issues that are not okay in any relationship – but they're beyond the scope of this book.

Domestic abuse or sexual assault are never the victim's fault – and if any of these things are happening to you, please seek professional assistance (you can call 1800 RESPECT or visit some of the resources listed at the back of this book):

- Your partner threatens to harm you, your pets, children, or other people
- They prevent you from seeing friends and family, or otherwise isolate you – limiting your freedom of movement, and cutting you off from your friends, family or community, or making you

feel guilty about socialising or going to work

- They threaten to leave, or to hurt themselves or you, unless you do what they say
- They constantly put you down, call you names, or do other things to degrade and humiliate you
- They pressure or force you into sexual activity
- They are jealous, follow you around, monitor your phone and media use, go through your stuff, or repeatedly try to contact you when you've said you don't want them to
- They take control of your financial affairs when you don't want them to, or prevent you from having access to money
- They push or hit you, drive dangerously to frighten you, or throw objects[6]

You're 'settling' because of panic about your age

Saying yes to a relationship – or, hell, even marriage – because society tells us we 'have' to be coupled up by a certain age can cause some of the most fabulous women to panic and settle for less-than-fabulous partners.

This pressure to couple up, even if it's with the wrong person, exists across every culture I know of, to varying extents. Psychotherapist Imi Lo has written about how in some East Asian cultures, while things are slowly changing, many women are still made to believe that they have an 'expiry date':

> In Japan, unmarried women 25-years-old or older are called the 'Christmas cake': buying a cake for Christmas is a Japanese tradition, but no one wants to eat it after December 25th. The label implies that these women have passed the 'freshness' of [their] youth and [are] therefore un-marriageable. Similarly, in China, those who do not have a husband by the age of 27 are called 'leftover women', with 'diminishing value in the dating market'.

Here in Australia, we may not use the term 'leftover women' (and the age of expected marriage is a little older) but the cultural norm certainly exists – silently yet somehow screamingly loud. It is reinforced through constant questions posed to single women about whether they've met anyone; those patronising looks of sympathy when women turn up solo to an event; through media storylines about fairy tale 'happy endings'; and through weird old-fashioned rituals like throwing the bouquet at the wedding (which are aimed only at women, since nobody seems to care whether single men are about to get married off.)

One problem with settling is that it's basically giving in to a cultural message that you're not okay on your own – which is BS. Another problem is that if you do actually want to meet someone right for you, wasting your time on Ms or Mr Wrong is just going to delay your meeting Ms or Mr Right.

So repeat after me: *don't say 'yes' to a relationship just because you're scared it's them or nobody; now or never.*

SIDE NOTE: So how do you know if you're settling?

Some big red flags

If you're looking for a relationship on a dating app, 'then there are red flag profiles that you should pass over quickly, such as the shirtless pic, no profile content, no shared interests, and blatantly sexual messaging', says relationship counsellor Samantha Burns. 'It's easy to swipe left on these since they are clear duds.'

For me, other instant deal-breakers include sexism, homophobia, racism and other 'isms' – and dudes who say things like 'contraception is only a woman's duty'. Also, white-guy dreadlocks. *Thank you, next!*

They're not at least an 80 per cent 'yes'

Dating someone imperfect is not 'settling'. Nobody is perfect, so waiting for someone who fulfils 100 per cent of your 'ideal partner' criteria is a losing game.

But as a general rule of thumb, online daters should feel about 80 per cent excited by a potential partner's online profile or message exchanges in order to move forward with a date or screening phone call, says Burns. 'Don't feel excited? Stop messaging and move onto someone with potential. This will help you decrease the number of one-and-done dates,' she adds.

If you're struggling to know whether you're 80 per cent interested, it can help to make a list of what you're actually looking for.

Keep it short – fewer than 12 requirements – and stick to general, core values and interests ('loves travel', 'wants a family'), not nit-picky superficial stuff that can change over time (like the car they drive, the suburb they live in, or whether they hate coriander, too).

You're not being yourself

If you feel a bit like that Missy Higgins lyric about a triangle trying to squeeze through a circle, you might be trying to change to suit your partner. It's a recipe for failure, says Burns. 'Don't be a chameleon, changing your colors based on who you're dating, or what you think they admire,' she says.

It's not only a lot of pressure to maintain this facade – you'll eventually let it slip, and 'your partner will feel duped or the differences in lifestyle won't be sustainable', says Burns. That means you will have just wasted your precious emotional energy investing inauthentically into a relationship.

Being yourself might involve geeking-out to science-fiction books. Or being really sexually adventurous. Or, equally, waiting months and months before you want to be sexually active with someone.

When I interviewed Abbie Chatfield – host of podcast *It's a Lot*, author of *So Let's Unpack That* (which abbreviates to *SLUT)*, and former *The Bachelor* contestant (who has spoken out beautifully against slut-shaming on the show) – she mentioned that she sometimes receives messages from fans, usually younger girls, saying, 'I don't feel comfortable having sex on the first date, does that make me a bad feminist?'

Abbie's advice? *You do you.*

'It's like, the point of this is to do whatever you feel like doing. Don't feel pressure from either side, but do speak up if you think something's wrong.'

♣

Speaking of not acting like yourself when dating, I'm reminded of the concept of 'the cool girl' introduced by author Gillian Flynn in her bestselling book *Gone Girl*. The cool girl, she explains, is a character that women try to act like in order to impress men. The cool girl doesn't nag. She's effortlessly slim and sexy, but drinks beer while she watches football with the boys. She's not uptight. She's funny, she's sexually adventurous, and she's cool with whatever. In other words, she's the persona I tried to adopt in my late teens and early 20s – much to the delight of the string of jocks and douchebags I dated in that era of my life.

Burns says your best bet, if you're seeking a true long-lasting relationship, is to be authentic, genuine, and vulnerable, and ultimately confident in who you are. No cool girl required.

'You want to be comfortable in your relationship, and by changing who you are or pretending to be someone you're not, you're dating from an unworthy mindset where you're placing all the emphasis on being chosen and seeking validation, instead of standing in your awesomeness,' she says.

It's no coincidence, I'm sure, that I first befriended my husband while being my weird, adventurous self – travelling in The Netherlands, and daggy-dancing in the mosh pit to some not-very-cool music. We started dating a few months later, once he'd well and truly got to know my real, uncool girl self.

You're doing the lion's share of housework and childcare

Attention: long-term, live-in, coupled-up types. Who books the cat's vet appointments at your house? Or buys an end-of-year card for the kindy teacher?

It's probably you, especially if you're in a heterosexual relationship in Australia. It's true that men are doing more housework than they once did (an average of 13.3 hours per week in 2016, up from 12.4 hours in 2002). But even in today's supposedly post-feminist society, women still take on the majority of household chores across the country, according to the latest Household, Income and Labour Dynamics in Australia (HILDA) survey.

This uneven division of labour is worse for couples who have kids, and applies even when both partners work full-time. Indeed, bread-winning mothers spend four hours more across domestic duties per week than bread-winning fathers, the 2019 HILDA survey found.[7] It's a lot for women to handle – and that's before we even delve into the ways that those expectations often butt up against pressures to be an 'ideal worker' (a whole other kettle of fish that we'll deal with later).

The challenges of juggling caring duties with paid work were compounded under coronavirus restrictions that forced many of us to work from home. A survey by Australian women's health organisation Jean Hailes asked women about their experiences during the first few months of the COVID-19 pandemic, and found that women aged 25–44 were most likely to report that they worked from home (42.6 per cent), that their home duties (19.2 per cent) and work hours (16.6 per cent) increased, and that they managed remote learning for children (14.6 per cent), 'which shows that this group of women found themselves busier than before COVID-19', the researchers concluded.[8]

How to even up housework

If the domestic work divides along gender lines in your house, I'm not blaming you: taking on the lion's share of this unpaid labour is an easy trap to fall into, even for egalitarian couples with the best will in the world. In fact, the stats show that even couples who split housework fairly evenly before babies enter the picture tend to find that things change once they have kids – with women shouldering the largest burden of unpaid work. (Mums, are you nodding along here? Or are you too busy pulling a pea out of somebody's nose, grilling sweet potato, and picking a sharp little Lego piece out of your foot at the same time?)

This is partly because women are mostly the ones taking parental leave – and they fall into the groove of becoming the 'default parent' and homemaker, a role that's hard to shrug off even once they re-enter the workforce. Once you're the one who knows exactly when the baby's vaccinations are due, or where the bottle cleaners are kept, you tend to remain the 'master' of those matters even when you're back at work.

The unpaid work that falls to mums is not just the physical doing of stuff, either – it's the knowing what needs to be done, the anticipating of chores and events that are coming up, and the planning for them – the 'mental load', it's been called. (This concept is perfectly illustrated by French comic artist Emma in her cartoon 'You Should Have Asked', which went absolutely bonkers when she published it in 2017, so strongly did it resonate with women readers.)[9]

I experienced the burden of the mental load one week while writing this book. My husband and I were trying to move house, so we decided to clean up and de-clutter before the agent came through for an inspection. As I dashed between rooms, vacuum cleaner in hand, I asked my husband if he could hide the kettle and a mouldy old vase. Minutes later, I found the kettle shoved, half-hidden, at the side of the microwave – not hidden at all but moved maybe 10 centimetres – and the mouldy vase hidden in a cupboard, smelly and filled with old petals.

I washed and moved the items myself – then spent another 45 minutes dashing around, ironing, hiding cords, and picking up fluff.

Later that afternoon, the agent having been and gone, my husband wondered aloud at how good the house looked. 'Those real-estate agents really make the place look good, don't they? They must have come in and moved the cords for the TV and put that kettle under the sink,' he remarked.

I couldn't help but quip that the cleaning fairy was, in fact, I.

♣

Enough about me. For Yes Women looking to say nope to carrying the lion's share of housework, the following tips can get you started.

(This bit's targeted specifically towards mothers – who carry the greatest load of domestic duties of all – and slightly towards heterosexual relationships, because the housework divide shows up most clearly in hetero relationships.)

Talk with your partner about expectations and assumptions

A frank conversation about division of labour is a good way to start making changes, according to psychologist Justine Alter, whom I interviewed for an *ABC Everyday* article about evening up housework with your partner.[10]

In your discussions with your partner, try naming the assumptions you might have both grown up with about who does what in the home. 'A common question we ask is: What was your family set-up? Did your mother work out of the home? What kind of family do you want to be when you have children yourselves?' says Alter, who specialises in life transitions and work-life balance.

Your next step: discuss what those assumptions are, and whether you want to try to flip any of them. Assumptions to pay attention to include: that a wife should buy birthday gifts for a husband's family; that a dad shouldn't be getting up to tend to the baby overnight because they're working the next day (*erm*, if the woman is looking after a baby the next day, that's also working!); and that a woman's career doesn't matter as much as a man's, so she should step back from the career ladder once she has kids (if your partner holds this belief

– beware. As Sheryl Sandberg, once said: 'The most important career choice you'll make is who you marry.').

Mix up the 'default parent' mould

One assumption that's particularly worth challenging is that the mum should always be the 'primary parent' – the one who takes a day of leave when the baby's sick, the one who does paperwork for kindy enrolments, and the one who plans the family's meals.

One kick-arse woman who's given thought to this assumption is Jamila Rizvi, journalist, presenter, political commentator, gender equality advocate and author of books including *The Motherhood* (and, once upon a time, my boss at *Mamamia*).

Rizvi and her husband have actively mixed up which parent gets nominated on forms and other life-admin relating to parenthood: 'one of the things they ask you when your kid gets enrolled in early childhood education is you have to write down parent one and parent two – and I wrote my husband as parent one', Rizvi tells me.

This wasn't because it was easier for her husband to pick their son up if he got sick. It was to actively share the mental load of having a child.

'I wanted him to be the point of contact. I wanted my husband to really understand that if work was being disrupted for me, he would get the call and he would have to call me and ask me to go and do it,' she says. 'But also he was responsible for all the Centrelink forms, and the permission slips, and the funny hat day, and the messages saying, "it's Halloween" and "it's lunchbox week" – I wanted him to be in control of that communication.'

Make a list and divide up chores

Another really practical tactic: sit down and make a list of all the tasks that go into keeping your household up and running. Try not to see it as a point-scoring exercise, but as a way of getting clear on who has time and energy and dividing tasks up in whatever way makes sense for you and your family (remember: your time is just as valuable as your partner's!).

This exercise makes the invisible work you do *visible* – and saves you from managing the family's to-do list, by assigning your partner complete responsibility for his or her tasks.

You might also want to read *Fair Play* by Eve Rodsky, who has game-ified this conversation by creating a card game that divides up 100 tasks within a partnership.[11]

Stop gatekeeping

When I interviewed Annabel Crabb, ABC journalist and author of *The Wife Drought*, about how women end up with such a heavy parenting load, she suggested that mums should stop 'gatekeeping'.

'You stop wordlessly expecting men to be shit at housework and raising children,' she told me in an interview for *Mamamia*.[12] 'I mean, how often do you hear "I'd never let my husband dress the children"?'

When Rizvi appointed her husband as 'parent one' on the day-care forms, she found it 'really hard to let go of early on, because I am quite an organised, take-care-of-everything person'. She also had to sit with the discomfort of seeing her husband miss the mark once or twice while he adjusted to carrying the mental load ('and I found it difficult because it meant that Rafi would often show up without a stupid hat on stupid hat day, and he'd be devastated', she says).

But 'it only took one or two times of Rafi being devastated for my husband to learn the lesson and go, "I can't hack that sad little face, and I will remember from now on."'

Simply resign

Here's one final, straightforward suggestion: 'You can do less stuff,' as Crabb told me in our interview.[13]

In other words, choose a task or two that the household can survive without – or that somebody else in the house can do – and simply quit it. Whether it's folding the socks into matching pairs after doing the laundry; making separate meals for your toddler (when she could really just chow down on whatever the grown-ups are eating); or bringing out the big guns when decorating for Christmas or Halloween – in most households, everyone will be fine with a couple of tasks scratched off your to-do list.

That's one approach taken by Rizvi. She quit laundry in her house – and she hasn't looked back.

'It's been six months since I've done any laundry that's not my own,' she tells me. 'Occasionally I do my own if I want something very specific washed at a time. But otherwise it's all my husband and son.'

SIDE NOTE: Don't get angry, get equal

The problem with reading up on the mental load and unequal division of domestic labour is that once you know about it, you see it everywhere. It's easy to get – rightfully – mad, and from there it's an easy jump to point-scoring, resentment and martyrdom.

Yes Women, my hope is that you won't simply begin noticing how much of the housework you take on, and then continue to do it, seethingly.

Instead, use your newfound knowledge (and/or feminist rage) to take action: get your partner on board with a division of labour in whatever way works for you.

In my household, my husband may be hopeless at kitchen-tidying – but we have implemented a few of the strategies above, and he takes ownership of a number of the substantial parenting and housework tasks.

Secure in that knowledge, I was able to laugh off the aforementioned tidying-up-by-moving-the-kettle-three-inches incident. Rather than harbouring a chip on my shoulder about how *I'm always the one cleaning the bloody house, dammit*, I could make a quip about the cleaning fairy, then remind myself of all the other domains he takes control of (grocery shopping, cooking dinner) and move on.

Chapter 11

Working 9 to 5 (requires saying nope to all that overtime)

When you say 'yes' to others, make sure you are not saying 'no' to yourself.

– Paulo Coelho[1]

Once upon a time, I was a very unhappy lawyer.

My legal career was brief but it taught me a lot: how to make spreadsheets as long and complex as they were boring. How to record time in six-minute increments.

And also: how to say yes to every work project that came my way.

When I first started out as a keen and fresh-faced legal trainee, a senior associate told me: 'When your boss asks you if you have capacity, the answer is always "yes".' I took that advice literally, plastering a bogus smile on my face whenever a new task was thrown my way.

Eager to please, I also put my hand up for an endless barrage of low-profile tasks with tight deadlines, and soon found my workdays crammed with unsatisfying, unchallenging 'busy work'. I was on committees; I baked brownies for the regular office afternoon tea; I signed up to the community engagement volunteer program.

I knew I was fortunate to have a secure job and a shiny glass office with city views – even the help of a legal assistant. I had a salary that I spent on smart little blazers with shoulder pads that made me feel like a Professional Career Woman out of a 90s movie. I bought scented handwash from a minimalist store that sold everything in tasteful amber bottles. I was living that bougie life.

But the reality was, I was miserable. I was stultifyingly bored – yet somehow also stressed by my relentless deadlines.

I'd figured that by saying yes to everything, I'd gain a reputation as an enthusiastic team player, and the promotions would follow. A door to more senior, fulfilling work should eventually swing open, and I'd be beckoned to work on cases that really felt like they mattered.

But the pat on the head I craved never came, and the promotion seemed nowhere on the horizon. Instead, I sorted through thousands upon thousands of black-and-white pages of tax jargon, and my dedication to this inane work went largely unnoticed.

After 18 months on the job, my morale was at rock-bottom. So I quit.

♣

The experience I had as a lawyer is nothing new, according to Jane Jackson, award-winning career coach, author of *Navigating Career Crossroads*, and host of *Your Career* podcast. Based in Sydney, Jackson has worked with more than 8000 clients across Hong Kong, San Francisco, London, Singapore and Sydney, and has 20 years of experience focusing on coaching senior executives through career changes and redundancy. So she knows her stuff.

Many of Jackson's clients have fallen into the trap of saying yes to 'earn their stripes' early in their career – only to end up resentful and burned out, she told me when I interviewed her for *ABC Everyday*.

'One of the reasons why most employees leave a job is a lack of appreciation, and little acknowledgement of all of the time and effort that they actually put into the work,' Jackson told me.[2] 'And if you struggle to say no, people don't respect your time' – so they just keep piling the work on.

Another risk of allowing your plate to pile up? Increased risk of burnout.

One study from the University of Montreal, published in the journal *Annals of Work Exposures and Health*, found that women suffer from alarmingly higher rates of burnout than men.[3]

Another study from the same university found that burnout symptoms in women were at their lowest levels at age 20, but then increased until ages 30 to 35. 'This result suggests that women's process of acquiring work mastery, combined with work–family conflicts, often higher for women than men, is stressful and leads to burnout symptoms,' the researchers noted.[4]

So common is burnout, in fact, that in 2019 the World Health Organization classified burnout as an official medical disorder and included it in the International Classification of Diseases.[5]

Being a Yes Woman in the workplace can be a blow to your success in another two ways, as well:

It undermines your success

Research also shows that 'agreeable' people – that'd be you, Yes Woman – tend to have lower incomes and lower occupational status (for example, they receive fewer promotions).[6]

Perhaps you tend to say yes to low-profile side projects. You hope you'll be recognised for your enthusiasm – but your people-pleasing behaviour just sees you thanklessly juggling a whole lot of extra work, while your managers focus their praise on cheesy old Mike from sales, who strategically focuses on high-profile, impactful work and gets promoted yearly. Dammit, Mike!

If you're a Yes Woman who endlessly puts your hands up for extra work, you might have ended up becoming a victim of your own competence. The more you demonstrate you can juggle multiple things, the more others demand of you.

And you might be delivering excellent work – but if you're consistently taking on a huge workload and managing to do it well, pretty soon that excellence becomes unremarkable.

What's more, this kind of Yes Woman behaviour often means you're doing a lot of multitasking – which can feel very effective, but ultimately doesn't work. Study after study has found that multitasking actually makes us less efficient, less effective, and stresses and damages the brain.[7] It causes us to be distracted – leaving us with little space for creative energy; for the time and space you need to make wise decisions, and to think of new ideas.

Which gets me thinking: it's little wonder that I didn't have the mental energy to write this book until I'd rested my brain in a hospital for four days. Right?

You neglect your most important work

Michelle Andrews, co-host of the wildly popular *Shameless* podcast and co-author of *The Space Between* (along with Zara McDonald) is also guilty of chronically saying yes.

'My instinct is to say yes to absolutely everything,' Michelle tells me, adding that she's always had something of a people-pleaser tendency. 'When someone asks me to do something, instead of thinking, "Is this best for me?" my instant thought is, "I don't want to let them down",' she says. 'I don't want to come off as too snobbish. I want this person to like me, and find me agreeable and easygoing.'

One thing that's helped Michelle get her Yes Woman ways under control? Her co-host Zara, who takes a different approach when she's asked to add extra work to her already over-heaped plate.

So what's Zara's secret? She simply asks herself if it's going to stop her from being the best version of herself because she'll be overloaded. 'All I think about is, I'll screw up all our further jobs because I'm not going to do it properly. I'm not going to be a good friend, I'm not going to be a good partner. I'm going to get to the point where I'm going to get resentful,' she says.

Now, when she's asked to do something for work, she considers how full her plate already is, and whether it can hold any more. If saying yes is going to tip her into overload, the answer's 'no'.

Without meaning to, Zara's hit on one of the re-framed beliefs we looked at earlier. Rather than the Yes Woman belief that 'busy is best',

Zara's flipped the script – reminding herself that busyness drains and dilutes us; it doesn't make us more effective.

Saying no at work (isn't only for managers)

Zara and Michelle have learned to say no early in their career – which is excellent, because it's a skill that's not only appropriate but important, even at the start of your career.

'If you're going to really respect yourself, it's something you need to really be aware of at all times, even when you're fresh out of uni,' career-coach Jane Jackson says. 'Of course you must put in the hard yards when you're younger to prove your ability, but you may set the boundaries at any age.'

This doesn't mean refusing work that's a core part of your job simply because you don't feel like it. But if you've already got a full work plate and you're asked to take on more; if you're regularly being asked to take on work outside your job description; if you're consistently working overtime to get your work done; if you're starting to really resent the amount of attendance or input expected of you; or if you feel like you're really not equipped to manage what's being asked of you – it's time to speak up.

Pushing back on your boss

When it comes to phrasing your 'no', Jackson suggests presenting your situation in a calm, factual, assertive way, and approaching your conversation in a manner that 'lets them know you're not being lazy, and really do want to get it done for them'.

You can do this in the moment, but it's often best to make a meeting and have a proper sit-down with your manager. Jackson suggests writing down the projects you're working on and their deadlines so you can ask for clarity around what your manager wants you to prioritise. 'It's a bit like triage in the hospital,' she suggests.

The idea is to let your manager know 'that you want to ensure that you have the time and capacity to do the very best job for them, so they'll understand that you are willing – however at this point, there just isn't enough time', says Jackson.

Try these phrases:

- 'I really appreciate your faith in my ability to get things done, but this is what's possible right now.'
- 'I've got two other things to get out the door today. I feel like I could do all three quickly, or just these two super well – which would you prefer?'[8]

If you're happy to do the work but your deadline is unreasonably tight, you can always suggest an alternative deadline:

- 'I'm not able to do it now because I have these other deadlines. What if I worked on it first thing on Monday?'
- 'Today isn't going to be possible, but we could put it on the list for next week. What do you think?'
- 'These are the deadlines for my current project – I'm really under the pump. I can do this, but I'll have to get to it tomorrow.'

If you can present your manager with another solution – perhaps another colleague has more capacity – by all means do that:

- 'As much as I love a challenge, I won't be able to give that the attention it needs today because I have to get this project out the door. I think Bill is close to finishing up his report, so he might have some capacity.'

It's important to keep a calm and confident tone, and avoid 'softening' your communication with a bunch of smiley-face emojis, apologies, or language like 'I was just wondering if …'

Pushing back on clients

The customer's always right. Right?

Actually, if a customer or client is asking for more than what they've paid for, they're in the wrong. Ditto if they're hassling you to get work done in a superhuman time frame.

Fortunately, there are ways of pushing back on those clients that will keep your professional reputation intact.

The best way of doing this, Jane Jackson tells me, is to set your terms and conditions in advance. 'You need to decide in advance what's right for you and what you'll accept,' she says. Then, before the client accepts the job, have him or her agree to the terms and conditions of service and the associated fee.

If they end up requesting work beyond the scope of the original agreement – this is known as 'scope creep', and it's irritatingly frequent – you can suggest:

> 'Unfortunately, that's not possible in the time left under our agreement.'

Or give them an option to purchase extra work:

> 'I wish I could help you out but that's not possible in the time and budget we've agreed on. Would you like to add another three hours to the job? The additional fee would be ...'

Depending on the nature of your work, you might want to set up a website outlining the services you offer, with a price list. You can require bookings and payments to go through your website, to avoid constantly having to explain and negotiate rates.

'By automating it, you don't struggle with the conversation about pricing, if it makes you feel uncomfortable,' Jackson says.

Pushing back on non-promotion-based work

Penny, 30, works in sports marketing in London – and tells me she's noticed that taking minutes at meetings is always delegated to one of the two women on her team. When both women were unavailable for the team-meeting one day, the men in the office came up with another solution: 'They literally suggested a manager from another team sit in on a meeting and take the minutes because she's a woman,' Penny recalls.

Sadie, 32, another Yes Woman I interviewed during my research, also noticed a gendered division of mundane tasks at her advertising job in Sydney. 'The office assistant was let go and there was no plan in place to cover her tasks, so naturally a few of the women had picked up a lot of the slack,' Sadie tells me.

The women were moved to desks near the entrance with a landline phone, so they were the ones fielding calls and greeting clients. 'Then, when the whole team went out for lunch together one day, the manager sent an email expressing his "disappointment" that the door was unmanned,' she says. 'The email was sent to the women in the office – including me, the most senior member of staff outside the directors – and all of the men were only CC-ed.'

As Penny and Sadie learned firsthand, extra work for women often takes the form of 'office housework', which has also been described as 'emotional labour of the workplace'. It can include the answering of phones, the refilling of water coolers, the stacking of mugs in the office dishwasher. In the Japanese business world, there's even a term for this phenomenon: ochakumi. Meaning 'tea squad', it refers to lower-ranking female office-workers being expected to make and serve tea to their male co-workers.[9]

This kind of practice sounds straight-out-of-the-1950s to me, but is still very common.

A 2018 study published in *Harvard Business Review* found women are 48 per cent more likely to volunteer for these 'non-promotable tasks' than men.[10] When the researchers conducted tests to check whether the women were putting their hands up for these tasks because they preferred that kind of work, or because they were naturally more altruistic, they ultimately found that neither of those were the motivators. Rather, 'the real driver was a shared understanding or expectation that women would volunteer more than men'.[11]

In other words, women sometimes take on these tasks because old-fashioned gender norms say that they should. We feel obligated to 'help' because it's Nice. And we end up overburdened, or sometimes just exploited.

This not only undermines our power, it also keeps us from spending our time and energy on our core job responsibilities. *Harvard Business Review* researchers put it adroitly: 'Women will continue to progress more slowly than men if they hold a portfolio of tasks that are less promotable.'[12]

♣

So what's the solution? Should we flat-out refuse to refill the water cooler?

Sydney-based Sadie – whose position is senior and permanent – felt comfortable enough in her role to directly respond to her manager's email, calling out his sexism and ending with the (rather iconic) line: 'You have an intern. Train him to answer the door.'

Dr Lois Frankel, author of *Nice Girls Don't Get the Corner Office*, takes particular aim at menial tasks involving food, presumably because cooking is associated with nurturing and housewifery: 'Don't volunteer to organize the company potluck lunch,' she advises. 'There are better things you want to be known for being good at.'[13]

But for some of us, the solution isn't as straightforward as flatly refusing office housework. As a study published in the *Journal of Applied Psychology* found, if women didn't do these 'altruistic' tasks in the workplace, they were viewed negatively, whereas men didn't suffer any penalisation. Which means as women, we may well face negative repercussions if we flatly refuse some of these tasks.

Frankly, we're damned if we do, damned if we don't.

The real solution to this gendered double-standard requires serious structural change led by all genders, at all levels of an organisation, of course. But at the individual level (until we've burned down the patriarchy, at least) your best bet may be to agree to some of these non-core tasks, but not all of them.

When it comes to baking a cake for the office afternoon tea, or arranging a birthday card for your colleague, you could unapologetically respond with, 'Wish I could help you out with this, but I'm flat out.' No need to feel guilty; no need to solve the problem for others.

If your boss asks you to do menial errands, try setting up a meeting with your manager and tell her or him that you don't want these tasks to take away from the core job you were hired to do. (If the requests continue, you might be in a toxic workplace – we'll deal with those in a minute.)

If you're being asked to take minutes in meetings, you could try pivoting to show that you're a good 'meeting manager', Frankel suggests: so, rather than just taking notes every meeting, make a checklist of meeting tasks and suggest that your team's administrative assistant be assigned them.[14]

Or alternatively, introduce a new custom: the newest person on the team, regardless of gender, is assigned to take control of those tasks.

'But it'll look so good on your CV!': when to accept 'hope labour'

Delilah, a 38-year-old academic in Sydney, has been saying yes to unpaid extra work since her late 20s, in the hope of becoming tenured. But after 10 years of doing all those things for free, she's no closer to that tenured job. 'I was led to believe, you need to do peer review, and mentor that person, and it's all stuff that will look great on your CV. But I've now realised that's bullshit, so I'm not doing any more,' she tells me.

This kind of work is sometimes known as 'hope labour' – you do it in the hope it'll lead to better, paid work or a promotion sometime down the line. Unpaid internships are a form of 'hope labour'. So, too, are many voluntary positions on work committees, in mentoring roles, as well as some types of speaking or writing engagements.

Delilah's feeling much freer now she's given up on all hope labour, and is considering a career switch. 'It is quite liberating when you look at the job and you go, I'm just going to do the job that I'm getting paid for. No, I'm not going to that committee meeting.'

Hope labour has, in recent years, been rightly criticised as sometimes exploitative and often problematic – in that it's only really viable for people with time and money to burn. (Who can afford to spend weeks or months in unpaid internships? Privileged kids whose families are paying their way through uni – that's who.)

But for some of us, giving up on hope labour altogether isn't a possibility.

The reality is that some job paths, unfairly, generally do require a certain amount of unpaid 'experience' before a promotion or paid work will materialise. (Journalism is one of them.)

If you're deciding whether to say yes to unpaid hope labour, I suggest asking yourself these questions:

- Is it a high-visibility, high-impact assignment (that is, your managers will see and notice the impact?)
- Does it clearly align with your professional goals?
- Is there a clear potential for advancement within the next 12 or 18 months if you do the hope labour?
- Will it significantly expand your network of contacts?

If the task doesn't tick off at least a couple of these points, give it a pass. You can respond to invitations or requests to undertake hope labour with phrases like this:

- 'Thanks for thinking of me, but I've got a lot on my plate this year, so I'm not able to do it.'
- 'I'm already at capacity this month, so I'll give it a pass. It sounds like an interesting initiative; best of luck with it.'

Protecting your work-life boundaries in the age of 'flexible work'

When I was hunting for a job in the middle of a pandemic-induced recession in Melbourne, I came across a job ad that said all the right things.

'Flexible work environment with working-from-home options!' it cheerfully exclaimed. 'Child-friendly work environment!'

As the parent of a toddler, I was after a job somewhere with fulfilling work that would also accommodate childcare drop-off times. So I applied for, and was offered, the gig – a senior media role at what seemed like a dream workplace.

There was just one problem: when I asked what the 'flexibility' entailed, it turned out it was code for 'we expect you to be on emails until bedtime'.

Yes, I'd be able to clock off by 5.30pm most days. But I'd have to be available to reply to email from 7am, and I'd be given a work phone that would ping with texts and calls throughout the evening. ('You can totally take an hour to feed your kid and drop her at day-care in the morning, though!' my would-be boss assured me cheerily.)

Yes, the workplace had cute perks like a day off for your birthday – but I'd also be on call every weekend.

Yes, I was able to work from home when I wanted – but when I did want to go into the office, I'd be expected to 'hot desk' amid the HR team, with no guarantee of a seat.

Yes, the workplace would allow me to bring my kid into the office if she was too sick to attend childcare. But honestly, I'd rather just take paid carer's leave than schlep my sick baby to a boardroom meeting. Wouldn't you?

♣

Flexibility in a workplace, when done right, is an essential part of helping us achieve work–life balance. Studies have shown that when workplaces are flexible, women are more likely to stay with a company and be a strong contributor to it.[15] There's also evidence that companies with high representation of women in the boardroom tend to perform better financially than those without female representation.[16] But there's a dark side to flexibility.

Research has found that full-time workers with flexible work arrangements often work three or more additional hours weekly, compared to those with inflexible schedules. This is partly because email, smartphones and laptops have increased the expectations for 'flexible workers' to be available anytime, anywhere.[17]

Throw in a trend in some industries towards 'results-oriented performance' (where performance is measured in terms of outcomes, not work hours) and an insecure job market, where workers feel they need to prove their dedication – and you can end up with a job that is 'boundary-less', says Dr Natalie Skinner, a senior research fellow at Flinders University who has researched work–life interference, stress and wellbeing in Australian workers. Skinner tells me that when the boundaries between work and life are blurred in this way, employees end up working during times that were once the sacred space of family or leisure.

Essentially, while flexibility was initially intended as a crucial part of helping employees find work–life balance, some companies have co-opted the term to suit their own focus on the bottom-line. Hence, when employers or politicians talk about flexibility, they usually mean 'flexibility by workers, not for workers', as Griffith University professor of employment relations David Peetz puts it. That might mean moving workers between activities and tasks depending on production needs; cutting or increasing a worker's hours, or classifying them as casuals or contractors.

The boundaries between work and life domains are now so blurred that some management types have suggested we stop talking about 'work–life balance' altogether, and instead embrace the concept of 'work–life integration'.[18] This concept is marked by permeable boundaries that allow for the integration of one role while present in the other role, 'such as scheduling dinner reservations on an app while at work or taking a work call while on vacation', as US management expert Dr Donna Weaver McCloskey writes.[19]

(Taken to the extreme, work–life integration takes the form of 'co-living' spaces: combined work and residential spaces geared towards the 'modern, flexible, "creative" worker who has bid farewell to the deskbound nine to five and instead jets around the world, dropping in to work remotely from exotic locations', as one *Guardian* article puts it.)[20]

The COVID work-from-home situation helped forge a new norm where work is now spilling much more into home life, clinical psychologist and educator Eileen Seah told me when I interviewed her. 'For example, people are thinking, "I'm not commuting as much and so I can work a little longer," or that their personal home space is literally the physical space in which they are working in and there's no spatial boundary.'

Sydney-based Seah went on to add: 'And employers or organisations might encroach more on employees' personal time and space (whether intentional or otherwise) such that a client needs to, more than ever, intentionally set up and prioritise work–life balance. If the work–life balance isn't front of mind, the boundaries can get invisible and murky.'

The problem for women is that work–life integration means you technically could be working at any time. And in times of job insecurity – say, a recession or a global pandemic – workers can feel even more pressured to demonstrate their dedication, availability and responsiveness, Natalie Skinner says.

'What has been observed for a long time is that this is really problematic for women,' she says. Women want to show dedication, but they're also responsible for most caring responsibilities – or what sociologist Arlie Hochschild calls 'the second shift'.

'I don't think flexibility solved that problem,' says Skinner. 'I suspect that the basic pattern remains, in terms of women being the primary caregivers and household managers, but now they're just integrating this in around their caregiving responsibilities.'

That can create stress and difficulties for women. Indeed, a study published in the *International Journal of Psychological Studies* found that employees using a work–life integration strategy experienced greater work–family conflict.[21] Meanwhile, employees who engaged in work-related activities beyond regular work hours found they had too little time to replenish their energy through leisure and sleep.[22]

Thus, during the coronavirus pandemic, many hetero couples with kids found that it was women who more often ended up working from the dining room table, trying to manage kids at home – while their partners holed up in the study.

Women are also more likely to work in casual or insecure roles (often they take these roles because they offer 'flexibility')[23] and found during the coronavirus crisis that they were without paid sick leave or carer's leave. When they lost jobs in greater numbers to men, those in the casualised workforce found themselves without a redundancy payout.[24]

When to say no to a 'flexible' workplace

So what, as a Yes Woman, can you do if your workplace's approach to flexibility is edging over your home-life boundary?

Seah tells me that it's best not to be rigid about those boundaries every time: if you can manage the occasional after-work call, go for it. She says:

> You can make choices and be flexible with personal boundaries, as long as you know what is workable in the long term, and what isn't going to work (for example, if you're the one who is consistently having to change your boundaries instead of a compromise between yourself and the other party).

But if you know a particular arrangement isn't going to work because it infringes too much on your home life, communicating assertively is your best shot at trying to get your needs met. In that situation, 'you could say, "If I do a 7pm meeting, I'm not going to come in as early the next day. However, could we try not to arrange for too many 7pm meetings in the future, all the time?",' Seah suggests.

And if you're offered a job – or a change to your current position – that claims to be 'flexible', don't accept without thinking it through. Asking yourself these questions can steer you as to whether your response is a yes or no:

- Who does the flexibility benefit? Is the flexibility demanded of you (because it benefits the employer) or is the flexibility an opportunity you can use if needed (benefitting you, the worker)?[25]
- If you take this job, does it come with expectations of blurred work–life boundaries? Will you be able to maintain strong enough boundaries needed to protect your mental wellbeing?

If the proposed job doesn't work for you, consider negotiating for conditions that suit you better. You could suggest an alternative like this:

> 'The job sounds like a great opportunity and I think I could bring great value to the role. However, because of my responsibilities outside of work, I'm not able to commit to an 8pm meeting each Monday night. Is there scope for me to sit that meeting out, and have the meeting minutes emailed to me the next day instead?'

Or try to get the flexibility written into your contract in a way that better suits you:

> 'If that's a standing meeting every Monday, perhaps my contract could specify that I work a long day on Monday – to accommodate that 8pm meeting – and then work a half-day on Friday. Let me know what you think.'

If the employer won't come to the table – and you're getting the sense that their idea of 'flexibility' is very much a one-way street – it could be that you need to tell the hiring manager a big fat 'nope'.

And in case you're wondering, I turned down that 'flexible' job that expected me to be glued to my emails at all hours – and I haven't looked back.

SIDE NOTE: You have rights here

Keep in mind that in Australia, it's unlawful for an employer to place undue influence or pressure on an employee to do certain things, including pressuring them to agree to an individual flexibility arrangement. It's also unlawful to coerce or pressure an employee to shift from a full-time to a casual work arrangement, as the Fair Work Ombudsman makes clear.[26]

And while it's legal for an employer to request an employee work reasonable overtime, it's only 'reasonable' if the request takes into account the employee's personal situation – including their family responsibilities – as well as whether they have already stated they can't ever work overtime. An employee can refuse to work overtime, if the request is unreasonable.[27]

If you're feeling pressured to accept endless extra hours, or a change in position that you think infringes your workplace rights, it's time to consider hitting up your union or a workplace lawyer.

Physical strategies to maintain work–life boundaries

Often, in situations where you find yourself responding to work requests on your screens at all hours, it's not because your boss is some kind of Machiavellian bully demanding this of you. Sometimes, he or she doesn't actually expect you to respond to those late-night emails until morning; it may just be the only time he or she has free. Or perhaps your boss is a workaholic who assumes everyone else is, too.

'Some managers, because they've been in environments where they've worked so hard, they assume that their team members can do the same thing,' says Hema Kangeson, a career coach who owns her own Melbourne business, inSpur. 'So you as a team member need to be brave enough to step up and have that conversation.'

If the emails can wait until morning (and let's be honest, unless you're Donald Trump's PR advisor, they probably can), you could adopt some practical guidelines to make sure you limit work communications after-hours.

'These can be set rules such as: I'm not going to respond to emails after a certain time; I'm going to turn off laptops after work; or I'm not going to have work emails on my personal phone,' says psychologist Eileen Seah.

And if you're working from home, you might also find it helpful to adopt a ritual at the end of each workday. 'A ritual can be a way of trying to set aside your workspace, and thinking, 'this is my home space now',' says Seah:

> Examples could be setting up an office space which you could close the door to (if possible), or packing away your work equipment and materials to put aside, or taking a walk outside of the home to simulate the 'commute' and switching from 'work' mode to 'personal or home' mode.

Saying no to toxic workplaces

Here are some things I've said yes to in my media career:

- Unpaid internships
- Walking the boss's dog while doing an unpaid internship
- Continuing with an unpaid internship after the blokes in the office joked they'd like to sniff my chair
- A job offer that paid next to nothing (but, hey, at least it paid, right?)
- A fancy new job title that came with no pay rise but a whole lot of responsibility
- Accepting a new job that promised a lovely central office … then working out of a coffee shop for months when it turned out there was no office
- Putting my name to opinion articles I didn't agree with
- Working in a job where my boss called out, 'Your tits look amazing in that dress!'
- Cutting my annual leave short (I was attending a close friend's wedding) because of a heavy guilt trip by my boss, who didn't approve of her employees taking leave
- Covering that same boss's responsibilities when they shortly thereafter decided to take six weeks annual leave

Although I didn't realise it at the time, many of the examples above happened when I was working at a toxic workplace. The hallmarks of this type of workplace, if you're not familiar, include a high staff turnover; poor communication from management; constant lack of clarity around projects; a lot of buck-passing when something goes wrong; passive-aggressive or abusive forms of communication; and negative effects on employees' wellbeing.

Hema Kangeson, who mostly coaches culturally diverse emerging leaders, tells me another toxic workplace red flag is 'performative allyship' – making a show of being 'allies' to marginalised groups, while actually doing little to help the cause – and 'performative diversity'. That is, workplaces that hire employees from diverse backgrounds because they 'tick a lot of boxes in terms of intersectionality', but then perpetuate the same old cycles of discrimination. In this sort of toxic workplace, 'Anything you call out, or anything you highlight or discuss, they don't even want to hear it, or they undermine it,' Kangeson says.

'Gaslighting' – a form of manipulation where the victim is led to question her own reality, memory or perceptions – is common in these workplaces, she adds. (Journalist, author and academic Ruby Hamad calls this 'gas-whiting' in her book, *White Tears/Brown Scars*.)

One of the many problems with toxic workplaces is they can make it feel impossible to say no. Employees often feel pressured or manipulated into taking on unreasonable workloads, and shamed or belittled if they can't meet those targets.

The sad truth is, assertive communication might not work with managers who are unreasonable and abusive. As a result, employees may feel resentful, and they may also begin to question whether they're the ones messing up. Their mental health, self-esteem and confidence can nosedive – making it harder to speak up for what they need.

If you're in a toxic work environment where the regular strategies to push back on unreasonable demands aren't effective, try these following strategies:

- **Speak up.** If you're dealing with discrimination or bullying, speak up to your manager, then HR and possibly a career coach or mentor, Kangeson suggests. But beware: if you're making a complaint, 'it's crucial to have solid evidence and solid examples' to maximise your chance of seeing any real solutions, she says.
- **Timebox it.** Accept that the culture may not change. Allocate a fixed time period (a 'timebox') within which you will see if things improve.
- **Move on.** Keep in mind that even with evidence, there are often repercussions for speaking up (and these can be worse for women of colour). If you're not seeing positive change within your timebox, it's time to leave. 'Trust me, the impact on your physical

and mental health is just not worth it,' says Kangeson. 'And a lot of the time, in these kinds of companies that are toxic, you are not going to be growing in your career as fast as you will be if you took a backseat, took some time off and did do something else with 10 per cent less money elsewhere.'

You're climbing the ladder. But who's climbing it with you?

'There's a special place in hell for women who don't help other women,' American politician and diplomat, and the first female US secretary of state, Madeleine Albright, apparently once said.

Honestly, I don't love her phrasing. Women face enough pressure to help others already without throwing in a threat of eternal damnation. But if you're someone who values helping other women – not because you feel you must, but because feminism or promoting gender equality matters to you – you might struggle with how often, and to what extent, you should say yes to requests to help other women.

It's a dilemma that author, commentator, and journalist Jane Caro AM has grappled with. 'As a feminist, I … feel a pressure to be tirelessly helpful to other women,' she wrote in a 2019 article for *Women's Agenda*.[28] '[E]ven among organisations that fight for greater diversity, even among feminists and feminist organisations there still seems to be a perception that being female and fighting for women's rights means we should do lots of things for, well, love.'

Sometimes, the decision to say yes to these requests comes naturally – if it's an organisation or a person who matters to us, and they can't get funding or support elsewhere; or if the request is quick and reasonable, for example.

But being a 'good feminist' certainly doesn't mean you have to say yes to any request for help from another woman, or to causes claiming to be feminist.

In particular, requests from rich corporations for women to contribute free labour to so-called feminist events – whether it's a speaking engagement, graphic design work or taking photos – can go straight in the 'no' pile (the irony is unbearable). Take your lead from Zara McDonald: she tells me she's regularly asked to give talks about 'women's empowerment', for free, to women within corporations. 'I have wanted to scream at my computer,' she says. 'I just write back and say we can't.'

Similarly, if a brand or company wants to involve you in a campaign or initiative that claims to support feminist values, pay careful attention to whether it actually walks the walk when it comes to those inclusive, progressive values. They may just be jumping on the recent 'fem-vertising' or 'purple-washing' trend that pays lip-service to feminism while perpetuating the same old systems of oppression.

A fashion brand that prints 'the future is female' t-shirts but relies on women's slave labour? They don't get your free photography skills. A cosmetics brand run by an openly transphobic millionaire? No free copywriting for you.

It's up to you how far you take this distinction; rarely are brands or individuals perfect. But I'd feel zero guilt about saying no to promoting a company which had entirely male leadership, or a company known for exploiting migrant workers. It makes sense, too, to eye with suspicion the large corporate International Women's Day events that charge $100 a ticket, take place at a time of day accessible only to senior executives, and feature only rich white women on their panels. They're evidence that initiatives aimed at 'diversity' and inclusion have often benefited white women – to the exclusion of others. As Ruby Hamad writes in *White Tears/Brown Scars*: 'For all the "I'm with her" and "the future is female" high-fiving floating around, it's becoming increasingly apparent that merely having more white women in powerful positions isn't going to result in a more just and equitable world.'[29]

And what about mentorships, requests for advice, or career questions from younger women?

Jane Caro's approach is to draw the line at having coffee with strangers to give career advice, or responding at length to people who approach her via social media. It's an approach driven partly by necessity: she's only one person, and it makes sense for her to prioritise requests that offer reward, or those that are truly for causes she believes in, or those that are quick, small asks.

But just as importantly, she points out that constantly saying yes to every request that pings into her inbox would be setting a bad example. It would be obscuring the fact that 'all of this is – in fact – work', she says. It would be reinforcing an age-old idea that women have a duty to do unpaid labour.

Carly Findlay OAM, Melbourne-based writer, speaker, appearance activist and author of *Say Hello*, points out that it's often women from marginalised groups who are targeted with work-for-free requests – which makes it all the more important to push back on requests for unpaid labour. 'My theory is, as a disabled woman, if you say yes to working for free then you are devaluing and not supporting your community,' she told me when I interviewed her.

> If you say yes to working for free in a marginalised community, we are so homogenised that everybody just thinks the whole community's the same and like-minded – and so I feel like you're raising the bar up when you say no, and you demand a fee, and that you're valuing your time in the wider community.

This applies to non-profits who claim they have no budget for speakers' fees: 'I get a lot of that: "Oh, we can't pay you but, hey, there's pizza for dinner!",' Findlay says, adding, 'You've got to push back on the "Oh, we don't have a budget" … You do have a budget when you're running an event, and speakers should come into that budget … They're paying their staff, they're paying the venue hire, they're paying the cleaner, they're paying the caterer.'

SIDE NOTE: Saying no to policies that keep women down

Here's another thing Yes Woman can learn to say no to: workplaces and policies that hold women back.

To some extent, saying no to these things assumes some degree of power: if you're the unpaid intern speaking up about an unpaid internship program, you're less likely to be heard than a manager voicing those same concerns. But often, 'The thing a lot of people forget is, they have a lot more power than they believe they have,' Kangeson says. 'Today if things don't work out, you can go to social media, you can go to support groups … so actually, you have a voice.'

Saying no to those workplaces or policies can include:

Calling out inequality where you see it

If the policies and processes in your workplace are directly or indirectly discriminatory, speak up. And make sure you're not only speaking up to promote policies aimed at helping white women lean in and prioritising the CEO level at work (too often, white feminists fail, for example, 'to show up when Black women are not being hired because of their names or fired for hairstyles', as US-based activist, cultural critic and author of *Hood Feminism* Mikki Kendall writes.[30]

Speaking up can be as simple as asking, 'Why are all the panelists at the events white and male?' And you don't need to be a manager to speak up, says Kangeson: at a number of workplaces, she's seen a powerful 'ripple effect' of positive change from non-managers simply calling attention to these concerns. And no, you don't have to be a woman from a marginalised community to point out policies that discriminate against them. In fact, white women, or those with other forms of privilege, 'actually have more of an opportunity to do this', Kangeson says.

Paying attention to who's making the hiring decisions

The phenomenon of 'similarity' or 'affinity bias' means that we tend to unconsciously like – and hire – people who remind us of ourselves. If you have any power to affect the makeup of a hiring panel, pay attention to diversity. If you have an all-male panel (or an all-white, all-able-bodied panel with no members of the LGBTQI community) the result can be an office populated with people who have personalities, educational backgrounds, or even ethnic backgrounds similar to the boss's, as my colleague Sana Qadar wrote for *ABC Everyday*.[31]

Finding allies or joining a professional association

'Sometimes, the next step is to build rapport with people in your team, or other teams and trying to change the dial that way,' says Kangeson. 'Maybe you're not a manager, but you know managers in another team. Get them to help you.'

Professional associations – including organisations targeted at women from particular cultural or racial groups, such as the Asian Australian Lawyers Association or African Australian Legal Network, if applicable – can be a good place to start. Your union may also be able to offer some advice or help with advocacy.

It's a structural problem, too

I don't want to tell women they can instantaneously shatter the glass ceiling by uttering 'no'. I don't want to suggest that by speaking assertively and setting boundaries at work, executive suites across the world will magically become populated with a diverse range of talented women. Because the truth is, it's systems of oppression – sexism, racism and all the rest – that allow some people to climb the career ladder faster than others (and keep some people off the ladder entirely).

'Practically, women are located in the impossible position of being required to perform the masculine, rational order of leadership whilst still being subject to feminine ideals,' writes Sydney-based Dr Alison Pullen, a professor of management and organisation studies at Macquarie University, who coined the term 'feminist leadership ethics'.[32] Pullen, who is also editor-in-chief of *Gender, Work &*

Organization, points to research that suggests that leadership creates significant anxieties for female managers because it puts them 'in the contradictory position of having to be both masculine and feminine at one and the same time', she explains.[33] 'An inability to do this means that whatever they do is unacceptable to the organisational status quo where the masculine has long been privileged.'[34]

So let me be clear: we won't get more female CEOs, close the gender pay gap, and witness a dramatic increase in parliamentary representation just by empowering women to say no at an individual level. The issue is so much bigger than that.

As Alison Pullen put it when I interviewed her:

> We're having similar conversations now as we had 25 years ago about women needing to put themselves forward for opportunities, women needing to be emancipated and empowered … I'm all for women going out there, being ambitious, being career-oriented, presenting themselves in whatever ways. But if you've got barriers institutionally, you can be as empowered as you want and you won't go anywhere.

♣

While I don't have all the solutions, one thing we can do is contribute to structural change in what small ways we can – and working on saying no can be a part of that. Pushing back on unpaid work or overtime and calling out injustices at work where we see them can be small rebukes to the stereotype that women have to be demure, Nice, and responsible for unpaid labour.

It's true that, as Kangeson says, voicing our concerns can also have a ripple effect – normalising discussion of these concerns, and inspiring others (perhaps even those in leadership roles) to make some changes.

Where we can, we can also say no to jobs and work that perpetuate the structural barriers that hold women down – in our culture, and in our organisations. That can include contributing to diversity and inclusion initiatives that aren't only about white women. And while we're at it, listening to what women from different communities say they need – and giving them the platform to speak and make decisions – rather than deciding for them. As Mikki Kendall writes, 'Sometimes being a good ally is about opening the door for someone instead of insisting that your voice is the only one that matters.'[35]

For women in leadership roles, saying no to oppressive structures also involves embracing Pullen's idea of 'feminist leadership ethics' – which requires not only supporting other women, but also taking care 'to not reproduce patterns of exploitation and oppression', she says.

Crucially, it's not only women who need to do the work to say no to these systems of oppression, either. When it comes to paying women fairly for their work, 'the onus really should be on the big companies to set the standard', as writer and activist Carly Findlay says.

Men, who disproportionately run those big companies and hold parliamentary positions, also need to lead this change – from creating strong policies and processes to help tackle gendered issues including sexual harassment and pregnancy discrimination; to supporting women to access affordable childcare and re-enter the workforce after having children; to tackling unconscious biases (by, for example, employing gender-blind recruitment processes); to ensuring workers of all genders, abilities, ethnicities and sexualities are paid equally for comparable work.

Without big companies, governments and men on board, saying no can only get us so far when it comes to reclaiming our time, energy and power at work.

Chapter 12

Mother, other or martyr?

Mothers have martyred themselves in their children's names since the beginning of time. We have lived as if she who disappears the most, loves the most.

– Glennon Doyle[1]

If you're a parent, you may have come across my least favourite children's book: *The Giving Tree* by Shel Silverstein.

My reservations about this book aren't about the drawings (which are beautiful), or the writing style (simple and poignant). Nope, my issue is that the book reads like a road map to destructive Yes Woman-like self-sacrifice – the type of endless giving that society demands of women, and particularly mothers.

If you haven't read *The Giving Tree*, here's the essence: there's a tree who loves a little boy. The kid climbs her trunk, swings from her branches, eats her apples and naps in her shade. When the boy grows into an adult, he tells the tree he doesn't just want to play with her anymore – he wants money to buy things, as well as a house and a boat.

So the tree sacrifices herself to make her boy happy. She implores him to take her apples and sell them for money, chop off her branches to build a house, and cut down her trunk to fashion a boat.

The boy strips her of the things that make her an apple tree – and off he goes. By the time the boy returns to the tree again, this time as an old man, the tree is no more than a stump in the ground. 'I wish that I could give you something … but I have nothing left. I am just an old stump. I am sorry,' utters the Giving Tree.

There's some debate about the true meaning of *The Giving Tree*, but a number of readers see it as a parable for self-sacrificial motherly love that knows no limits. One online review remarks that the story 'really parallels how a parent feels about their kids ... how we sacrifice everything we have, everything we are just to see a smile on our kids' faces [because] there is nothing you won't do for your babies', while another suggests the book 'shows that sometimes love and sacrifice go hand in hand'.[2]

Which makes me uneasy, to say the least. Not because I believe parenthood shouldn't involve a level of sacrifice. Anyone with a small being in their home knows it's a gig that requires patience, kindness and a whole lot of giving. All mums know about listening to endless repeats of The Wiggles albums instead of Triple J, and (for those of us who carried the pregnancy) drinking sparkling water instead of sparkling wine for nine long months – not to mention enduring chafing, tearing and drooping of our formerly nubile bodies.

But the fact that parenthood involves sacrifice doesn't mean that mothers have to be the ones doing all the sacrificing. Nor does it mean that we must offer up our every last resource until we're a stump in the ground. (On this point, I recommend *Down Girl* by Kate Manne for a particularly adroit feminist critique of *The Giving Tree*.)

Motherhood doesn't have to be about endless sacrifice that leaves you drained and incapacitated – but that's a message our culture often gives new parents through stories and stereotypes. We grow up watching TV mums playing dutiful homemakers who tirelessly put up with their befuddled husbands: Marge Simpson in *The Simpsons*, Debra Barone in *Everybody Loves Raymond*, Jane Jetson in *The Jetsons*. Even when pop culture does interrogate those expectations about mums having to do everything perfectly, the storylines often end up reinforcing these old tropes. (The film *Bad Moms*, for example, turns on the premise that mums have failed to meet the expectations laid out for 'good mums' even when they do relatively benign things like quitting the PTA or having a night out with the girls – inadvertently buttressing the very ideals the film tries to invert.)

When a woman gets pregnant, she's bombarded with comments, expectations and gifts that subtly position her own needs as less important than the baby's. Well-meaning family and friends give gifts to ensure the baby has the best of everything, while very few think to gift the grumpy pregnant woman something to soothe her sore, growing body (*What do I have to do to get a massage voucher around here?*). Then, as well as being told to not so much as glance at any food items that may, in very rare cases, contain harmful bacteria – deli meats, soft-serve ice cream, soft cheeses and sushi, to name a few – she's often told erroneously to avoid practices that haven't even been proven to harm the baby, such as hair-dyeing or lying on her right side.

The training in self-sacrifice goes on. Relatives tell pregnant women, 'Go see a movie now while you can' – setting a tacit expectation that the mother won't be handing off the kid to a partner, grandparent or babysitter to catch a film with a friend. When Mother's Day rolls around each year, grocery store shelves are lined with cards that say things like 'You sacrificed so much for us, mum!' while quotes on Pinterest say things like, 'A mother is a person who, seeing there are only four pieces of the pie for five people, promptly announces she never did care for pie.'[3]

And, of course, as children's book author Laurel Snyder has said, 'When you give a new mother ten copies of *The Giving Tree*, it does send a message to the mother that we are supposed to be this person.'[4]

All this is a long way of saying that it's easy to absorb the message that self-care sits at the bottom of a 'Nice' new mother's to-do list. I'd go so far as to say that nowhere is the cult of female sacrifice more powerful than in the realm of motherhood. So it's no wonder one study found that at six months postpartum, the vast majority of women were completing their desired or usual levels of baby and household activities, but more than 80 per cent had not yet fully resumed their usual self-care activities.[5]

The women who say no to mothering

Most of this chapter looks at how to say no to unrealistic expectations of motherhood – the type that demand we give and give and give until we have nothing left. But first, let's spend a moment looking at the decision some women make to say no to motherhood altogether.

For some women who are voluntarily childless – also known as 'childfree by choice' – it's unattainable, perfectionist mothering standards that turn them off parenthood altogether, according to Melbourne-based psychotherapist, researcher and academic Dr Zoë Krupka.[6]

'It's that attitude of self-sacrifice, and particularly an attitude of, "You're not meant to have any needs anymore,"' once you become pregnant and become a mother, Krupka told me when I interviewed her. (This is an alarming attitude, she adds, because in pregnancy you 'actually have more needs than most people'.)

One Yes Woman who's always found those expectations daunting is Bettina, 37, from Adelaide. The marketing executive tells me she decided in her 20s never to have kids after witnessing her three older sisters 'tearing their hair out' in their struggle to perfectly balance motherhood with part-time work.

'It looked like a losing game to me; here they were, these smart and capable and loving women, and they were always feeling less-than both at work and at home, and still expected to give up everything and never do anything for themselves,' says Bettina. 'Deciding not to have children, ever, was almost like my way of pre-emptively opting out of the worst parts of the expectation that women will be perfect.'

Other women choose to bypass parenthood for other reasons: they never felt a maternal urge; were concerned about the environmental cost of having children; had health concerns that took priority over child-rearing; wanted to focus on retaining a romantic relationship without the shared obligation of childrearing;[7] or they simply disliked kids. Some are put off by the 'intense social criticism of mothers that makes it a particularly unattractive option', as Dr Krupka suggested when interviewed on ABC podcast *Ladies, We Need to Talk*.[8]

For 55-year-old Carol from Melbourne, being childfree was about making space for career, creative pursuits and self-actualisation. 'My childhood dreams were about creative expression of artistic gifts, and I saw that as incompatible with relationship and marriage and children, in many ways,' she told me in interview.

Carol also said she drew on her 'feminist consciousness' early in life when deciding to actively reject marriage and motherhood as normative markers of womanhood. 'I do recall at uni doing research on women writers in the 19th century, and compiling lists on those who were married, those who were married with children, and those who were single,' she says. When she noticed her list of successful writers was filled with childfree women, her instinctive response was, 'Yep, that's how it is.'

These days, Carol juggles writing and teaching, and feels that, as a mother, she wouldn't have been able to hold down her career. 'Adding children into that mix – I personally would have found very difficult,' she says.

Whatever the reason, saying no to motherhood takes guts. Going childfree goes against the societal script about women existing to provide care to others – a script that says womanhood is synonymous with motherhood. As well as feeling stigmatised,[9] many childfree women often feel expected to constantly justify their position. As researcher Kristin Park puts it, they're required to 'engage in information control and stigma management techniques, tailored to particular audiences, to manage their "deviant" identities'.[10]

The decision not to have children requires 'a constant coming out', says Krupka: the childfree woman has to constantly field questions about whether she has children and, later in life, grandchildren. 'I think the courage that comes with not having children is about bumping up against this persistent criticism, isolation and exclusion for the rest of your life,' she explains.

Lillian, a 33-year-old librarian from the Illawarra region of NSW, has felt keenly this sense of having to manage or explain her 'deviant' identity. 'At parties and events, whether you have children just seems to be part of the things people ask – and when you say no, it gets awkward,' she says.

She's begun to dread those conversations, particularly because they often involve follow-up remarks 'like, "What's wrong with you?" or "Oh, you don't know what life's about," or "You don't know what love is until you have a baby,"' she tells me.

Family members can be just as bad. 'I've been married for ten years now and every single one of those ten years, my older sister has been giving me a hard time about the fact we don't have children,' Lillian says.

Perth-based Abigail, 40, has had a similar experience: 'I have a Hungarian family, so the expectation's there that at a certain age you get married and make babies,' she says. 'My dad cried when I first told him [I didn't want kids], and it's been ten years of constantly telling my mother "no".'

Constantly confronting these kinds of statements can be difficult – particularly for Yes Women, with their dread of disappointing others.

'I'm still not as brave as I would like to be when it comes to publicly owning my choice to not have kids,' says Lillian, who says she's a people-pleasing perfectionist. 'I still baulk at my sister's comments; I do still shy away from it a little bit, and I always dread being asked about it by that stranger at the party.'

One thing that has helped Lillian feel more confident about expressing her decision not to have kids is 'reading a lot of feminist literature' that explores a more expansive view of womanhood. 'I'm reading Lindy West at the moment and poetry by Rupi Kaur and Amanda Lovelace – these are women who I think are incredibly brave, and they tend to go against the grain,' she says. 'It makes me think there's nothing selfish about these women, which is a common thing people say about women without kids, and then I think, it's not selfish that I want to take a different path either.'

Krupka agrees that reading up on the structures that prescribe restrictive roles for women can be helpful for those who choose to go childfree. 'I'm a really big believer in how supportive it can be to understand the structural context for what you're experiencing,' she says.

'I think what can be really helpful for women who choose not to have children is to understand that what they're bumping up against is the very limited idea of what it is to be a woman,' she adds. 'And I think once you understand that, there's a freedom in understanding, "Well, of course I'm more than that. Every woman is more than that."'

♣

Most childfree women I spoke to acknowledged that saying no to motherhood has allowed them to say yes to other aspects of their life: a high-flying career in several cases; a passion for scuba diving, creative pursuits and world travel, and a rewarding grown-up relationship in others. For many, throwing off the societal expectation of parenthood has created time and space for other personal priorities. It's been nothing short of empowering.

But several childfree women I spoke to – especially the ones who identified as people-pleasers – said they were dogged by the persistent belief that they 'should' be outshining their more maternal friends in these areas, being unhindered by childrearing duties.

Lillian said that her people-pleasing goes into overdrive when it comes to her career: 'I tend to over-commit at work,' she says. 'It's partly because my friends with kids are working part-time, so I feel like I have to push to be that really career-oriented friend. It's stupid, but working in a high-pressured job and always being busy at work makes me feel a little bit more validated in my decision not to have kids.'

Krupka has a message for childfree women who feel themselves 'falling into that trap' of thinking other parts of life have to substitute for the children they've decided not to have: 'You don't have to say, "Well, I have my job," or "I'm a great auntie." It's like, you don't have to be a great auntie, you just have a life. You just are,' she says.

In other words, if you're childfree by choice, it's great that you've recognised motherhood isn't right for you and thrown off that societal expectation. But you might have to work hard not to internalise another societal message commonly swallowed by Yes Women: that if you're not a mother, you must be a doubly hard worker.

It's about resisting 'that neoliberal idea that you've got to be productive, or that your life's purpose has to be more than just being a human being on the planet', Krupka says. 'That's just so devaluing of everybody really, that idea.'

Intensive mothering: one big guilt trip

Back to women who do choose to become mothers. Learning to say no is huge for mums – and that's especially the case because we live in an age of super-involved, hyper-vigilant, child-centred parenting, known as 'intensive mothering'. It's a cultural child-rearing trend that has only really taken grip in our society in the past few decades, and it involves constantly attempting to decipher the child's wishes and needs, then trying to meet them at almost any cost.

Intensive motherhood is underpinned by beliefs that the mother is the essential parent; that the time she spends with her kids is critical for positive cognitive, behavioural and academic outcomes; that good child-rearing requires placing the child's needs before all else; and that parenting has to be an exhausting, challenging job.[11] Basically, its motto seems to be: 'If you're not stressed out, you're doing it wrong'.

I know many mums who ascribe to this style of parenthood. They're the ones who feel guilty leaving their partner with the toddler for a couple of hours on a Saturday, or haven't nipped out to a cafe to see a friend in two years – not because they don't have resources to arrange babysitting support, but because of guilt, or fear of judgement, or an internalised belief that their new role is to say yes to whatever they believed their baby asked of them.

One mum told me she barely left her home for six months after the birth because she 'felt bad' that she might be 'forcing him out of the home, where he's more comfortable'. (If her newborn could talk, I'm fairly sure he'd say he wouldn't mind popping to a cafe in a pram while his mum grabbed a croissant.)

I don't blame these mums. It's easy to subscribe to intensive mothering without actively choosing to, because in modern Western society it's often presented as the norm. But intensive mothering is particularly dangerous for Yes Women, whose issues with guilt around looking after their own needs can mean they take intensive mothering to extremes. Many Yes Women also fear the shame that might follow if we fall short of these expectations.

The problem is, trying to perfectly execute intensive motherhood is a losing battle, because the demands of parenting today are more full-on than ever.

In previous generations, mums were of course expected to serve their family, but they could at least send their kids out to ride bikes all afternoon without hovering nearby, ready to whisk their offspring off to their afternoon dance class before helping with their Japanese homework.

Most of us work outside the home, but somehow mothers in Western countries are actually spending *more* time with their kids today than they have since the mid-1960s, according to one University of California study.[12] The study's co-author, sociologist Judith Treas, has specifically called out the role of the 'intensive parenting' ideology in fuelling this trend: 'These beliefs have taken hold among the best-educated residents of Western countries and are also diffusing to their counterparts who have less schooling,' she says.

In the US, women with male partners also still perform about twice as much childcare and housework as their partners, meaning women are basically doing more with less time.[13]

Adding to mums' workloads, I've recently noticed a resurgence of a type of domesticity reminiscent of the 1950s and before, now popularised by Instagram and exacerbated by COVID-19 lockdowns: a return to vegetable-garden growing, bread-baking, crafting and knitting. This branch of intensive mothering is sometimes known as 'urban homesteading', and it's associated with mothers encouraging families to live a sustainable lifestyle that emphasises household self-provisioning, incorporating practices such as gardening and urban agriculture, canning and pickling, and a range of DIY and craft projects.[14] (Personally, I have a long history of getting sucked into these kinds of 'intensive mothering' expectations – sewing tiny Liberty-print sets for my newborn, knitting hats, planting a vegetable garden so my toddler could watch me dig up her dinner.)

If you haven't figured it out yet, saying yes to intensive mothering isn't only fuelled by guilt (and conservative gender roles), but also driven by perfectionism. In the world of intensive mothering, all efforts have to be executed to perfection: intensive mothers believe their role is to devotedly foster every opportunity for their child's growth and happiness, and they fear that falling short could stunt their child's attachment, development or future wellbeing.

In a deeply relatable article for *New Stateman*, journalist Sophie McBain suggests that millennials who first developed perfectionist traits in response to our work culture and social media interactions are now finding those anxieties playing a role in how they raise their children. She writes:

> My friends and I prepared for motherhood by piling our bedside tables high with parenting books. We learned about the Wonder Weeks and the Ferber method. We bought slings so we could be like the Ye'kuana tribespeople of the Venezuelan rainforest,

> whose babies never cry. We lost hours googling the safest car seats and the most educational toys and the bottle teats that best resemble human nipples. And when our babies refused to play along, by going on hunger strikes or screaming all night, we riffled through our dog-eared baby books to work out how we'd messed up. Of course it was all our fault.[15]

Taking these expectations to extremes is the parenting method known as 'attachment parenting', an increasingly fashionable offshoot of intensive parenting that promotes baby-wearing, co-sleeping and long-term breastfeeding.[16]

For some women, attachment parenting is joyous, empowering and feels exactly right. But for some – and I would argue for Yes Women particularly – this brand of intensive parenting and the sacrifices it requires can feel like one big guilt trip; or, as UK journalist Hadley Freeman writes: 'maternal masochism' that 'puts its thumb right on the maternal pressure point, by asking how much of yourself you are willing to give up for your child'. It plays on mothers' worst fears by suggesting that 'anything less than constant devotion will cause your baby emotional harm'.[17]

My point here is not to throw shade at attachment parenting – I know some terrific mums who subscribe to this style of parenting. Instead, I want to reassure you that you can do … well, a lot *less* and still be a good mum with a securely attached baby.

SIDE NOTE: Intensive mothering and mental health

Saying no to intensive mothering might also save your sanity.

When we're worrying ourselves sick about trying to do everything right by our babies, we sacrifice our wellbeing. This should come as no surprise to you, given the impacts of chronic stress we looked at earlier in the book – but there are a few terrifying studies into how stress affects parents (particularly 'intensive mothering' parents) in particular, so let's take a look.

Dr Lisa Forbes, an assistant clinical professor at the University of Colorado Denver, whose work focuses on working mothers, gender roles and mental health, has criticised intensive mothering ideals because they 'set expectations for mothers that recruit them into inequitable parental partnerships and create challenges for their wellbeing, health, and relational fitness'.[18]

A 2012 US study published in the *Journal of Child and Family Studies* assessed how strongly a group of mothers held intensive-mothering beliefs (by asking them to rate how strongly they agreed with statements such as, 'Children's needs should come before their parents'.'). The researchers found that the parents with intensive mothering beliefs had poorer mental health outcomes. What's more, the authors concluded that when women believed they – as a mother – were the essential parent, they were more likely to have lower life satisfaction.[19]

So if intensive mothering is related to so many negative mental health outcomes, why do women do it?

Researchers from the University of Virginia have suggested that it's because many women think that it makes them better mothers, and so they are willing to sacrifice their own mental health to enhance their children's cognitive and socio-emotional outcomes.[20] But they point out that there's no actual data to support that assumption.

On the contrary, 'young children of over-involved or over-protective parents often experience internalising disorders[21] [and] research clearly indicates that the children of women with poor mental health … are at higher risk for negative outcomes'.[22] The researchers concluded that, given aspects of intensive parenting are associated with negative maternal mental health, 'then intensive parenting may have the opposite effect on children from what parents intend'.

Some researchers also argue that when women feel they must subsume their needs to the needs of their child, they lose a sense of personal freedom, which may result in women experiencing negative mental health outcomes.[23]

That old saying, 'happy mum, happy baby', seems to have some truth to it, then.

Let's talk about telling your kids no

For many Yes Women, literally saying no to their kids is a challenge. We don't want to deal with their tantrums. We feel bad about letting our kids down, or we fear not being available enough for them – perhaps because we've been busy at work, or otherwise distracted – so we say yes to their requests out of guilt.

The cult of intensive mothering would also have us believe that saying no to many of our kids' requests – to them having our undivided attention 24/7, to sharing our beds, to singing them 'Twinkle Twinkle' for the 12th time before bed – will somehow leave them feeling unheard or misunderstood.

For many months, I lived in that guilt-trap. As my daughter grew from baby to toddler, she began to request my involvement in play, and I'd pride myself on dropping everything, getting down on the floor for some hands and knees time and getting into whatever game she demanded of me. It wasn't until I began interviewing experts about saying no to kids that I realised it can actually benefit kids for their parents to say no.

In fact, it's your job as a parent to set boundaries, according to Georgina Manning, director of Wellbeing for Kids, and a registered counsellor and psychotherapist based in Melbourne. 'I have this saying that if we're saying no regularly, we're on the right track,' she says.

This isn't about refusing our kids' every request in order to teach them a lesson; it's about setting boundaries. 'Children's job is to push those boundaries with parents … they like to see where it is, where it starts, how fluid it is, or whether it is something that's solid,' Manning says.

And as a parent, your job is to set boundaries with them – whether it's making it clear they're not allowed mobile phones in their bedrooms, or ensuring their diet consists of more than popcorn and ice cream.

You might even have to let them down sometimes (say, if you're not available for every Saturday soccer game).

'It's okay to set limits with our children and say, "Hey, I've got this on, but I'll come to this game, and Dad will go to that one,"' says Manning.

Same goes if your kid wants to do six extracurricular activities, and the drop-offs and cost and time is going to be more than you can manage: feel free to tell them that's not happening. 'A child might say, "I want to do this and I want to do basketball and I also want to do soccer, and tennis and footy." And we might say, "What do you want to focus on this year? Let's find something you really want to stick to [and] at this stage there's just one,"' Manning says.

You'll be doing them a favour: having some free time around extracurricular activities will allow your family to have the space for the free play and recuperation that's often needed.

Sort your glass balls from your plastic balls

Having a baby can be a radicalising experience.[24] For many women, I believe it's not until they have a baby that they realise our society isn't set up to fit with family life, it's set up to enhance economic productivity – and as a result, mothers often feel they're not capable or hard-working enough.[25] Ironically, some become feminists at the very moment they don't have spare time to engage in activism, as journalist Helen Lewis points out.[26]

Women today are facing a time crisis: none of us have enough of it, and working mothers are among the most time-poor people in the world. That's especially true for single mums, who bear an especially intense responsibility for a multitude of roles.[27]

So what's the solution?

For Yes Women who try hard to please others and live up to societal standards expected of them, the challenge is to meet the necessary sacrifices of parenting (you know, to make sure your children are fed and rested) while saying nope to all the extra BS expectations around women giving up their health, identity or lives to have kids.

It's easier said than done, because the system isn't set up for us. As journalist Brigid Schulte notes in her book *Overwhelmed*: 'When women began working in a man's world, their lives changed completely. Yet workplace cultures, government policies and cultural attitudes, by and large, still act as though it is, or should be, 1950 in Middle America.'[28]

Essentially, as author and journalist Amy Westervelt sums up in her book *Forget 'Having It All'*, we're expected to parent as if we don't have jobs, and work as though we don't have kids.

As is often the case, it's the system – not our individual behaviour – that most needs to change, and there are crucial economic and legal reforms needed to support this. But in terms of doing our best with what we have on the individual level in our everyday lives, we can focus on prioritisation.

The best advice I've read on this comes from author Nora Roberts, who was asked in an author Q&A how to balance writing and kids.[29] She said the trick to juggling is to think of each of the balls you have in the air as either plastic or glass.[30] You can afford to drop a plastic ball, because it bounces and stays in one piece. But if you drop a glass ball, it shatters irreparably. The trick is to distinguish between which balls are plastic and which are glass, then focus on catching the glass ones.

Plastic balls I've felt free to drop (or throw entirely away, frankly) include cutting my kid's sandwiches into cutesy animal shapes, taking Instagram pics to show everyone how goddamn adorable she is, enrolling in baby swim lessons (until she's a bit older, at least) and sourcing only organic food for her to eat.

Glass balls, for me, include making time for soothing cuddles when she's hurt or scared, making sure she gets vaccinated on time, providing mostly nutritious food, being available for transition times (such as starting at a new day-care) and prioritising time for books, songs and screen-free play.

Aim to be a 'good enough' – not a perfect – mother

For Yes Women, overcoming the intensive motherhood trap starts with lowering expectations.

I'm not suggesting you adopt a Moira Rose of *Schitt's Creek* persona and forget your daughter's middle name – but you could add a sprinkle of Lorelai Gilmore (who orders takeaway pizza when she can't be stuffed doing the Martha Stewart thing in the kitchen) or Rainbow Johnson from *Black-ish* (who has a great career because she finds it fulfilling) to your understanding of what a great mum is.

There's no doubt that the relationship a baby has with their primary caregiver – usually the mother – has a big impact on the infant's future development.[31] But this relationship doesn't have to be flawless 24/7 for your kids to grow up healthy and happy. It's all about quality, not quantity.

In fact, according to a 2015 study published in the *Journal of Marriage and Family*,[32] the amount of time mums spend with their kids has no bearing on the behavioural and emotional outcomes in younger children. In fact, mums who spent time with their children while overwhelmed, rattled with guilt or sleep-deprived, actually did more harm than good.[33] 'We can be at all those Saturday kids sports' games and we can be distracted, or we can be mindful and say, "I'm only going to go to one soccer game but I'm really going to be present, I'm not on my phone,"' as Georgina Manning, director of Wellbeing for Kids, tells me.

Researchers also say there's actually no reason to beat yourself up if you don't respond instantaneously to any sign of displeasure from your little ones. In fact, little frequent interruptions to your attention are alright – they are known as 'rupture and repair' by researchers. 'We can't be fully present all the time, that's impractical,' says Manning:

> I think that kids don't need as much as we think they need, in regard to the amount of attention. It's the quality of attention. So they need to be able to feel safe to come back to you, have their cups refilled, know that you're really attuned, and you're really present with them, and then they feel strong and safe to go out and explore the world.

To put it simply, the bar isn't as high as you might think. Some attachment theory experts say that if the primary caregiver can be reliable, available, warm and responsive at least 30 per cent of the time, and really follow their cues and be present with the child in those moments, the kids will be okay.[34]

Ditch the competitive parenting

Intensive parenting beliefs hold that mums should consistently provide intellectual stimulation for their child. You may have internalised that belief via the weirdly competitive messaging you receive from the media, Facebook, and maybe that slightly unbearable member of your mothers' group.

Manning says she's come across a lot of competitive parenting in her line of work, and she finds that it exhausts and daunts parents. 'There's this huge pressure that we have to be there and attentive for everything, otherwise we're not a loving mother, father, whatever,' she says.

Melissa Milkie, of the University of Toronto, and her colleague Catharine Warner, of the University of Maryland, have pointed out that these 'intensive mothering' expectations have even been expanded to include 'status safeguarding' – the work mothers do to 'ensure that a child's future social and economic status in a competitive marketplace is sustained or improved'.[35] In a time of economic uncertainty with relatively fewer good jobs (compared to previous generations), mums bend over backwards to create thriving, successful, unique children who are 'set to achieve a similar or better place in the social hierarchy compared with [their] parents'.

Which is why we have parents, even in cities in Australia with great public school systems, paying hundreds of dollars to list their kids on private-school waiting lists from the day after birth.

Some of us (*guilty!*) spend hours researching which childcare centres offer the most enriching activities, and securing access to toys that perfectly match each month's developmental stage. (Baby swim lessons, music and rhyme sessions, book-reading hours and sensory play classes are all common in my neighbourhood.)

As the children grow up, this 'status safeguarding' work also involves serious intervention if the child is falling off that path or not getting good grades or not getting enough attention from teachers. (Should we get a tutor? Send an email of concern to the teacher? Seek a child psychologist's opinion about why our kid is shy at parties?)

You might call this 'helicopter parenting' – and it is. But it's also what's expected of middle-class parents in Australia today, and it adds another layer of perfectionistic pressure that we have to work hard to say no to.

So repeat after me:

To be a good mother, you don't need to send your kids to school with a gourmet lunch every day.

You don't need to make sure they're dressed in all the latest trends.

You don't need to enrol them in Kumon classes, karate, ballet and a bilingual kindergarten to give them 'the best chance in life' (in fact, that kind of over-stimulation can be exhausting for them).

You don't need to spend your Saturdays making pasta necklaces, baking and converting your lounge room into a finger-painting zone.

And you certainly don't need to do any of these things to impress other parents, to post on social media about it, or to prove anything to yourself about what a good parent you are.

One fabulous woman who's consciously decided to pull back from

'Instagram-ifying' her kids is Bekah Martinez, co-host of popular podcast *Chatty Broads* and former contestant on *The Bachelor US*. 'I sometimes feel pressure from Instagram and other influencers for my kids to look put together, to always have their hair done, to always have matching cute outfits,' Bekah says. 'And I've chosen not to do that for my own sanity. But also because I want my kids to be able to play freely and get dirty outside and enjoy being a kid.'

Hear, hear.

♣

In the end, says psychotherapist Georgina Manning, intensive parenting is completely unsustainable, and 'heartbreaking for the parent, for the child, and for the family'. Instead of buying into this competitive parenting culture, she says, families could be 'just living, being in the flow, letting children play and taking the pressure off'. 'Balance' might be a corny word, but it's an important one, she says.

> I think that those extra things can be really enriching for children, but at what cost? Is there any time left for the children to have free play – not directed, outcome-based competitive stuff – every day? And is there time left for the parent and their wellbeing? If there's not time for those two things, something has to give.

SIDE NOTE: Three ways saying no can actually benefit your kids

You're teaching them resilience and empathy

When your answer's not always yes, you're teaching your kids how to handle delayed gratification, an essential skill as they get older, says Georgina Manning.

She's not talking about denying your toddler basic needs like food, but if your kid is demanding a certain toy, or another chocolate biscuit, or an episode of *Play School* before bed, they'll need to learn that they can't always get what they want immediately (unless you're keen on having a Veruca Salt on your hands).

By learning to sit with uncomfortable emotions, you're also building their resilience. 'It really helps children to be able to manage those different emotions, feeling uncomfortable, frustrated,' Manning says. 'And it's wider than that, because … it also comes into what we're teaching children about life, [as in] life's not always easy. It can also be quite difficult.'

When I interviewed Hobart-based child psychiatrist Dr Nicola Beamish for an *ABC Everyday* article about how much attention toddlers really need, she reassured me with a similar view.[36] Having to wait while a parent does something else, says Beamish, can actually teach toddlers that parents have their own mind and their own emotional needs, which helps them develop empathy.

You're fostering independent play

The 'circle of security' model describes how children constantly go out to explore the world, then circle back to their parent for comfort and protection. Secure attachment involves letting them go out and have that play.[37] That doesn't mean you should pop your kid in the sandpit and disappear for an hour, but it does mean it's healthy to let your kid investigate the world around them without a parent hovering or directing the play.

'It's about stepping back and letting your kid drive that interaction,' says Beamish. 'It's about asking yourself: "Does my child have a need that has to be met? Or are there times where they're happy doing their own thing?"'

You're a role model, mama

Saying no can also be a powerful way of modelling self-care for your kids.

'We know that children are always looking up to their parents for guidance, that role modelling,' says Manning. And they don't only absorb the explicit lessons we verbalise to our kids – they notice the way we prioritise and live our lives, too.

'They're learning about the world, about yourself and how you value yourself and your energy, and how you take care of yourself, how you value your interests,' Manning says. 'If you are running yourself thin as a female more than a male ... then children see that. If parents don't have self-care time, then children see that,' she adds.

'We're role modelling those boundaries, so that we're not an endless cup of love that doesn't run out ... And this teaches children about their own wellbeing. How do they refill their own cups, how do they replenish?'

American author Glennon Doyle has tackled a similar theme in her bestselling book *Untamed*, in which she tells the story of learning that a good mother is not one who slowly dies for her children, but one who shows them how to fully live.

Growing up, she 'was taught that mothers were to be martyrs', she says.[38] But as a parent, she made a decision: 'I'm going to create my own ideal, which is that mothers are models.'

She draws on the philosophy of Swiss psychologist Carl Jung, who once said that the greatest psychological influence on a child is 'the unlived life of the parent', to suggest that: 'Children will only allow themselves to live as fully as a parent lived ... So the duty of a parent is to not accept any life or relationship we wouldn't want our child to live.'

As mothers, our duty is not to endlessly self-sacrifice, Doyle says, but 'to accept nothing less true or beautiful than what we would accept for our own children'.

Chapter 13

Are you saving the world yet?

We threw away all our conventional notions of what was 'ladylike' and 'good form', and we applied to our methods the one test question: will it help?

– Emmeline Pankhurst[1]

I was touring a day-care centre when the eco-guilt set in.

The centre director was a proud environmentalist – and she made it clear that compliance with the centre's sustainability principles were heavily expected, if not enforced, among families attending the centre.

'Of course, we only use cloth nappies here,' she told me, leading me through an idyllic outdoor play area including a chicken coop, compost bin and a veggie patch. 'You're welcome to bring disposable nappies, but we'll change your baby into cloth nappies when they arrive. And then we'll send the dirty disposable nappies home with you – we don't want to contribute to the landfill here.'

The centre director went on to list the other guidelines she encouraged families to abide by: compulsory parents' 'working bees' to help plant the outdoor spaces. Strict policies about the types of toys children were allowed to bring from home (plastic toys, and toy soldiers, were a strict no-no.) Oh, and the centre closed at 5.30pm sharp, to promote family harmony in the evenings.

A large part of me admired the centre being run in such a principled way. But I also left the tour feeling wracked with self-doubt. Was I really so behind the times that I hadn't got around cloth nappies? What kind of workaholic was I that I couldn't guarantee my work would always wrap up by 5pm, allowing me to pick up my daughter before the centre shut its doors?

Oh, the shame!

I went home and googled 'disposable nappies and landfill'. Then I felt like a shit human being. Then I asked my husband whether he thought we should commit to cloth nappies – to which his immediate reaction was 'that seems too hard and too stinky'. Then I went to bed, adding it to my list of 'ethical life changes to research and budget for' (a mental spreadsheet with about 25 tabs, in case you're wondering).

Yes women and 'ethical guilt'

I'm not alone in questioning whether my life choices are ethical enough. Many women I surveyed for this book described a similar creeping sense of 'ethical guilt'. Often – but not always – this guilt centres on environmental concerns: reusable plastic, ethically made clothing, calculating the carbon emissions of travel, and eating less meat.

Very often, this guilt is wrapped up in perfectionism ('I make some ethical choices, but beat myself up for not making *every* ethical choice') and people-pleasing ('what will people think if I don't live an eco-friendly lifestyle?')

Laila, 29, who lives in New York, tells me she carries a reusable tote bag to go grocery shopping. But 'every time a package from an online delivery has unnecessary bubble wrap, or a drink is served to me with a plastic straw before I get a chance to say "No straw, please!" my soul dies a little because I feel personally responsible for killing a turtle,' she says.

Several women told me they worried their period products weren't sustainable: 'I have two menstrual cups but find them painful to use. I don't use them regularly and use disposable products – I feel like a quitter,' says Kayleigh, 27.

Some women dedicated their lives' work to making the world a better place – but found their boundless dedication to charity work had left them depleted and overwhelmed.

Others described their 'ethical guilt' in terms of feeling horrified that others might judge them.

'I sometimes cheat with my recyclable rubbish if my other bin is full – and I got a red tag on my bin from the Council once and all the neighbours knew. The guilt was horrible,' says Bel, 71, from Melbourne.

'We don't compost because we don't have a garden and I feel very bad about that. And I'm super worried about what other people think,' 26-year-old Kelly, from Darwin, tells me.

Carmen, 33, from regional Victoria, used to be a vegetarian, but following medical advice began eating meat after struggling for more than a year to conceive. 'I was pregnant soon after,' says Carmen – but she felt 'constant guilt through Instagram and vegan accounts I follow'.

How to do good without burning out

I'm not arguing that Yes Women should forget about living ethical lives. Like anyone who believes in science and cares about the planet, I'm deeply concerned about climate change, and recognise that the planet needs us all to make more eco-friendly choices. I also acknowledge the vital work people in the nonprofit sector and 'helping professions' do in improving the world (where would we be without the aid workers, the social workers, the nurses, the teachers, the counsellors?) I also recognise that I live a life of privilege – and to some extent, I believe that comes with a duty to share some of my fortune where I can.

But what concerns me is the thread of guilt and self-flagellation that ran through the anecdotes women shared with me about their attempts to live ethical lives. The Yes Women I spoke to often felt mortified and selfish if they left the house lights on when they went out, accidentally bought non-free-range pork or chucked their recyclables in the wrong bin. They also often shouldered all the burden for their family's 'good deeds' – being more likely than their partners to take care of the recycling, the donating and the volunteering in the family.

That's why this chapter digs into how a Yes Woman can do good in the world – without ending up burned out, stressed out and no good to anyone.

Here's what can help.

Find your cause(s)

As a Yes Woman, you want to do everything perfectly. But it's important to separate our ethical concerns from our perfectionistic streaks. That means accepting that it's *just not possible* to live an ethically perfect life.

There are always going to be trade-offs, because you'll have to work around your budget, your physical ability to get to the store or access internet delivery services, as well as your capacity for taking on the mental load of researching ethical options, says Dr Michal Carrington, a senior marketing lecturer at the University of Melbourne.

We're also, quite simply, constrained by the system we live in: 'There's a trade-off in terms of standing at the supermarket, looking at the shelf, and thinking, "well, I'm really passionate about organic, but I'm also passionate about local [and] this local product isn't organic," and vice versa,' Carrington explains. That's not to say we shouldn't try to make the best decisions we can – but it's about accepting that sometimes we can't make all the right choices, every time.

To use another example, unless you wear entirely homemade or vintage clothes, you've almost certainly shopped from a brand that's complicit in forced labour.[2] And the last time you signed a virtual petition on your smartphone? Sorry, but the device itself was probably made in a sweatshop that may have used child labour.[3]

But this leaves me wondering: if each of us makes trade-offs, how are we each meant to work out *what* to trade off? There's no single answer. Ethicists, climate lobbyists, and animal rights activists will all have different answers.

For Australian philosopher Peter Singer, living an ethical life means doing 'the most good you can do' given your means and life circumstances.[4] For Singer, an ethical decision isn't just volunteering for any charitable cause or giving money to a busker on the street – it's about thoughtfully weighing up where your actions or money can have the most impact, and making your decision.

For Carrington, passion and personal connection to a cause is also important. Generally, the cause you're most likely to stick with will be the one 'you're most passionate about it,' she says. It's also important to consider whether you have the financial means to devote yourself to a cause, and how much you can actually do as an individual before you feel fatigued and overwhelmed.

It may be that you have capacity to volunteer once a month for a single cause, or it might be that you're able to overhaul your entire family's shopping habits; ultimately, deciding what your ethical trade-off looks like is a very personal decision. Your own trade-offs might involve always choosing free-range eggs at the supermarket, but sometimes buying your sneakers from a chain store with an iffy environmental record. Or cycling whenever you can, but buying your kid a vaguely sexist toy because she *reeeeeally* wants it for Christmas.

Let's keep in mind that some ethical consumption choices have elitist overtones, with many sustainable options requiring a fair amount of disposable income (not to mention 'the leisure time to research the purchasing decisions you make, the luxury to turn up your nose at 95% of what you're offered, and, arguably, a post-graduate degree in chemistry to understand the true meaning behind ingredient labels', as Alden Wicker, journalist and sustainable fashion expert, wrote for *Quartz*).[5]

For Melbourne-based Yoruba, a 31-year-old part-time teacher and mother of one, the financial burden of buying 'ethically' has precluded her from buying the locally grown, organic food she'd prefer. Rather than beating herself up about buying factory-farmed meat for the family, she avoids buying new clothes for her kid, shopping at op shops instead, and works in a 'giving' profession with young children.

Run on passion, not guilt

Guilt isn't a good motivator, according to Carrington – and she's studied ethical consumption and consumer behaviour for years at the University of Melbourne, so she knows her stuff. Rather than making the world a better place, guilt just makes you feel bad.

It's far better for your wellbeing and the world if you make informed choices (which we'll get to in a minute), and then feel at peace with the decisions you've made.

It's healthier – and more effective – to make ethical decisions based on empathy and passion, not guilt or shame.

Put your individual acts into context

Can't stop self-flagellating when it comes to ethical decisions? It may help to put your individual choices into context. Because the reality is, while we feel guilty about the gap between our ethical attitudes and our actual actions (sometimes called 'the ethical consumption gap'), there are larger forces causing significantly worse damage to the world.

Desecration of sacred cultural sites by multinational oil companies. The illegal wildlife trade. Deforestation. The rise of economic inequality. Exploitative and abusive labour conditions in many parts of the world. Animal cruelty in industrialised farming.

These are issues on a massive scale caused by large corporations and governments – which are largely run by men, by the way.

Which sometimes makes me wonder if focusing on tampons and nappies and dishwasher detergent is, to some extent, a distraction from these major environmental threats.

I asked Carrington what she thinks about this. Do individuals have a responsibility to make the world a better place? Or is it corporations and governments who need to take the lead?

Her answer is, well, a little bit of both – but she definitely believes there's no use in individuals just sitting around feeling guilty.

'The individual can and should play an important role' in making ethical consumption choices, Carrington says. But it's also important to acknowledge that the individual is just one cog in a massive machine – a fact that often gets overlooked in conversations about ethical decisions, partly because 'companies and governments as well have become really good at placing the responsibility solely on the shoulders of the shopper', she adds.

It's a tactic Carrington calls 'the responsibilisation of the individual', and it perpetuates the idea that we can change the world through our individual choices.

Think, for example, about government PR campaigns urging families take shorter showers during the drought – seemingly obscuring the fact that industry, not individuals, consume the vast majority (88 per cent) of water in Australia. (Cotton producers use between 600 and 20,000 litres of water to grow the lint for a basic cotton t-shirt, for example, while the average water use per person per day in Sydney is just 324 litres.)[6]

In reality, our individual choices do have some impact – but arguably, it's more important to effectively lobby for politicians and companies to commit to climate action than to lose sleep over an occasional extra minute in the shower.

Ultimately, burdening yourself as an individual undercuts your effectiveness. Your individual actions should be balanced by societal and collective action.

Share the eco-burden with men in your life

Research shows that women tend to shoulder more ethical guilt than men.

Consider this: a study by market intelligence agency Mintel found that in the UK, while 71 per cent of women increased their commitment to ethical living, just 59 per cent of men say they began living more ethically between 2017 and 2018.[7] The same study found that men (67 per cent) were considerably less likely than women

(77 per cent) to be committed to regular recycling. Women were also more likely to try to use less water, save on or compost food waste, and regularly turn the heating off or down when they are not at home.[8]

The study's authors concluded that the results indicated an 'eco gender gap', revealing that men are less likely to pursue environmentally friendly behaviours than their female counterparts.

Closer to home, Michal Carrington has found in her research that women seem to be more concerned about slave labour – particularly when children and women are involved. She tells me women seem to be more active in ethical shopping in a broader sense, too.

Women are also more likely to volunteer than men,[9] and in politics, women are also at the forefront of environmental activism – with probably the highest-profile climate campaigners being Greta Thunberg and Alexandria Ocasio-Cortez.

So why do women say yes to these ethical causes more than men?

When it comes to buying environmental products, this could partly be because, as Mintel's research found, many women still tend to take charge of the running of the household – with chores such as grocery shopping, cleaning and laundry falling under that banner.[10]

Gendered social roles about 'Niceness' and communal values (caring about others and the wider community) being considered 'feminine' also seem to be partly to blame. Research has found that, ridiculously enough, some men feel that caring for the environment somehow undermines their masculinity. It's a phenomenon that researchers call the 'green-feminine stereotype'.

A study by researchers from Penn State in the US found that men could be disinclined to carry a reusable shopping bag for fear of being perceived as effeminate.[11] The same concern has been expressed as a factor in men's reluctance to adopt vegetarian or vegan diets.[12] In a series of experiments involving participants from across the US and China, researchers found that 'men and women both judged eco-friendly products, behaviours, and consumers as more feminine than their non-green counterparts'.[13]

Misogyny has even been identified as a factor in climate denial. A study by Swedish researchers, published in the *International Journal for Masculinity Studies* in 2014, found that: 'For climate sceptics, it was not the environment that was threatened; it was a certain kind of modern industrial society built and dominated by their form of masculinity.'[14]

So women – as society's 'givers', of whom we expect 'Niceness' and community-minded values – are expected to shoulder the burden of 'ethical living': the eco-friendly purchasing, the recycling, the community volunteering. In short, society has decided that 'ethical living' falls within women's portfolio.

There are interesting and depressing consequences of this gendered division of ethical behaviour. Research has found that not only are women held to a higher moral standard than men – they actually suffer disproportionate punishment when they violate this prescription, too.[15]

Take this 2016 study out of the US, for example. Researchers Jessica A Kennedy, Mary-Hunter McDonnell and Nicole Stephens concocted an experiment to test whether women might be judged more harshly for unethical behaviour. The researchers manipulated the gender of a manager in a hypothetical scenario, telling volunteers about a hospital administrator who deliberately filed a false reimbursement claim.

Some of the volunteers were told the 40-year-old administrator responsible for this fraud was named 'Jack Moranty', while others were told the administrator was 'Jill Moranty'. Apart from the name, all the other details were identical. The volunteers were then asked to recommend a jail sentence for this unethical administrator – and guess what? The average recommended sentence was around 80 days for Jack and around 130 days for Jill. That's nearly two months extra jail time, just because of the culprit's gender.[16]

There are other studies that show women seem to be judged worse when they fall short on other ethical matters, too. A whopping

92 per cent of women believe they face worse and more frequent criticism than men for cheating on their spouse, according to a study by married-dating site Ashley Madison.[17]

And while I doubt anyone has formally studied this, I'd put money on the fact that women are judged more harshly when they refuse to volunteer at a school fundraiser, or if they choose eggs from chooks in cages rather than free-range, or if they slam the door in the face of a door-to-door charity fundraiser.

All of which is to say: it shouldn't be on women to make sure the world's an ethical place.

Remember how we talked about dividing up emotional labour in a relationship, in Chapter 10? If you have a male partner, one assumption worth tackling as part of that process is the idea that you, as the woman, will take care of the household's ethical imprint.

Take care of yourself, too

For activists, nonprofit workers, and others working hard to change the world, self-care is crucial. Studies have shown that 90 per cent of charity workers felt stress, overwhelm or burnout over the past year.[18] Workers – such as teachers, social workers and nurses – who deal with people are also prone to burnout, with teaching having 'the highest burnout rate of any public service job', researchers have found.[19]

Emergency service workers such as paramedics, nurses and doctors, who continually work in high-stress conditions, are also at risk. Consider, for example, that burnout is experienced by 75 per cent of residents (doctors) and 67 per cent of mental health workers.[20,21]

Burnout is also common among activists – and is particularly rife among Black racial justice activists. That's not only because they are fighting a centuries-old fight, but also because they're experiencing something called 'racial battle fatigue', which US-based activist, author and burnout educator Dr Paul Gorski says is the 'cumulative impact of experiencing racism day to day'.[22]

One problem causing activism burnout is that 'the cultures of these movements often disregard the importance of self-care, seeing it as self-indulgence, putting activists at even higher risks of burnout', Gorski writes.[23]

When I interviewed a range of inspirational feminists for an *ABC Everyday* article on how to stay energised during the #MeToo movement, they each gave thoughtful responses about how they looked after themselves.[24]

Melbourne actor and writer Carissa Lee told me that as an Indigenous woman self-care is essential because, 'I'm trying to be active in the fight for our mob, as well as the feminist movement.' She makes a point of surrounding herself with 'strong, diverse women I can vent to', catching up with friends, and relying on her supportive partner to buoy her up through tough times.

Zoya Patel, a Canberra-based writer and editor who founded the online journal *Feminartsy*, told me that she similarly relies on her 'fellow feminists' to bolster her. 'I spend a lot of time connecting with my group chats,' she says. 'I often vent through those mediums, and I like that social media allows you to feel that solidarity straight away.'

It's also important to keep up your other interests outside of advocacy, so that being a warrior for women is not all-encompassing.[25]

Gorski, who has researched what works to mitigate burnout experiences in activists, has found that mindfulness practices such as yoga, tai chi, and meditation can help head off burnout. His research into social justice educators who tried these methods revealed 'a shared perception that, beyond helping to sustain their activism, mindfulness made them more effective activists'.[26]

Of course, if you're an activist or nonprofit worker or someone else doing good in the world, it's important to protect your own needs – and that of your work – by saying no.

Racial justice educator Rachel Ricketts talked about how 'no' is a large part of the work she does to help the BIPOC community heal from internalised trauma and challenge white supremacy. 'Saying no is a critical boundary-setting practice for [both cisgender and transgender] women, especially Black and Indigenous women,' she tells reporter Jess Sims in an article for *Health*.[27]

'Black women are expected to work harder, longer, and better than everybody else for less pay and less respect,' Ricketts says. 'Saying no allows us to prioritize ourselves rather than prioritizing everyone else, as we have been socialized to do.'

Do something kind for somebody else (and don't tell anyone about it)

Many Yes Women do good in the world because they're passionate, because they care deeply about a cause, and because they feel a sense of burning injustice. To those change-makers, I say: all power to you.

But sometimes, people do more 'good things' when others are around to witness them. One study set up an experiment in a coffee shop, and found that 70 per cent of consumers were happy to pay more for fair-trade coffee when they placed their order in earshot of other customers.[28] The customers wanted to keep up appearances, even when they didn't know the person listening in, the researchers found.

If that sounds like you, it's time to cut it out. Don't add 'posting a social justice hashtag' to your to-do list because you want to look like a good person. Don't waste the energy explaining that you feel 'so bad' about forgetting your keep cup because your colleagues will judge you. Performative 'ethical guilt' is boring, takes up time and energy you don't have – and doesn't help anyone.

Instead, consider finding a cause you care about, stick with that, and say nope to performing 'good deeds' out of guilt and vanity.

When you can't 'do good' 24/7

Ethical living can take up time – but it doesn't have to be an enormous time-suck. You don't need to volunteer every Saturday, switch careers to nonprofit fundraising, or donate your eggs in order to do good in the world.

As a short-on-time Yes Woman, you might want to also consider these options for taking ethical action – which don't come with a significant time commitment:

Writing letters

For every letter that a retailer gets, their assumption is that there are at least one thousand other people out there with the same complaint. (That's according to marketing lecturer Michal Carrington, who used to work for retailers.) So don't underestimate the power of a letter to a manufacturer or government – they might just take it more seriously than you'd expect.

Voting for parties that represent your values and ethical views

And lobby your friends to vote, too.

Just consuming less

Rather than obsessing over whether you're buying eco-friendly brands, consider easy ways to reduce the amount you buy overall. (Do you really need fabric softener, or that third pair of sneakers? Could you join the library rather than buying new books for your kids?)

Automating it

Peter Singer argues in his book *The Most Good You Can Do* that there are many ways to be an 'effective altruist' (a term he uses to describe a person who does 'the most good they can do'). For some effective altruists, doing good means working in a well-paid job (in, say, finance or manufacturing) – and then donating a significant part of that income to the most effective charities.[29] As Singer puts it, 'the more you earn, the more you can donate'.[30]

Even if you earn an average salary, making regular financial donations isn't out of the question. If you take a look through your monthly spending on a recent bank statement, you might just find that you're blowing money on items you could do without.

For Yes Women who can afford this option, it can be incredibly time-efficient: you can automate your internet banking to deposit a portion of your pay cheque into charitable funds every month. Sure, there is a certain amount of mental energy you'll need to expend upfront deciding which cause to donate to. (Websites such as *The Life You Can Save*, *ChangePath* and *GiveWell* have searchable online databases that can help with your search.)

But once you've decided where your automated donations will go each month, you can kiss goodbye to ethical guilt – freeing up the time and energy you may have otherwise spent fretting over where, and how, to do good in the world.

Chapter 14

Pretty (tired)

> Prettiness is not a rent you pay for occupying a space marked female.
>
> – Erin McKean[1]

The young women raise their arms high over the roof of the red 4WD, whooping and cheering as the vehicle slows to a stop outside the mansion.

Clad in the tiniest swimsuits imaginable, the women – all but one are white – strut into a garishly decorated, newly built villa.

The young women's glossy lips slide around the rims of tall flutes of champagne served poolside. The camera zooms in on the young women's rears, momentarily going into slow-motion to emphasise the bikini briefs wedged high up their backsides. Their legs, arms and bottoms are shiny, as if they've been oiled from head to toe.

It's season one of Australian reality series *Love Island*, and this is prime-time television in the 2020s.

Welcome to the hyper-sexy beauty standards of today, ladies.

I watched *Love Island* for weeks when the first season aired in Australia. It was my nightly unwind routine, my guilty pleasure.

But then I stopped – because I started to feel like shit about my own body. After an evening sprawled on the couch, watching the blow-dried, whippet-thin-but-somehow-also-toned *Love Island* beauties on the screen in front of me, I popped to the bathroom and scowled at the jiggle in my arms that had emerged sometime in my mid-20s. I regarded my short, brittle fingernails with disdain. I even idly googled botox.

As the weeks wore on, this little dance of self-scrutiny became a nightly mental tug-of-war. I'd start by admiring the contestants' fit figures and flawless skin. I'd quickly move on to comparing myself with them – and coming up screamingly short. And then I'd launch into an internal debate between two parts of my brain.

The reasonable, kind part of my mind soothingly reminded me that not everyone can have the proportions of a bikini model (and assured me that, anyway, I was only seeing these women after they'd been styled and spray-tanned.) Meanwhile, my screechy inner voice noted with disgust that I had thick ankles and still didn't know the first thing about contour makeup.

I feel embarrassed – like a bad feminist, even – admitting that a reality show made me care so much about my looks. But I will, because I know I'm not alone: research has been showing for years that the unrealistic images of beauty popularised by the media generally make women less satisfied with their bodies.[2]

In especially bad news for Yes Women, research has found that perfectionists, in particular, are vulnerable to negative body image[3] and tend to be more appearance-oriented than non-perfectionists. We also know that Yes Women tend to be particularly influenced by social expectations – and there's no avoiding the fact that some of the most intense (and most gendered) social expectations around are centred on beauty ideals. For Yes Women, good enough isn't ever good enough, and we can find ourselves pouring huge amounts of time and angst – not to mention money – into looking the way we believe we should look.

Making things even tougher for us perfectionistic Yes Women: we're living in an age where, in many ways, these media images of beautiful women are more unrealistic – and more populous – than ever.

Think about it: decades ago, bypassing the magazine aisle was enough to avoid comparing yourself with models, and even the most beautiful women in movies had yellowing teeth or the occasional stray hair. Beauty ideals still plagued women – and while they were problematically Eurocentric (as they remain today), many markers of 'beauty' in a woman were more achievable; we could spot a touch of cellulite on a TV star and remind ourselves these women were mortals.

Unlike the otherworldly beauties of *Love Island*, whose thighs are as smooth as their unwrinkled foreheads.

Yes Women and the politics of beauty

Ideals of feminine beauty have changed over cultures and centuries. The most familiar model to women these days, repeated through decades' worth of entertainment and art, is the very thin, usually white, ultra-feminised woman.

So where do these expectations come from?

Interestingly, they come from very similar places to all other Yes Woman expectations: from patriarchy, racism and capitalism.

Starving, straight, white females

Capitalism has a lot to answer for when it comes to the unrealistic beauty ideals women are expected to care about (and devote their precious time, money, and 'yes-es') to attaining.

As Clementine Ford writes in her book *Fight Like a Girl*:

> No matter what we do, we'll never succeed in attaining the 'perfect' body or the 'perfect' face. This isn't just because perfection is an unattainable goal; it's because capitalism relies on people being constantly unhappy so it can keep selling us the promise that consumerism will make our lives better.[4]

You know those parts of your body you hate? Deep down, we all realise they're not inherently 'flawed'. You've only been told they are because advertisers make money off making women feel shit about themselves – and because we live in a society that tells us our appearance is the most important thing about us. Removed from those messages, the parts of your body have no inherent value. You don't have 'a good nose' or 'a bad nose' – you just have a nose.

Beauty ideals are not only upheld by capitalism – they're also determined by racist values. Yep, Western colonialism – and systemic racism – have meant that Eurocentric beauty standards have essentially become global beauty standards, as reporter Jessica DeFino argues.[5] For many women of colour, the beauty and fashion industries and the media still seem to send a clear message that whiteness equals beauty; that the way they look isn't normal, desirable or enough. Even in India, almost all Indian actresses and models are fair-skinned.[6] Look at any mainstream fashion magazine, runway or billboard and you're likely to be blinded by the white.

Beauty products and fashions are arguably often made with white women in mind – just look at garments being regularly labelled 'nude', when they're clearly porcelain- or beige-coloured.

These difficulties continue in the makeup aisle: a 2016 Superdrug survey found that 70 per cent of Asian and Black women felt their beauty needs weren't met by high street brands[7] (that's why it was so celebrated when Rihanna introduced Fenty Beauty, which offers shades and colours to match all skin tones).

And for most of my living memory, a cursory glance at runways and billboards has presented whiteness as the apex of female beauty. At the 2015 Fall New York Fashion Week, more than three-quarters of runway models (77.4 per cent) were white – despite the fact that fewer than 43 per cent of New York residents are white.[8] Black models on those runways accounted for 8.7 per cent, Asian models made up 8.5 per cent, and Latina women less than 4 per cent[9] – while on the real-life city streets, 29 per cent of residents are Hispanic or Latino, more than 24 per cent are Black or African American, and almost 14 per cent are Asian.[10]

The fact that Angolan model Maria Borges made history in 2015 by appearing with her natural hair on the annual Victoria's Secret runway – a show that (when it still existed) was widely regarded as a showcase of the most stunning models – says a lot about how long it's taken to even start a conversation about diversity in the industry.[11]

There's been a slow shift towards representation of more diverse forms of beauty in the last few years, though. By spring 2019, more than one-third of all runway models across New York, London, Milan and Paris fashion weeks were models of colour, according to a report by *The Fashion Spot*.[12] Women's magazines are also slowly becoming better at featuring women of colour on their covers, at least in the US.[13] But even today, many models of colour who do succeed tend to have fairer skin and typically European features such as light eyes, straightish hair, and a narrow nose: models of colour in media,[14] have to be 'a white girl dipped in chocolate', as a magazine editor once described supermodel Iman back in 1976.[15]

These concerns were echoed by a number of Yes Women of colour I heard from in researching for this book – such as Nimala, a 29-year-old New-York based communications professional with Sri Lankan heritage, who struggled with her skin colour for many years because of restrictive beauty standards. 'Growing up in Sri Lankan culture, I noticed how light skin was the ideal standard of beauty. It was preferred, regarded as more attractive, and in turn came with advantages,' she tells me.

She remembers, as a child, attending Sri Lankan dance class, and noticing that the dancers with lighter skin were placed in the front row or featured more prominently.

'That example stands out to me as that's when I began to identify light skin with privilege, opportunity, success,' she says.

She noticed that relatives in Sri Lanka, when looking to set up their daughter or son with a partner, sought a 'fair' match. She was also told she was 'pretty, even though you're dark' – as if her skin tone was a blemish to be overcome.

'I tried really hard to change something that I couldn't really change – researching things, trying different products and remedies, avoiding the sun, not wearing certain colours, writing myself off from pursuing things because I felt disadvantaged to begin with,' she says. When relatives or friends offered natural solutions to lighten her skin, such as using aloe or papaya or sandalwood, 'I definitely bought into it … and was interested for a while,' she says.

'I felt that way until my early 20s when I started to feel comfortable with the way I looked and realised the problem was not me,' she added.

⁂

As well as being rooted in racism, these beauty standards are entrenched in heteronormative beliefs. At their core is this essential idea of what a woman is and should be: cisgendered, straight and primed for an old-school male gaze.

We're expected to jump through hoops to meet this narrow ideal of femininity – and anyone who doesn't fit within that ideal, or chooses to present in a way that doesn't conform, can feel excluded from or devalued by society.

People of all sexualities and gender identities can feel influenced and oppressed by these narrow expectations. But these ideals can be especially problematic for queer and trans people. Taylor, a 27-year-old trans non-binary person who uses 'they/them' pronouns, described their ambivalence towards these traditional feminine beauty ideals – which they saw as reflecting 'compulsory heterosexuality'.

'I'm thinking about whether I want to do top surgery or a breast reduction [because] my boobs give me awful staggering gender dysphoria,' Taylor says. But Taylor is constantly aware of the voice of society whispering, 'you have to be sexually palatable … if you cut off your tits, the average man is not going to be interested in you, and your big boobs were the things that boys in high school told you were your greatest asset.'

There's also a fear of misogynistic, transphobic repercussions that can arise from rejecting these beauty ideals, Taylor says – and indeed, studies have shown that people who reject heteronormative beauty ideals (such as women who refuse to shave their legs) are met with 'homophobia and heterosexism from others as well as hostility'.[16]

'If I cut my tits off and I have the gayest fucking haircut, it makes me more visible,' Taylor says. 'If you move away from the more traditional look of femininity, you're moving away from the traditional vestige of safety; the safety of knowing the patriarchal handbook back to front.'

So when you're considering who you're shaving your legs for, or dyeing your hair for, or slathering that foundation on for, it's worth considering the extent to which beauty ideals rooted in 'compulsory heterosexuality' have played a part.

From ultra-thin to the rise of the toned, curvy-bummed, ultra-groomed woman

Beyond the focus on being straight and white, the specifics of the 'ideal' female beauty have shifted a little over time – and with each shift, I believe Yes Women are increasingly bogged down by the need to look a certain way.

Consider this: if you're a millennial like me, you grew up seeing the ultra-thin, 'heroin chic' aesthetic take centre stage in popular media. Now you're a grown-ish woman, and you still probably equate thinness with beauty – but the look has changed over time to arguably become harder to achieve.

Models have been thin for decades, but today's models are more so. In 1986 the average model weighed 8 per cent less than the average woman, and by 2006, they weighed 23 per cent less.[17] The body weight percentage has continued to fall since then: by 2016, the average model had a BMI of 17.3 – well below the World Health Organization's definition of 'malnourished'.[18] Today, some of the highest paid models in the world are Kendall Jenner and Karlie Kloss, with reported BMIs of 16 and 17 respectively.[19]

Many of us perfectionists struggle not to compare ourselves to runway models (and then beat ourselves up when we inevitably fall short). And we're fighting a losing battle, as this current media ideal of thinness for women is achievable by less than five per cent of the female population.[20] Even runway models don't naturally look as whippet-thin as they appear on the catwalk, with many relying on unhealthy practices: prescription drugs, laxatives, daily colonics, cigarettes, and even injections to suppress their appetite and speed up thyroid function, as Russian model and actor Kira Dikhtyar has said in interviews.[21]

For everyday women to hold themselves to the same standard of thinness that is difficult to achieve even for the professionals, whose wages rely on them adhering to it, is clearly absurd. But I've absolutely said yep to calorie-counting apps and crash diets with the sole goal of looking skinnier (health be damned).

Today, reality stars and fitness 'influencers' on Instagram are rising alongside cover girls and supermodels when it comes to setting the beauty standards. The look they promote? Still very slender and still very white – but with the addition of incredible toning, rock-hard abs, full lips, and often curvy bums or boobs to boot. They also invariably showcase intense grooming – thick, perfectly pencilled-in eyebrows; contoured cheeks; chiselled noses and cheekbones; full lips.

If you don't know the look to which I'm referring, find Jen Selter's Instagram, which is packed with photos of the fitness influencer doing yoga in front of pristine beachscapes, her impossibly pert derrière often clad in a thong bikini (I mention her derrière because she makes a point of centring much of her content on it; she's even sometimes captioned her photos 'just another photo of my booty with a view').[22]

Reality TV royalty the Kardashian sisters spruik a similar aesthetic. Their gym selfies (seen by hundreds of millions of Instagram followers) invariably showcase teeny-tiny waists, unbelievably rounded bosoms and bums, a full face of makeup, plumped-up lips and not a hair out of place.

Some critics suggest the Kardashians' beauty styles contain

elements of cultural appropriation, 'making cutesy trends out of the cornrows, wigs, and extensions that have been part of black beauty culture for decades and, in some cases, centuries', as Zan Romanoff writes for *BuzzFeed News*. Pointing to Kylie Kardashian's enhanced lips and the Kardashians' collective celebration of the derrière, Romanoff points out that the Kardashians 'wear black bodies' and have 'taken these features and styles and turned them into trends; they've received approbation and gotten extraordinarily wealthy in part because they can wear blackness without having to actually be black'.[23]

In my role at *ABC Everyday*, I did some reporting around girls' body image and social media. When I interviewed University of Canberra clinical psychologist and assistant professor of psychology Vivienne Lewis about the effect that social media can have on girls' self-esteem, she expressed concern that the look young women are chasing today is 'thin, toned and fit' all at once.[24] You might assume that this fit, toned aesthetic is healthier than the 90s ideal of stick-thin or heroin chic. But Lewis told me that even if the pretext of an influencer's brand is 'fitness' – not thinness or beauty – the message can still be negative.

'At the end of the day, the message [that the girls viewing those images] really take home is, "I should look that particular way". You don't see many adolescents striving to have better hearts or better lung capacity,' Lewis says.

Indeed, after 10 minutes scrolling through Jen Selter's Instagram account, it's her tiny waist and round bum that I compare myself to (Instagram is a visual medium, more given to showcasing the way somebody looks than their cardio health, after all.) I'm not alone, either: research has found that thin 'fitness inspo' images don't actually motivate participants to engage in higher levels of exercise than non-fitness 'thinspiration' images – but they do lead to increased body dissatisfaction among university-aged girls.[25]

Instagram and self-objectification

You might think that feeling better about the way we look involves unfollowing fitness influencers, switching off reality TV, and walking on by the magazine aisle at Coles.

If only it were that easy.

Today, it's not just airbrushed models in ads or 'influencers' who are posing by Lake Como in a bikini anymore – it's that girl you haven't seen since high school. Or your next-door neighbour. Or that woman from your mothers' group. She's probably using one of a dozen cheap-and-easy slimming photo apps to filter and tweak and 'Facetune' her image so it looks like a model's.

With the rise of Instagram and its attendant editing apps, the boundary between advertisement and real-life happy snap has been blurred. Now, even non-celebrities are urged to refine their 'personal brand',[26] as if each of us is a corporation to be marketed. We're invited to manipulate and manage our own image – sometimes under the illusion that it's somehow subversive or liberating to be the ones defining the way our image is shown.[27] (Personally, I'm not sure I buy it. But more on that later.)

Apart from the requirement to be white, thin and toned, there's also all the other stuff – plumped-up lips, botoxed crow's feet, flawless nails, spray-on effect eyebrows – we're expected to nail these days.

Our television screens feature more cosmetically enhanced and highly groomed women than in previous decades: those *Love Island* beauties with their hair extensions and their pert, oiled-up buttocks, for example. Jia Tolentino, a staff writer at *The New Yorker*, expertly sums up this new 'ideal woman'. In her book *Trick Mirror*, Tolentino states that the new ideal woman focuses on meticulous improvement of her image:

> The work formerly carried out by makeup has been embedded directly into her face: her cheekbones or lips have been plumped up, or some lines have been filled in, and her eyelashes are

> lengthened every four weeks by a professional wielding individual lashes and glue. The same is true of her body, which no longer requires the traditional enhancements of clothing or strategic underwear; it has been pre-shaped by exercise that ensures there is little to conceal or rearrange.[28]

There's also a particular look that women of colour and Black women are expected to fulfil. For 18-year-old student Salma, from Oxford in the UK, one source of perfectionistic pressure comes from the fact that the media has become 'obsessed with a particular aesthetic' for mixed-race and Black women. 'We are only deemed attractive if we have tiny waists and large hips and lips,' Salma told *The Guardian* in an article on women and perfectionism.[29] 'Over the past few months I have started to become very self-conscious about my lips, which are not as full and beautiful as other Black women's. I don't have plans to get plastic surgery, but if I did get anything done it would be lip fillers because it just seems to be a fashion thing now – [a] lot of celebrities get it done.'

This isn't a dig at models or women on reality TV. They can do what they want with their bodies. But when every media source we see promotes an ideal of beauty that requires artificial eyelashes, nails, hair, liposculpture, lip fillers, boob jobs and even 'beautification' processes of the vulva (ouch), we begin to normalise this ultra-enhanced, hyper-sexualised form of physical beauty. At some level, we ingest the message that this form of physical perfection is attainable.

Against this backdrop, it's no surprise that extreme and often painful beautification measures are on the rise. Lip fillers and anal bleaching (yep) are no longer the domain of women whose job it is to fulfil these beauty standards or turn others on: the popularity of lip fillers surged 44 per cent in the six years to 2016,[30] and there's been a 23 per cent surge in the number of women seeking anal bleaching – the trend resulting from popular reality stars discussing the procedure, according to one *Glamour* article.[31] Bum implants involving fat-grafting (taking unwanted fat from one area like the stomach and adding it to the backside) was the hottest growing cosmetic surgery trend in 2019, surging 19 per cent from 2018, according to a report by the American Society of Plastic Surgeons.[32]

An article published in peer-reviewed medical journal *JAMA Facial Plastic Surgery* even deemed this the 'era of filtered photographs'. 'These filters and edits have become the norm, altering people's perception of beauty worldwide,' the authors remarked.[33] Millennials, in particular, tell doctors they want to look as good in person as they do through their Snapchat filters, as doctors reported to CNBC for a 2019 article about Instagram driving plastic surgery among millennials.[34]

♣

This trend towards marketing ourselves – towards 'self-presentation and self-surveillance' – is aptly dissected by Jia Tolentino. She points out that it's now easy enough to 'engage women's scepticism towards ads and magazine covers, images produced by professionals'. The problem, she writes, is that 'it is harder for us to suspect images produced by our peers, and nearly impossible to get us to suspect the images we produce of ourselves, for our own pleasure and benefit'.[35]

Tolentino is essentially expanding here on the feminist theory of self-objectification: the idea, first proposed in the 90s by US researchers Barbara Fredrickson and Tomi-Ann Roberts, that 'sexually objectifying experiences encountered by girls and women accumulate over time, eventually leading them to internalize the sexual objectification and turn it on themselves', as US psychology professor Rachel Calogero explains it.[36] In this way, Fredrickson and Roberts argue, girls and women in Westernised societies come to see themselves through a 'veil of sexism'.

This compulsion to edit and market ourselves – to objectify ourselves – and to constantly compare ourselves to others leads us to constantly body-monitor, or 'body check'; our relationship with our body becomes shaped by constant comparison to societal standards, and we can also develop feelings of shame, anxiety, disordered eating, depression, and sexual dysfunction.[37]

Just 30 minutes a day scrolling Instagram can make women fixate negatively on their weight and appearance, according to a study by the University of New South Wales and Macquarie University,[38] and studies have also shown our perception of wellbeing and life satisfaction may be undermined by Facebook.[39]

How to decide what beauty ideals to say yes to

None of this is to say that beautification procedures are inherently bad. I'm not interested in demonising all beauty practices: sometimes, it can feel great to pop on a bright red lippie, try a new hair mask, or get a pedi.

But for Yes Women who struggle to set limits on other people's expectations on them, society's obsession with female beauty can be an exhausting rabbit hole that sucks up our time – and makes us feel crap, not better, about ourselves. That's why it's important we consciously decide how much time, energy and money we'd like to pour into beauty, diet culture and grooming – and interrogate the extent to which we really want to engage with those expectations.

One incredible woman who has said no to beauty standards is Bekah Martinez of *The Bachelor (US)* and *Chatty Broads* podcast fame. When I got in touch to ask about whether she struggled to say no to any beauty standards in particular, she told me she's given up removing body hair.

'Growing up I was always super insecure about my leg and armpit hair. I would get anxiety whenever I was with friends or at swim parties and I wasn't completely shaved,' she told me:

> This was a crippling insecurity for me growing up and when I became a mom I wanted my kids to have an example of their mom existing in her natural body without shame. So when I completely stopped shaving I felt like I was working to overcome

my insecurity and rewriting the narrative about the things that make my body beautiful.

It's taken time and hard work, though: 'It's been a long journey to make myself feel comfortable, but it's worth it to work against unrealistic standards that the beauty industry profits from,' she said.

♣

Pushing back on these beauty standards is often easier said than done though, right? That's why I've laid out a few pointers that Yes Women can use to distinguish between practices that genuinely feel good – and those that feel onerous, as if they're sapping time and energy better used elsewhere.

Look at your 'flaws' for what they are

As with the Yes Woman myths we looked at earlier, once you've started to challenge your assumed beliefs, they lose power. So next time you start to obsess about a specific 'flaw' of yours, step back and question what makes you think it even is a flaw. Chances are you'll find that there's nothing inherently wrong with it: there are social and political reasons you're being made to feel this way.

Shall I give you a personal example? Oh, go on then – let's talk about my 'hip dips'.

I spent many years staring at what I believed to be a grievous bodily flaw: the gentle inward curve between the hip bone and thigh. For years, I wondered why my hip dips (also known as 'violin hips') weren't a neat, curved bracket.

They drove me crazy.

I went on a mission to rid myself of my curvy situation: I dieted. I wore Spanx. I avoided pencil skirts. I covertly googled 'how to get rid of hip dips' and did a ton of leg and glute exercises.

It wasn't until I researched human anatomy that I realised hip dips are normal. Completely, utterly normal. They're not an indication that you're unhealthy, or out of shape; they're literally a part of the bone structure that's more visible in some women than others. No amount of diet, or exercise, or even surgery can remove them – and what's more, throughout history most women haven't wanted to. Because what we now call 'hip dips' has historically been seen as a lovely, normal, womanly part of the female figure (and still is, if you look at some of the gorgeous women sporting hip dips: Jessica Alba, Rihanna, Bella Hadid, Kate Moss and Marilyn Monroe).

It was only when Instagram culture made up a name for them, and fitness influencers and dubious sports articles started posting about how to 'cure them', that they suddenly got added to the list of 'bits us women have to hate about our bodies'.

It may not be 'hip dips' that bother you, of course. It might be your cellulite, or your feet, or your grey hair, or your tummy, or your breasts – take your pick of a hundred different beauty expectations relating to all parts of the human physique. Whatever body part you focus on, it probably wasn't considered a flaw until advertisers made it out to be. (Cellulite wasn't really talked about widely until 1973, when *Vogue* magazine introduced readers to the word. Before that, that bumpy orange-peel effect was actually considered a normal part of the female form.)[40]

Learning more about the systems of power making you feel bad about your physical appearance can help, regardless of what physical feature you're focused on.

While we're speaking of reading up, remember Nimala, the New York-based communications professional with Sri Lankan heritage?

Diving into study on structural racism and privilege helped her overcome a decades-long feeling of insecurity about her skin colour.

'I learnt about structural racism, privilege, colorism, inequality and it put my personal examples into context for me. It took a really long time to unlearn all of that and my perception of myself completely changed,' she tells me. 'Today I completely reject the idea that my skin colour makes me less attractive,' Nimala tells me. 'I no longer feel like I'm competing in a race that I will never be able to win. It feels very liberating.'

Calculate how much (time, effort and dollars) your beauty and diet routine is costing

Ever since I was 14, I've been getting my hair coloured blonde. I have thick hair, and it takes four hours each time I visit the salon – which my colourist urges me to do every eight weeks.

When you add it up, I have spent 3536 hours of my life having my hair dyed. That's 147 days – almost five whole months.

(My husband, by comparison, spends exactly 20 minutes in the salon every three months getting a trim. And that, my friend, is the 'gender beauty gap' – the increased time and money that women spend on grooming and beauty compared to men.)

♣

For your sake, I hope you don't spend four hours in a salon chair every few weeks.

But whatever your circumstances, as a Yes Woman it's worth considering which parts of your beauty regimen take up the most time and energy. This is as simple as sitting down with a calculator, a bank statement and a calendar showing appointments for the last three months or so, and working out how much your beauty efforts are costing you. Include on the list an estimate of the time and money you spend on everything from hair (colour, extensions, relaxant, toning) and makeup, to hair removal, skin treatments, skin tanning or lightening, teeth whitening, injectables, and so on.

Consciously decide what's worth it

So what next?

I'm not about to tell you to chuck your eyeliner in the bin and swear off shaving your legs forever (although literally do that if you're feeling it).

Once you've scrutinised your own beauty and dieting regimen, it's up to you to make an informed choice about which bits are worth your while – and to say no to practices that hinder you. This doesn't mean that you stop caring about how you look. But it does mean that you have a choice about which beauty ideals you partake in, and which you don't.

If you spend money on makeup because it's fun, and you love it, go ahead and say yep to those practices. (Fake tan, come right on in! Shellac manicures, come at me.) But if you're leaning on your beauty routine because you don't feel okay, normal or acceptable without it – it's likely you're saying yes to beauty ideals for more problematic reasons: because you struggle with poor body image or are plagued by a sense that you 'have to' look a certain way.

Those feelings are signals it may be time to ditch some of the routines and work on developing a better self-image – so you can use your valuable time, energy and money on things that really matter to you and make you feel good.

Of course, society is more forgiving of certain people relaxing beauty standards than others. Mikki Kendall, in *Hood Feminism*, points out: 'While a messy bun might be considered sloppy chic for white girls, any hint that a Black woman has failed to put effort into her appearance is met with ardent disapproval both inside her community and outside it.' She adds, 'In order to be pretty in a white-centered aesthetic or in a Black one you have to look as if you spend at least some time in the beauty parlor, or at least with a good kitchen beautician.'[41]

It's possible to reject Eurocentric beauty standards – Kendall did so as an adult by embracing her natural hair after an entire childhood of having her hair 'tamed' – but it means making a more radical statement, and facing potentially greater repercussions.[42] Research from Duke University in 2020 showed that Black women with natural hairstyles, such as afros, braids or twists, are often perceived as less professional than Black women with straightened hair, and were not recommended as frequently for interviews compared with three other types of candidates.[43]

That's discouraging – but as more women speak out and work to decentre Eurocentric ideals of beauty, there have been signs of positive change. At the time of writing, Miss Universe Australia has been won by women of colour three years running. The 2020 winner Maria Thattil – who is Melbourne-born and of Indian heritage – says she believes she's part of a growing collective of women of colour redefining Australian beauty standards – and has been 'inundated' with messages of support from other women of colour who feel encouraged by seeing more diversity within the beauty industry. [44] 'Many say that seeing this kind of representation is inspiring, and has spurred in them a sense of self-belief that they too can take up and create space,' Thattil says.[45]

Who am I actually doing this for?

Working out what you actually want to say yes to involves asking yourselves some frank questions about the motivations behind each item on your beauty routine. Specifically: do you diet, wear makeup, and get hot wax stripped off your body for yourself – or for other people?

Many women say their beauty routines are all about feeling their best, most confident, freshest, most professional selves.

But for many of us, the answer is murkier – because none of us live in a vacuum; we've absorbed ideas (from advertising and elsewhere) about what makes us feel our best, most confident, freshest and most professional self. So what might feel like a personal choice is informed by politics and cultural influences. As journalist Yumi Stynes has pointed out for *ABC Everyday*, most of us engage in at least some beauty practices for other reasons. 'We're playing in a space that rewards beautiful women and discredits plain ones. Women head into workspaces that implicitly – and sometimes explicitly – demand that we look "groomed",' she writes.[46]

After decades living among those messages and practising these practices without question, it can be difficult to unpick our own feelings of self-worth from the sexist, internalised ideals swirling around us of what is 'beautiful'.

So how do you work out what feels good for you and what you're only doing out of a sense of 'should' (and internalised ideas about what women should look like)?

One tactic is to consider a break for a day, week or month to see the difference those changes make to your time, money and energy: sometimes, stepping off the treadmill of grooming, beautifying, preening and dieting can give you perspective on how much of yourself you're really pouring into beautification.

Case in point: journalist Katie Cunningham – whose self-esteem struggles manifest 'as a perfectionism in matters of personal grooming' – noticed that having a forced break from her beauty regimen during the first lockdowns of the coronavirus pandemic in 2020 felt liberating. '[W]ith salons ordered to close, my finely tuned schedule was no more. And so, with a shrug, I simply gave up on the whole thing,' she wrote in an article for *The Guardian*.[47] 'To my surprise, it's felt like exhaling.'

While Cunningham described no plans to give up makeup forever, she reflects that the months-long pause from caring about her appearance has caused her to question her perfectionistic mindset: 'I used to think striving for perfection was the only solution to my insecurities; I now know there is a truer peace in not giving them brain space at all.'

Similarly, Yumi Stynes gave up on buying makeup and beauty products for the month of May 2020 – and, after spending zero that month on makeup, she compared it to the same month a year prior, and found she had spent at least $200 on makeup.[48]

It's also worth considering the headspace your beauty regimen is taking up. The American Psychological Association has found that girls' preoccupation with appearance ties up cognitive resources, 'meaning girls will have less time and mental energy for other pursuits' such as schoolwork.[49]

The same holds true for adults. In a passage from *The Beauty Myth*, which I still think about regularly, Naomi Wolf wrote about what she might have done instead if she had not spent her time counting calories:

> What if she [the young woman] doesn't worry about her body and eats enough for all the growing she has to do? She might rip her stockings and slam-dance on a forged ID to see the Pogues, and walk home barefoot, holding her shoes, alone at dawn; she might babysit in a battered-women's shelter once a month; she might skateboard down Lombard Street with its seven hairpin turns, or fall in love with her best friend and do something about it, or lose herself for hours gazing into test tubes with her hair a mess, or climb a promontory with the girls and get drunk at the top ...[50]

Only engage in selfie culture that feels good for you

While you're deciding which beauty practices are worth it, one area worth special attention is the posting (and editing) of photos of yourself on social media.

Social media is fuel to the flames in women's perfectionism: it makes perfection appear attainable by inundating us with many, many more images that are, quite literally, edited for perfection. While there has always been pressure on women to be attractive, 'for the first time in history, we are getting to see far more "perfect" people than ordinary people now that computer imaging produces perfection in a nanosecond,' as journalist Caryl Rivers and research psychologist Rosalind Barnett note in their book *The New Soft War on Women*.[51]

Essentially, on Instagram and Facebook we're bombarded with the highlight reels of other people's lives – and for us Yes Women, it can feel near-impossible not to compare our regular, warts-and-all lives with the picture-perfect images on our screens.

Our body image, as we've already covered, suffers markedly from this constant social media comparison. Additionally, researchers from Berlin have found that our Facebook friends tending to come from similar backgrounds to ours means that the negative effects of social comparison are heightened. ('I guess it's not as depressing to measure yourself against a Hollywood movie star as against the girl you went to primary school with,' journalist Jill Stark muses in her book *Happy Never After*.)[52] This phenomenon is perfectly summed up by 18-year-old Miranda, from Cambridge, quoted in an article by Sarah Marsh in *The Guardian*:

> I certainly feel the pressure to be perfect and it has got to the point where it's damaging my health. Social media is the main culprit. I had to delete my Instagram account because it would actually make me cry. I am a mature person with a firm grip on reality, but I have so many peers whose lives seem so perfect and sociable that it left me feeling worthless and lonely.[53]

Despite these effects, selfie culture can feel particularly enticing because it's often positioned these days as women empowering themselves – reclaiming the male gaze and taking agency of their own image and sexuality, as British sociologist and feminist cultural theorist Rosalind Gill writes.[54]

The problem is that, while women's bodies are being presented as their key source of validation, they're simultaneously expected to conform to increasingly narrower standards of beauty and sexual attractiveness in order to achieve such validation.[55]

Kim Kardashian was a forerunner in seizing the 'empowerment' trope in relation to nude selfies. In 2016, after copping flack for posting a naked selfie online, she wrote on her website: 'I am empowered by my body. I am empowered by my sexuality. I am empowered by feeling comfortable in my skin. I am empowered by showing the world my flaws and not being afraid of what anyone is going to say about me.'

This sparked debate among feminists old and new: American lawyer and writer Jill Filipovic pointed out that while there's absolutely nothing wrong with feeling good about how you look in a naked selfie, 'succeeding in sexiness isn't real power', adding, 'Women and girls will be empowered – powerful, even – when "everything it means to be a woman" has nothing to do with looking pretty in a picture.'[56]

Some pointed out that Kardashian's nude selfies are indeed empowering – for her, personally – in the sense that she's capitalised on a system that rewards women for adhering to a narrow, hyper-sexy beauty ideal. We live in a world that's obsessed with women's looks and sex – why not cash in?[57]

♣

Regardless of whether you believe smokin' selfies are empowering, it's a good idea to step back and assess whether, for you, social media is a worthwhile use of your time and energy.

If you're an Instagram person, is the filtering and editing and posting making you feel great – or fuelling your Yes Woman need for approval?

For me, it's the latter – which is why I deleted the app off my phone a few weeks after my burnout episode. I realised that taking, filtering and posting Instagram photos had become an enormous time-suck that directly hooked me into an approval-seeking, insecure, anxious way of being.

But for other women, taking selfies is a fun pastime, a way of expressing themselves – or a money-maker – that's worth their energy.

One woman who's absolutely killing it on Instagram is Abbie Chatfield. Chatfield posts selfies regularly to her Instagram account – which has more than 280,000 followers – and is an outspoken feminist. I asked Chatfield whether she thinks we, as women, can use social media to reclaim our image – or is it just another vehicle that is mostly used to play to the male gaze?

She told me it all comes down to intention.

'I think it depends how you're using it,' says Chatfield. 'I make a point to be like, "fuck you" to the male gaze.' That said, there's nothing wrong with a smokin' bikini photo, she adds. 'If you do want to do a thirst trap, fucking do it,' she says. (Amen to that.)

She also doesn't want to shame women who make money off the male gaze. 'If you do have a whole Instagram account and you're making money on OnlyFans – and that's entirely off the male gaze – that's amazing.' (For the unacquainted, OnlyFans is a website where content creators earn money from users – 'fans' – who subscribe to their content, which is often, but not exclusively, softcore or hardcore porn.)

Where it gets more problematic, she suggests, is when you're posting selfies out of insecurity and a need for validation – or as she puts it, 'editing yourself to what you think is a societal expectation of what men want and then uploading that for validation.'

If you realise social media is becoming a validation-seeking trap for you, give these tips a whirl:

- **Remove stimuli that brings you down**. Unfollow those diet-focused fitness influencers, humblebraggers and old friends with irritatingly glossy lives, so you'll be less likely to desire their seemingly perfect (and probably highly edited) lives/jobs/abs. While you're at it, delete whatever apps make you feel crap about yourself when scrolling.
- **Consider keeping your own Instagram account private**, so it's only visible to close friends and family. Use that space to be your authentic, unimpressive self or to share life updates – no filters required.
- **Keep reminding yourself of this:** social media only features the highlights – not all the mundane pyjamas-and-hangover moments – from your acquaintances' lives. That girl on the yacht probably has

really bad IBS or terrible taste in men – she just didn't mention that in her latest post about how #blessed she is.

You radical, you

I'm about to tell you to do something that sounds tame but is actually very radical:

It's time to accept that the way you look isn't a measure of your worth.

It's time to accept that you don't need hair dye, or injectables, or diets, or high heels, or Brazilian waxes to feel worthy or attractive – not just because beauty comes in all different forms, but because you are worth more than just your physical appearance. Because you are worthy no matter what you look like.

I use the word 'radical' because we live in a world where entire industries and systems are built on women feeling shit about the way they look and saying yes to expectations that are exhausting, pricey, and often painful. And as Mikki Kendall argues, beauty is political – especially for Black women and women of colour.[58]

Sonya Renee Taylor, poet and founder of *The Body Is Not An Apology*, similarly argues that accepting our bodies is a political act.

> Every time you call truce with your body, you interrupt a system of violence and power that profits off of your self-hate. Every time you interrogate the beliefs and biases … you interrupt a system that profits off the way that you feel about other bodies and the systems of comparison that we live in.[59]

Now, it's worth acknowledging that understanding the reasons you feel bad about your body won't totally stop you feeling bad about your body. (Sorry.)

Research has found that 'feminist cognitive strategies' such as reading up on structural sexism aren't enough to fully combat deeply engrained societal notions of beauty: we're up against a billion-dollar beauty products industry, which is founded on women feeling the need to conform to certain standards of appearance, after all![60,61]

But that same research also found that these strategies can go some way to helping you feel good about your appearance. So be gentle with yourself: you may still have creeping feelings of inadequacy from time to time, but being aware of – and challenging – that toxic thinking about your body is still worthwhile.

After all, every time you make an active choice to ignore a beauty standard and focus on celebrating and pursuing what you're actually passionate about, you're challenging the status quo – which is empowering for other women and girls in your life, too.

♣

So how do you call a truce with your body and your appearance?

It's all about mentally calling out the damaging messages – catching yourself before buying into a beauty practice just because you feel you 'should'.

Actively think 'fuck off' every time you encounter messages telling you to be something else, look another way, or lose weight for aesthetic reasons, suggests Taryn Brumfitt, Australian writer, film director, and founder of the Body Image Movement.

'Women are smart, intelligent and fabulous, with so much to contribute to the world, yet so many of us are anchored down by thoughts we have about ourselves,' she writes in her book *Embrace*. 'So, we have a choice. We can either let this misrepresentation own us or we bow out of the race by saying "Fuck off". We exercise our right to not buy into the bullshit. We are taking back our power.'[62]

Mentally telling these messages to bugger off creates room in our lives, and space in our brain, to deal with the things we actually care about. As British actor and activist Jameela Jamil once said, 'I'm fucking tired of seeing women just ignore what's amazing about them and their lives and their achievements, just because they don't have a bloody thigh gap.'[63]

I echo that sentiment wholeheartedly. How great would it be if we redirected our focus, time and energy to more interesting, authentic things?

I tried it myself – and reaped the benefits over the year I spent writing this book.

When people ask me how I found the time to hold down a job, write a book and parent a toddler, one answer is that I'm quite strict on what I won't spend time on – especially when it comes to the way I look. A year ago, eyelash extensions, Instagram photos, shellac manicures and blonde highlights were my norm: today, I'm off Instagram, I only get manicures and other beauty treatments for very special occasions, and I've even transitioned to an easy-to-manage ombré hairstyle that only requires two quick salon visits a year.

I want to acknowledge here that it's much harder for other people with different demands to find this time – for example, if you need to work three jobs for financial reasons, or if you can't get childcare. But in my own personal situation, I've been fortunate enough to find that saying no to the demands of grooming and dieting has freed up a hell of a lot of time.

You know this book you're currently reading? I literally wrote the proposal for it – the pitch document I sent to the publisher – in the time I would normally have spent in a salon chair over just two or three appointments.

And you know what? I haven't missed my old, packed-with-highlights hairstyle one bit. I have bigger things to focus on.

Chapter 15

Preparing for pushback and driving change

> [Y]ou have to get over any kind of attachment to perfectionism. Or to being liked by everybody all the time, or understood by everybody all the time.
>
> – bell hooks[1]

'No' is one of the first words my daughter learned to say.

Children learn to say the word early because it's in our natures to stand up for our own needs, to recognise injustice, and to push back on what doesn't feel good for us.

But as girls go through life, so many of us unlearn that word. We swallow the myth that women aren't allowed to disappoint other people. We internalise the old-fashioned belief that for a woman to put her needs first is unthinkable, abhorrent. We learn to care desperately about what others might think and whether we're doing life 'right'. We lose hold of our priorities and we lose sight of our deepest values.

The feisty, self-confident little girls we were as toddlers slowly become shackled by the compulsion to please others, to be everything to everyone, and to do it all correctly. We begin to say yes much more than no. And as we've seen throughout this book, that compulsion can silence us, harm us and hold us back.

Then as Yes Women, we run ourselves ragged. We're endlessly busy, juggling multiple roles, and trying to excel at all of them – which is why more of us, compared to men, end up as perfectionists and people-pleasers. More of us end up anxious and highly stressed, or – for a few of us, including myself – we can even end up burned out and hospitalised.

Saying no is harder for some

One solution to all this, as this book has argued, is to start to throw off the stifling pressure on us to be 'Nice' – and to disentangle our ideas of femininity with an obligation to be these things. But I'm not suggesting that's an easy task – nor one that can be undertaken by all women in the same way. Audre Lorde once wrote that the 'transformation of silence into language and action is an act of self-revelation, and that always seems fraught with danger' – and it's worth acknowledging that this danger is greater for some of us (including Lorde herself) than others.[2]

It is, of course, easier to say no to expectations when you're an able-bodied, straight, cisgendered, relatively well-off, educated white woman. I'm aware that I fit into those categories – and because this book draws on my own life, it's been difficult to decentre my own experiences while writing it; while I've interviewed and surveyed a diverse cross-section of women in my research, that's no substitute for lived experience.

Ultimately, though, I hope this book will help women in some small way to fight the 'tyranny of Niceness' – because, as Helen Lewis notes, that 'is, and has always been, one of the most potent forces holding women back.'[3]

March like a girl: what comes next?

I want to be clear that I don't believe individual women learning to say no is the key to gender equality. It simply isn't enough, on its own, to create meaningful systemic change.

In fact, I am wary of career and self-help advice instructing women to just be a little more confident, just ask for a pay rise, to dress a little less provocatively – as if our individual choices or failings are to blame for the discrimination or lack of advancement women experience. I do not wish to add 'just say no' to this laundry list of advice thrust upon women.

I don't want to shift responsibility for women's 'yes-es' entirely onto women.

Because the truth is, we are socialised into Niceness by a system of patriarchy. We are, as Simone de Beauvoir described, 'the second sex' – positioned in society as secondary and lesser than the 'default' male model of personhood.[4] We are up against not just individual challenges, but larger systems of oppression: sexism, as well as racism and economic inequality, to name a few.

So, rather than a few of us saying no in isolation, a more powerful driver of change is for many women to join their voices together in saying no as a group – driving collective action and feminist advocacy, and bringing about new laws and policies.

Some of these collective 'no-es' can (and should) be about everyday, seemingly lighter expectations and assumptions – that women's orgasms aren't as important as men's, that women must remove body hair, that women should be the ones to take leave from work when the kids get sick. Saying no to everyday pressures can bring about small wins such as allowing us to not give a damn about how we look on Instagram; it can also free up more space for important activities such as looking after our health, or reading books, or running for office – or whatever else floats our particular boats.

Other collective 'no-es' are bigger and more groundbreaking. Just think: 150 years ago, women couldn't control their fertility, work after marriage, vote, or own property – and it was loud, collective 'no-es' by feminists that brought about those wins. In other arenas, collective 'no-es' – sometimes sparked by an individual 'no' that set off a movement – have been equally powerful.

When Rosa Parks, an African American seamstress, refused to give up her seat to a white man on a bus in 1955, she helped launch the civil rights movement.

When Tarana Burke spoke out, in 2006, against the pervasiveness of sexual abuse and assault in society, she coined the phrase 'Me Too', which became a global hashtag and feminist movement when other women joined their voices to the cause.

When Greta Thunberg began protesting outside Swedish Parliament at age 15, she began a global school climate strike movement and brought more than 10 million people together worldwide to demand action on climate change.

Closer to home, Australians said no to old laws that prevented same-sex couples from marrying – with women driving the vote more than men.[5] More women than men are trade union members in Australia – and they use their collective voice in industries and occupations such as nursing and teaching to continue to fight for better pay and conditions.[6]

And in the US, when Joe Biden and Kamala Harris were voted in and Donald Trump was voted out in 2020, women – especially Black women – voters supported Biden at higher rates than men.[7]

♣

While women can do powerful things when we combine our individual 'no-es' into a collective voice, we can't always do it alone. We need men – everyone from business leaders and politicians to partners and economists – to join us in saying no to injustice at a systemic level.

Society is stuck between an old world, where women were expected to say yes to caring for others at home, and the new world, where parents are expected to work and workers are expected to parent. The system still isn't set up for working mums. We fear punishment for saying no to either our work or our children, so we each constantly struggle to assert our individual boundaries. As a society, we need decisions and policies that hold some of these boundaries – these 'no-es' in place for us – so that each woman doesn't have to individually fight a battle against all the 'yes-es' that are demanded of her.

We need economic and legal reforms that help protect women's time, energy and resources: from free (or affordable) universal childcare, to generous parental leave for people of all genders, to more government funding to help with adult social care (so women don't bear the brunt of caring in an ageing society).

We need laws and employment policies that guarantee women

– and industries dominated by women – are paid fair wages; have enough work, and not too much work; work predictable hours; that women have job security – partly so they can stand up against harassment or discrimination without fearing retribution.

We need workplace cultures that don't make women choose between success and their wellbeing. As Arianna Huffington writes, the science shows 'this is a false choice – when we prioritise our well-being, we're actually better and more productive at work'.[8]

This systemic change needs to tackle not just sexism, but the potent combination of sexism, racism and economic inequality that keeps so many women down. This might include laws and policies aimed at improving wages and working conditions for jobs often filled by migrant women. It might include bolstering discrimination laws. It might mean including more women at leadership levels – and not just 'white, middle-class women, who have the smallest gaps when it comes to their opportunities versus those of white men', as Liv Little has argued in *The Guardian*.[9]

We need changes to the way women are portrayed in media. That could include portraying women of all backgrounds standing assertively in positions of power, figuratively flipping the bird to the old-fashioned gender stereotypes that require women to 'be Nice or face the consequences'. It could include media representation of women who look after their own needs first and aren't dubbed selfish or strange. And as Abbie Chatfield put it in an interview for this book, 'I think we do need to have more sexually liberated women [in media] but not make it a thing – just like, "[T]his is a woman enjoying her life and this is how women enjoy sex, and there are different ways you can enjoy sex and being free and dressing how you want to dress and doing what you want to do."'

Ultimately, as Kate Manne writes in her thoroughly researched book *Down Girl*, we need leaders to understand the inherent biases of the system and work to change them.[10] Not just one part of the system, but 'the whole elephant', as writer and lawyer Caroline Fredrickson once put it, when talking about the challenges that working-class women in particular faced.[11]

Without tackling 'the whole elephant', our individual efforts to say no to sexist expectations can only get us so far.

Notes from a recovered(ish) Yes Woman

Let's zoom in from the big picture and return our focus to the small piece of the puzzle that this book reckons with – women learning to say no as a tool to begin taking back their time, energy and resources.

It's a tool I've been learning to use over the last year throughout the process of writing this book – and I've felt the changes as the book has progressed. Writing a book is a form of speaking out – and so I simply couldn't dip my toe into the controversial arena of feminist writing in this way, without inherently stepping out of the 'good girls' line' to some extent.

I started writing *The Yes Woman* when I was, indeed, still a Yes Woman. Today, I'm more of a No Woman-in-progress. (Watch this space.)

When I take a moment to look back at myself a year ago – almost 12 months to the day, I sat in that ugly suburban mental health ward for mums and babies – I realise how much I've changed for the better since actively resolving to unlearn the word 'yes'.

I rarely bother with recording special moments or good-hair days on social media. I've allowed friendships that don't serve me to drift, refocusing that time on nurturing the friends I adore. I've left a bunch of group chats to cut down on the dreaded ping of phone notifications. I've made a firm decision not to feel guilty about being a working parent – letting go of a lot of the intensive parenting expectations that sucked me into tornadoes of guilt in my first few months as a mother.

Burning out wasn't fun – but it was the circuit-breaker I needed. It pushed me to ask whether I really had to be everything to everyone. The answer, of course, was 'no'.

♣

I'd be lying if I said I was totally cured from my Yes Women ways – but I'm getting better. And if I tried to be 'perfect' at kicking my perfectionism, I'd be a big old hypocrite.

I still do a lot. Too much, really: while writing this book, I was raising a toddler; moving house; recovering from a stay in a psych ward; changing medications; returning to work; being told I would be made redundant; interviewing for new jobs; trying to lose my 'baby weight'; making new friends at my mums' group; being told I wouldn't be made redundant after all; helping plan my mum's second wedding; having three surgeries for my health – and all this was bookended by coronavirus-induced Melbourne lockdowns.

But saying yes to lots of things isn't the Yes Woman's core problem – the real problem is saying yes to things that aren't priorities.

The difference is that today I'm busy with things I actually really want (or need) to do. And in the year since my burnout, I've genuinely learned to say no to a bucketload of things – which has freed up my time and energy, enabling me to do everything I listed above, the vast majority of which really matters to me.

I still trip up – after all, as Arianna Huffington observes, the world we live in provides endless neon lights directing us towards superficial, distracting, ultimately unrewarding time-sucks (*ahem* – phone scrolling, caring about our 'hip dips', Instagram).[12]

But much of the time, I'm able to hold that compulsion to say yes to all that BS at bay – both by using the tactics I've outlined in this book, as well as with the help of a good therapist and medication to treat my generalised anxiety disorder (thank you, modern medicine).

Let's do this thing

A gratifying thing has happened since I began telling people I was writing a book focused on overcoming perfectionism, people-pleasing and the compulsion to say yes: women have affirmed to me that they, too, want to start saying no more. It's clear to me the will is there to kick our Yes Women ways: we're collectively yearning to jump off the treadmill of anxiety, people-pleasing and perfectionism. We've realised that if we only chase recognition, validation and perfection, we'll always feel we don't have enough – that we *are* not enough.

In learning to say no, I have started to live more boldly and fully; you can do the same. But – at the risk of sounding totally new-age wellness guru – saying no is not only a gift you can give yourself: it can also contribute to a world in which women aren't expected to give up their time, energy and power solely for others.

While we won't succeed as individuals alone, we equally won't succeed only with policies, ideas and words. We need Yes Women to find their 'no' so they can inspire other women to do the same. I was quite taken by the way Imi Lo expressed this same thought. She wrote that the ability to say no to oppressive gender stereotypes is not a selfish act – rather, it is a 'gift' to the world:

> As one moves towards authenticity, what she actualizes along the way are gifts to the public and collective life … Being able to thrive as who she is, even when it means for a while she stands on the fringe of society, she open doors for all the creative, intelligent and sensitive girls who come after her. Ultimately, it is a courageous and noble act.[13]

So I urge you, recovering Yes Woman, to go out in the world and show how a new way of being – with boundaries, with intentional decisions behind what we're saying yes to – can work.

Because, really, are we going to let sexist, old-fashioned ideas about what a woman should be continue to shackle and limit us?

Nah. Nope. No chance. No freaking way, baby.

Author's note

This book is called *The Yes Woman*, and it draws on research about how women, more than men, experience people-pleasing, perfectionism and difficulties saying no.

Throughout this book, I make the distinction between men and women because we live in a society that tends to divide us, rather strictly and compulsorily, into those two categories, and ascribe us roles and responsibilities accordingly. I recognise that this gender binary is problematic in many ways – and presents particular difficulties for trans and non-binary folks. By using the term 'Yes Woman', it's not my intention to suggest only two genders exist. I also want to be clear that when I talk about women, I mean to do so as inclusively as possible. Whether cis or trans, pretty much all women have come up against gendered stereotypes and expectations equating womanhood with 'Niceness' and agreeableness, and all of us can be shaped by the other forces of Yes Woman behaviour I examine in this book.

Throughout the book, I make generalisations like 'women are disadvantaged in these ways' and 'women are more prone to people-pleasing'. Clearly, there are exceptions to all generalisations. Not every example will apply to every woman; not every woman is disadvantaged relative to every man; and not every woman is a Yes Woman. It's also worth noting that, while this is a woman-centred book, much of my research and examples throughout this book will also apply to non-binary folks, to men and to people with other gender identities.

This book focuses largely on cultures in which I've lived – in Australia, the United States, and the United Kingdom – because this book contains elements of memoir. But I'm aware that even within the countries I have lived, there are many experiences I can't speak to – for example, the challenges of saying no will be different and greater for Aboriginal and Torres Straight Islander women, for women with disabilities, for LGBTQI women, and for myriad others with overlapping life experiences. I'm well aware that I don't have the requisite authority and lived experience to cover, in detail, the ways in which saying no is experienced by many others.

I also want to acknowledge that in some places in the world, some of the 'no-es' I have advocated – exercising the right to free speech, choosing who you marry, to name just two – put women at risk of persecution, prosecution or even death. In writing a book about how (mostly Western) women can learn to say no, it is not my intention to suggest this is the biggest issue feminism must tackle. Clearly, it is not.

But I believe gender equality issues exist on a spectrum, and many can matter at once. So I hope that the message of this book is taken in the spirit in which it is intended – which is that each woman who throws off her Yes Woman ways is playing a small part in a much larger movement of change.

A quick note about my research: I surveyed and interviewed more than 200 people for this book through phone interviews, email exchanges and online surveys. This isn't an academic work nor a newspaper report, so while I've presented quotes accurately and in context, I've taken some creative liberties to make the book flow – by occasionally combining two or more interviewees with similar experiences into an amalgamated 'case study', and, in many instances, by changing names, job titles, ages and/or locations for privacy. In four specific instances, I've even created a new character 'case study' based on my research, to illustrate a point. (I've flagged these as they arise throughout the book.)

One last note. The book delves into my own struggles with mental ill-health, and recounts how my own Yes Woman ways have fuelled my own anxiety and burnout (as well as those of many other women). I don't contend that all women who feel exhausted, overcommitted and obligated to say yes have a mental disorder – in many ways, the feelings of overwhelm I describe are understandable reactions to societal expectations and competing time pressures.

What's more, the causes of mental ill health are many, and it's important to steer clear of oversimplifying topics in this realm – so to be clear, this book is intended to contribute my own experience to a wider conversation about why some women are exhausted, overwhelmed and anxious. It's not a comprehensive explainer of all things to do with perfectionism and people-pleasing, and it's certainly not diagnostic – I'll leave that to the experts.

Speaking of experts, the psychologists, therapists and researchers I interview throughout this book are giving general advice on issues such as managing anxiety, setting boundaries, and the causes of perfectionism – I haven't asked them to endorse my Yes Woman theory in full. And, of course, the advice and insights the experts and I offer in this book are for general information only. *For detailed personal advice, please do see a qualified medical practitioner who knows your medical history. And consider therapy. All of the therapy.*

Acknowledgements

I am so grateful for the support of the entire team at Affirm Press, who took a gamble on me as a first-time author and guided me through the publication process with warmth and wisdom.

I owe particular thanks to Affirm's publishing director Martin Hughes, who was one of the first to believe in *The Yes Woman*. You 'got' this book and me as an author on a fundamental level from the get-go. I couldn't have asked for a better publishing house than yours; it made the process of creating this book a joy.

Thanks also to my talented editors Ruby Ashby-Orr and Kevin O'Brien. Ruby, your astute eye helped transform this book from a jumbled sample chapter to a pacey, readable thing I can be proud of. It's been a pleasure to work with someone so lightning-fast, yet remarkably patient. Kevin, you took over seamlessly when Ruby went on parental leave, guiding me through the later stages of this whole book thing with reassuring professionalism and some spot-on practical suggestions. I'm deeply grateful.

Thanks also to Affirm's publicity team, including Laura McNicol Smith and Rosanna Hunt, who expertly executed the mammoth task of getting this thing out and into the world (and made the scary prospect of promoting myself feel so much less scary) and to the talented Grace Breen, who passed on my initial pitch and set the ball rolling. My gratitude also to publishing coordinator Susie Kennewell, who walked me through several nitty gritty parts of the publishing process I would have otherwise had no clue how to tackle. Thanks also to sales and marketing director Kieran Rogers, and sales and distribution coordinator Lauren Ravida for actually getting this thing sold!

Thanks to my copyeditor, Lesley Halm, who whipped these

words into shape with insight and sensitivity, Jenni Kauppi, who contributed further invaluable and much appreciated thoughts on the text, the outrageously talented Christian Bachelier – professional photographer and my stepdad – for the perfect author photo, and Alissa Dinallo for the eye-catching cover design. I never thought orange would win me over, but you made it happen.

I am also indebted to the wise and generous early draft readers and hand holders, including my thoughtful and politically attuned sister Lola, my outrageously clever mum Gael and my endlessly talented *Kill Your Darlings* mentor Ruby Hamad. This book is so much better thanks to you. Ruby, your whip-smart insights helped shape this book, and you gently asked all the right questions, preventing me from making a couple of embarrassing blunders. (I also credit you with suggesting 'Nice with a capital N'!)

Thank you to the following experts, thinkers, feminists and authors for taking time from your busy schedules to share your professional insights through phone interviews: Cass Dunn, Rashida Dungarwalla, Jane Jackson, Imi Lo, Kimberley Norris, Eileen Seah, Brenda Dolieslager, Nicole Perry, Krasi Kirova, Hema Kangeson, Ann Stoneson, Zoë Krupka, Hannah Korrel, Larissa Waters, Alice Pung, Carissa Lee, Arianna Huffington, Bekah Martinez, Michal Carrington, Natalie Skinner, Georgina Manning, Alison Pullen, Sally Goldner, Grace Lee, Samantha Burns, Kate Leaver, Jamila Rizvi, Carly Findlay, Abbie Chatfield, Zara McDonald and Michelle Andrews. Your expertise was invaluable in grounding my reporting and anecdotes. I admire you all deeply and am warmed by your support for this project and your willingness to give your time to a first-time author like me. (Thank you, also, Tanya Plibersek, for the best rejection letter ever.)

A heartfelt thanks to Bianca Lapins and Jaimee Damon from the media team at SANE Australia for reading an excerpt of this book and advising me on how to report responsibly and minimise stigma.

An enormous thank you to the 200-plus women who generously

shared their experiences with me in person, over the phone, via direct message, email and anonymous surveys. Your willingness to open up about some of your most intimate thoughts and feelings formed the backbone of this book. Thank you for trusting me with your stories.

I also owe a debt of gratitude to the thoughts and words of so many brilliant writers and thinkers whose work I drew from when writing *The Yes Woman*. They are too many to list, but I'd like to especially pay tribute to the late Dr Harriet Braiker, whose work on the 'type E woman' who tries to be 'everything to everyone' was an early precursor to *The Yes Woman* and resonated strongly with my own experiences.

Thank you also to Yarra Libraries for making your books available to me when I was researching this book during COVID-19 lockdowns. Your free online offerings saved my skin.

I have been privileged to work with a number of wonderful editors throughout my career who have helped hone my writing, editing and research skills and built my confidence. Thank you to *ABC Everyday* editor Bhakthi Puvanenthiran, Sonya Gee and the other fabulous deputy editors, Farz Edraki, Jo Joyce and Christian Harimanow. Thanks also to Tim Fisher, ABC alumni and my digital journalism teacher from way back, who allowed me to write stories I'm passionate about and helped me rein in my em-dash usage, and my former editor Claudine Ryan for driving me to be a more rigorous women's health reporter. Many thanks to Jamila Rizvi, who was editor-in-chief when I was a baby journalist at *Mamamia* and has generously provided career advice and references ever since, and Mia Freedman, who gave me my very first media job back when I first made the switch from lawyer to journalist.

I deeply appreciate the work of Mirna Falan, a brilliant psychologist who has helped me on a personal level to say no and set boundaries.

This project would have stayed a pipedream without the incredible childcare support offered by loving family members, particularly when childcare arrangements were up in the air during COVID-19 lockdowns. Thank you to my marvellous, generous in-laws, Miranda and John, my loving mum Gael and stepdad Christian, for caring for Olive so beautifully, and my sister Lola for stepping in when we were day-care-less in 2020.

Endless gratitude and love to my parents for raising their daughters to question the status quo and raise our voices when we need to, and for supporting me through the hardest times in my life. What an enormous privilege to have parents who have always believed in me and equipped me with the education and resources I needed to chase the career of my dreams. Mum, thank you for being my OG feminist and journalistic inspiration, for knowing me inside and out and for always offering sage advice in life and work. Dad, thank you for helping to foster my love of books and the arts, for instilling in me an appreciation for vigorous research and sound logic, for your woke-before-your-time approach to gender roles, and for your gentle guidance.

And to my sisters, Anna and Lola, you are a daily source of love, humour, support, advice and top-notch group chats and you had some killer suggestions about who to interview for this project (particular shout-out here to Anna's encyclopaedic knowledge of former *The Bachelor* cast members). You both pumped up my ego when I doubted myself or got 'mum guilt' for taking time to work on the book.

To the other special women in my circle, both in Australia and abroad: you are too many to name but particular mention goes to the wonderful BJ, my incredible HLP Daisy, and my oldest and dear friend Vic. You have all supported me with words/love/memes over the years and I'm a better person just by virtue of being in your orbit. There is no way to write this without coming off revoltingly cheesy, but you all inspired me just by being magnificent, creative, intelligent, compassionate humans who live your truth. Thank you for understanding when I said 'no' to dinner, drinks and everything else fun when I was head down, bum up, writing this thing.

To my endlessly delightful daughter Olive, who shared her mum with this 'book baby' for a year while I wrote, thank you. I am incredibly lucky to have you.

And finally, to my ever-patient husband Ben. You are the kindest man in the world. Thank you for eternally supporting me, for all the nights you made dinner while I wrote this thing (okay, even when I *wasn't* writing this thing), for being my sounding board, for taking full parenting responsibilities during my at-home 'writing retreats', and for supporting me while I learned to say no. I couldn't ask for a better partner in love and life.

Notes and references

Chapter 1: This is what a Yes Woman looks like

1 Gloria Steinem, interview by Oprah Winfrey, *Oprah's Next Chapter*, YouTube Video, 3:52 minutes (published by Oprah Winfrey Network).

2 Harriet Braiker, *The Type E* Woman: how to overcome the stress of being everything to everybody* (iUniverse, 2002).

3 Sheryl Sandberg, *Lean In: women, work, and the will to lead* (Knopf, 2013), p. 43.

4 The exact statistics on self-identified people-pleasers are 54.4 per cent of women and 40.3 per cent of men – although, note that these figures focused on overweight and obese participants. From Robert Kushner and Seung Choi, 'Prevalence of Unhealthy Lifestyle Patterns Among Overweight and Obese Adults', *Obesity* 18, no. 6 (2010). My own anonymous surveys found even higher levels of all these characteristics: a whopping 88 per cent of respondents said they were people-pleasers; 71 per cent said they were perfectionists; and 74 per cent had trouble saying no to favours, invitations and requests that didn't serve them. (Granted, people-pleasers are probably more likely to agree to being surveyed – so you could argue my respondents were self-selecting.)

5 The exact figures are 33 per cent for women and 21 per cent for men. From Medibio, *Australia's Biggest Mental Health Check-In*, 2017, (https://www.medianet.com.au/releases/140342/).

6 Katharine Ridgway O'Brien, 'Just Saying "No": an examination of gender differences in the ability to decline requests in the workplace', Diss., Rice University (2014). As expected, women indicated that they had chronic difficulty saying no, more so than men.

7 William J. Goode, 'A theory of role strain'. *American Sociological Review*, 25 (1960).

8 Research commissioned by TVBed.com, 'Average mum gets just 17 minutes of "me time",' (6 February 2014) (https://www.swnsdigital.com/2014/02/me-time/).

9 Cleveland Clinic, 'Women and Stress' (13 February 2019), (https://my.clevelandclinic.org/health/articles/5545-women-and-stress); and Melissa Milkie, Sara Sarah and Suzanne Bianchi, 'Taking on the Second Shift: Time Allocations and Time Pressures of U.S. Parents with Preschoolers', *Social Forces* 88, no. 2 (2009).

10 Kei M. Nomaguchi, Melissa A Milkie, Suzanne M Bianchi, 'Time Strains and Psychological Well-Being: Do Dual-Earner Mothers and Fathers Differ?' *Journal of Family Issues* 26, no. 6 (2005).

11 *Stress in America* survey, The Harris Poll on behalf of the American Psychological Association (2019).

12 In the United States and Western Europe. From Olivia Remes et al, 'A Systematic Review of Reviews on the Prevalence of Anxiety Disorders in Adult Populations', *Brain and Behaviour* 6, no. 7 (2016).

13 American Psychological Association, 'Gender and Stress', 2010, (https://www.apa.org/news/press/releases/stress/2010/gender-stress).

14 Olivia Remes, 'Women are far more anxious than men – here's the science', *The*

Conversation, 10 June 2016, (https://theconversation.com/women-are-far-more-anxious-than-men-heres-the-science-60458).

15 These mental illnesses had been diagnosed in 13.4 per cent of women aged 35–54, and 12.8 per cent of women aged 15–34 in 2009. Those figures jumped up significantly – to 19.4 and 20.1 per cent respectively in those age groups – as of 2017. Melbourne Institute, University of Melbourne, the Household, Income and Labour Dynamics in Australia (HILDA) survey, 2019, (https://melbourneinstitute.unimelb.edu.au/__data/assets/pdf_file/0011/3127664/HILDA-Statistical-Report-2019.pdf).

16 There are certain factors that make a woman more likely to suffer from any of the above afflictions: for example, brain chemistry and hormone fluctuations may affect women differently to men, and women are also more likely to experience physical and mental abuse, which has been linked to the development of anxiety disorders. From Olivia Remes, 'Women are far more anxious than men – here's the science' *The Conversation,* 10 June 2016, (https://theconversation.com/women-are-far-more-anxious-than-men-heres-the-science-60458).

17 Tamara J Ferguson, Susan L Crowley, 'Gender Differences in the Organization of Guilt and Shame', *Sex Roles* 37 (1997).

18 She was talking about perfectionism and people-pleasing; 'Yes Woman' is my own term.

19 Soraya Chemaly, *Rage Becomes Her: the power of women's anger* (Atria, 2018), introduction: xxii.

20 This term can be confusing, because some 'Mother and Baby Units' are also known as 'Early Parenting Centres' (sometimes colloquially called 'sleep schools' because they offer residential programs dealing with infant sleep disorders.) For clarity, I was voluntarily admitted to a different sort of unit – a residential perinatal mental health unit – which is specifically for mums dealing with mental health challenges related to pregnancy, birth and early parenthood.

21 Harriet Braiker, *The Type E* Woman: how to overcome the stress of being everything to everybody* (iUniverse, 2002).

22 Anne Summers, *The Misogyny Factor* (NewSouth, 2013).

Chapter 2: (Not) born this way: how culture makes us Nice

1 Clinical and consultant psychologist Brenda Dolieslager, interview with the author, April 2020.

2 Taylor Swift, cited in Lana Wilson, *Miss Americana*. Netflix (2020).

3 Alan Feingold, 'Gender Differences in Personality: a meta-analysis,' *Psychological Bulletin* 116, (1994)–; Paul T. Costa, Antonio Terracciano and Robert R McCrae, 'Gender Differences in Personality Traits Across Cultures: robust and surprising findings,' *Journal of Personality and Social Psychology* 81, no. 2, (2001).

4 David Schmitt, Juri Allik, Robert McCrae, 'The Geographic Distribution of Big Five Personality Traits: patterns and profiles of human self-description across 56 nations', *Journal of Cross-Cultural Psychology* 38, no. 2 (2007); David Schmitt, Anu Realo, Martin Voracek, Juri Allik, 'Why Can't a Man Be More Like a Woman? Sex Differences in Big Five Personality Traits across 55 Cultures', *Journal of Personality and Social Psychology* 96, no. 1 (2009) (https://pubmed.ncbi.nlm.nih.gov/18179326/).

5 Erin B McClure, 'A meta-analytic review of sex differences in facial expression processing and their development in infants, children, and adolescents', *Psychological Bulletin* 126, no. 3 (2000).

6 Jennifer Connellan, Simon Baron-Cohen, Sally Wheelwright, Anna Batki, Jag Ahluwalia, 'Sex differences in human neonatal social perception', *Infant Behavior and Development* 23, no. 1 (2000).

7 Caryl Rivers and Rosalind C Barnett, *The New Soft War on Women: how the myth of female ascendance is hurting women, men – and our economy* (Penguin, 2015).

8 The Rosalind Franklin University of Medicine and Science. 'Male/female brain differences? Big data says not so much', *ScienceDaily*, 29 October 2015, (www.sciencedaily.com/releases/2015/10/151029185544.htm).

9 Soraya Chemaly, *Rage Becomes Her: the power of women's anger* (Simon & Schuster, 2018).

10 Peter Glick and Susan Fiske, 'The Ambivalent Sexism Inventory: Differentiating Hostile and Benevolent Sexism', *Journal of Personality and Social Psychology* 70, no. 3 (1996).

11 Mary R Jackman, *The Velvet Glove: paternalism and conflict in gender, class, and race relations* (University of California Press, 1994).

12 Adapted from Brené Brown, *I Thought it Was Just Me (but it isn't)* (Penguin, 2007).

13 Judith Butler, 'Performative Acts and Gender Constitution: an essay in phenomenology and feminist theory'. In: Sue-Ellen Case (ed.) *Performing Feminisms: Feminist Critical Theory and Theatre* 40, no. 4, Baltimore, (The Johns Hopkins University Press 1988).

14 Igi Moon, '"Boying" the Boy and "Girling" the Girl: from affective interpellation to trans-emotionality', *Sexualities* 22, nos. 1–2, (2019).

15 Kate Long, Tweet, 3 November 2019, (https://twitter.com/volewriter/status/1190666248780238853).

16 Alison Nash and Rosemary Krawczyk, who inventoried the toys of more than 200 US kids in 1994. Cited in Cordelia Fine, *Delusions of Gender: the real science behind sex differences* (Icon, 2005).

17 Cordelia Fine, *Delusions of Gender: the real science behind sex differences* (Icon, 2005), 239.

18 Diane Ruble and Carol Lynn Martin, 'Patterns of Gender Development', *Annual Review of Psychology* 61 (2010).

19 Lin Bian, Sarah-Jane Leslie and Andrei Cimpian, 'Gender Stereotypes About Intellectual Ability Emerge Early and Influence Children's Interests', *Science* 355, no. 6323 (2017).

20 Stefanie Preissner, *Can I Say No?* (Hachette, 2020), 21.

21 Julie De Azevedo Hanks, *Assertiveness Guide for Women: how to communicate your needs, set healthy boundaries, and transform your relationships* (New Harbinger Publications, 2016).

22 Myra Sadker and David Sadker, *Failing at Fairness: how America's schools cheat girls*, (Scribner, 1995).

23 Jeffrey Rubin, Frank J Provenzano and Zella Luria, 'The Eye of the Beholder: parents' views on sex of newborns', *American Journal of Orthopsychiatry* 44, no. 4 (1974), 512–519.

24 Iris Marion Young, 'Throwing Like a Girl: a phenomenology of feminine body comportment motility and spatiality', *Human Studies* 3, no. 2 (1980) 137–156.

25 Lori Lakin Hutcherson, *Good Black News*, July 14 2016 (https://goodblacknews.org/2016/07/14/editorial-what-i-said-when-my-white-friend-asked-for-my-black-opinion-on-white-privilege/).

26 Imi Lo, 'The Non-Conforming Asian Women', *Psychology Today*, 13 July 2018,

(https://www.psychologytoday.com/us/blog/living-emotional-intensity/201807/the-non-conforming-asian-women).

27 Jill Filipovic, *The H-Spot: the feminist pursuit of happiness* (PublicAffairs, 2018).

28 Kate Manne, *Down Girl: the logic of misogyny* (Penguin Books, 2018), 22.

29 Emily Kane, *The Gender Trap: parents and the pitfalls of raising boys and girls* (NYU Press, 2012).

30 Ibid.

31 Cited in Cordelia Fine, *Delusions of Gender: the real science behind sex differences* (Icon, 2005), and Helen Lewis, *Difficult Women: a history of feminism in 11 fights* (Jonathan Cape, 2020), 298.

32 Cordelia Fine, *Delusions of Gender: the real science behind sex differences* (Icon, 2005).

33 Mark S Allen & Davina A Robson, 'Personality and Sexual Orientation: new data and meta-analysis', *The Journal of Sex Research* 57, no. 8 (2020).

34 Full disclosure: 'Stace' is a made-up character, based on this column about the effects of growing up telling the lie of 'I'm straight': Adam D Blum, 'Gay People Have Been Taught to be People-Pleasing Pushovers,' *The Advocate*, 2 March 2019, (https://www.advocate.com/love-and-sex/2019/3/02/gay-people-have-been-taught-be-people-pleasing-push-overs).

35 When I asked Sally Goldner if she was a perfectionist, her response was emphatic: 'I plead guilty to being a past president, vice-president, treasurer and secretary of the perfectionists' club,' she told me. ('It is necessary to hold all four roles,' she joked as an aside.)

36 Ben A Barres, 'Does Gender Matter?' *Nature* 442, no. 13 (2016).

37 Cited in Elizabeth Svodoba, 'Ben Barres: a transgender scientist shares his story', *Spectrum News*, 14 November 2018, (https://www.spectrumnews.org/news/ben-barres-transgender-scientist-shares-story/).

38 Jill Filipovic, *The H-Spot: the feminist pursuit of happiness* (PublicAffairs, 2018).

39 Kate Manne writes that 'misogyny should be understood primarily as the "law enforcement" branch of a patriarchal order, which has the overall function of policing and enforcing its governing norms and expectations'. See: Kate Manne, *Down Girl: the logic of misogyny* (Penguin Books, 2018), 78.

40 Rachel Simmons, *Odd Girl Out: the hidden culture of aggression in girls* (Mariner Books, 2003).

41 Ibid.

42 Victoria L Brescoll, Eric Luis Uhlmann, 'Can an Angry Woman Get Ahead? Status conferral, gender, and expression of emotion in the workplace', *Psychological Science* 19, no. 3 (2008), 268–275. See also: Madeleine E Heilman, 'Information as a Deterrent Against Sex Discrimination: the effects of applicant sex and information type on preliminary employment decisions', *Organizational Behavior and Human Performance* 33, no. 2 (1984).

43 Ibid.

44 Caryl Rivers and Rosalind C Barnett, *The New Soft War on Women: how the myth of female ascendance is hurting women, men – and our economy* (Penguin, 2015).

45 Riana Duncan, *Punch Limited*, 1988 (https://punch.photoshelter.com/image/I0000eHEXGJ_wImQ).

46 Inter-Parliamentary Union, 'Sexism, harassment and violence against women parliamentarians', October 2016 (https://www.ipu.org/file/2425/download?token=0H5YdXVB).

47 Steph Harmon and Amaani Siddeek, '"It took on a life of its own": the story behind Julia Gillard's misogyny speech,' *The Guardian*, 7 February 2020, (https://www.

theguardian.com/tv-and-radio/2020/feb/07/it-took-on-a-life-of-its-own-the-story-behind-julia-gillards-misogyny-speech).

48 Soraya Chemaly, *Rage Becomes Her: the power of women's anger* (Simon & Schuster, 2018).

49 Kate Manne, *Down Girl: the logic of misogyny* (Penguin, 2019), p. 261.

50 Brené Brown, *I Thought it Was Just Me (but it isn't)* (Penguin, 2007).

51 Michael McGowan and Paul Karp, 'Sarah Hanson-Young Awarded $120,000 Damages in Defamation Case Against David Leyonhjelm', *The Guardian*, 25 November 2019, (https://www.theguardian.com/australia-news/2019/nov/25/sarah-hanson-young-awarded-120000-damages-defamation-david-leyonhjelm).

52 Tara Moss, *Speaking Out: a 21-st century handbook for women and girls* (Harper Collins, 2016).

53 Gender Equity Victoria and the Media Entertainment & Arts Alliance, 'Don't Read the Comments: enhancing online safety for women working in the media', 2019, (https://www.genvic.org.au/wp-content/uploads/2019/10/GV_MEAA_PolicyDoc_V5_WEB.pdf).

54 Anastasia Powell, Nicola Henry, Asher Flynn and Scott Adrian, 'Image-Based Sexual Abuse: the extent, nature, and predictors of perpetration in a community sample of Australian residents', *Computers in Human Behavior*, vol. 92, (2019) 393–402.

55 It was rapper, writer, and actor Adam Briggs who made this comment on the podcast. He added: 'There's nothing more threatening to a male, especially a white male, than a Black female.' See: 'episode 1: Hustle, Baby, Hustle', *Pretty for an Aboriginal*, 14 September 2017.

56 Moya Bailey coined the term with indie artist, creator and writer Trudy in 2008. Source: Moya Bailey, 'On Misogynoir: citation, erasure, and plagiarism', *Feminist Media Studies* 18, no. 4, (2018).

57 I have capitalised 'Black' in a racial, ethnic or cultural sense to convey an essential and shared sense of history, identity and community among people who identify as Black, including those in the African diaspora and within Africa, in accordance with AP Style Guide (https://apnews.com/article/archive-race-and-ethnicity-9105661462).

58 National Association of Black Journalists, 'NABJ denounces Herald Sun cartoon of Serena Williams and Naomi Osaka', *NABJ News & Press*, 10 September 2018 (https://www.nabj.org/news/417612/NABJ-denounces-Herald-Sun-cartoon-of-Serena-Williams-and-Naomi-Osaka.htm).

59 Amy Held, 'Controversial Serena Williams Cartoon Ruled 'Non-Racist' By Australia's Press Council,' *NPR*, 25 February 2019, (https://www.npr.org/2019/02/25/697672690/controversial-serena-cartoon-ruled-non-racist-by-australia-s-governing-press-bod).

60 Tara Mohr, *Playing Big: find your voice, your mission, your message* (Avery Publishing Group, 2014).

61 Ibid.

62 Audre Lorde, 'The Transformation of Silence into Language and Action', paper delivered at the Modern Language Association's 'Lesbian and Literature Panel', Chicago, Illinois, 28 December 1977. First Published in *Sinister Wisdom* 6 (1978) and *The Cancer Journals* (Spinsters, Ink, San Francisco, 1980).

63 Ibid.

64 Rachel Simmons, *Odd Girl Out: the Hidden Culture of Aggression in Girls* (Mariner Books, 2002).

Chapter 3: I guess this is growing up: your family, your brain and other reasons you say yes

1 Suzanne Gerber, 'Why Even Strong Women Sometimes Have a Hard Time Saying No', *Next Avenue*, 1 March 2012, (http://www.nextavenue.org/blog/why-even-strong-womensometimes-have-hard-time-saying-no).

2 I haven't asked these women to take the self-test or asked if they identify as Yes Women personally, so I'm not claiming they're Yes Women necessarily. However, each has told me they've dealt with perfectionism, people-pleasing and/or difficulty saying no in their own lives – all of which I refer to as 'Yes Women tendencies' throughout this book.

3 Carissa Lee, her words, video, 16 July 2017, (https://www.herwords.com.au/episodes-all/carissa-lee).

4 Arianna Huffington, 'It's Time to End Perfection Anxiety Once and For All,' *Thrive Global*, 11 June 2019, (https://thriveglobal.com/stories/how-to-stop-perfection-anxiety-tips-arianna-huffington/).

5 Emily L Lyman and Suniya S Luthar, 'Further Evidence on the "Costs of Privilege": perfectionism in high-achieving youth at socioeconomic extremes', *Psychology in the Schools* 51, no. 9 (2014).

6 Melissa Benn, *What Should We Tell our Daughters? The Pleasures and Pressures of Growing Up Female* (Hodder & Stoughton, 2013).

7 E.g. Alain de Botton, *Status Anxiety* (Pantheon, 2004); Michael Marmot, 'Status syndrome', *Significance* 1 (2004); and Kristin Scott, Diane M Martin and John W Schouten 'Marketing and the New Materialism', *Journal of Macromarketing* 34, (2014). Cited in Thomas Curran & Andrew P Hill, 'Perfectionism Is Increasing Over Time: a meta-analysis of birth cohort differences from 1989 to 2016', *Psychological Bulletin* 145, no. 4 (2017).

8 Mohammad Ali Besharat and Shahriar Shahidi, 'Perfectionism, Anger, and Anger Rumination', *International Journal of Psychology* 45, no. 6 (2010).

9 Socially prescribed perfectionism is strongly linked to people-pleasing tendencies, psychologist Kimberley Norris told me when I interviewed her for this book.

10 Thomas Frank, *Listen Liberal: or what ever happened to the party of the people?* (Metropolitan Books, 2016). Cited in Thomas Curran & Andrew P Hill, 'Perfectionism Is Increasing Over Time: a meta-analysis of birth cohort differences from 1989 to 2016', *Psychological Bulletin* 145, no. 4 (2017).

11 Paul L Hewitt, Gordon L Flett, G & Samuel F Mikail, *Perfectionism: a relational approach to conceptualization, assessment, and treatment* (Guilford Press, 2017). Cited in Thomas Curran & Andrew P Hill, 'Perfectionism Is Increasing Over Time: a meta-analysis of birth cohort differences from 1989 to 2016', *Psychological Bulletin* 145, no. 4 (2017).

12 Martin Smith, Simon Sherry, Vanja Vidovic, 'Perfectionism and the Five-Factor Model of Personality: a meta-analytic review', *Pers Soc Psychol Rev* 23, no. 4 (2019).

13 Katharine Ridgway O'Brien, 'Just Saying "No": an examination of gender differences in the ability to decline requests in the workplace', Diss., Rice University (2014).

14 'Highly sensitive person' traits that can overlap with Yes Woman tendencies include finding that other people's moods affect you; a feeling that your nervous system is so frazzled that you need to go off by yourself; see Elaine Aron, 'The Highly Sensitive Person,' (https://hsperson.com).

15 Imi Lo, 'What is emotional intensity?' *Eggshell Therapy and Coaching*, (https://www.eggshelltherapy.com/emotional-intensity/).

16 Ernest Hartmann, *Boundaries of the mind: a new psychology of personality* (Basic Books, 1991).
17 Dr Jessamy Hibberd, *The Imposter Cure: how to stop feeling like a fraud and escape the mind-trap of imposter syndrome* (Octopus, 2019).
18 Sahaj Kohli, Twitter thread, 20 August 2020, (https://twitter.com/SahajKohli/status/1296176544797335553).
19 Sahaj Kohli, tweet, 20 August 2020, (https://twitter.com/SahajKohli/status/1296176544797335553).
20 Ibid.
21 Thomas Curran & Andrew P Hill, 'Perfectionism Is Increasing Over Time: a meta-analysis of birth cohort differences from 1989 to 2016', *Psychological Bulletin* 145, no. 4 (2017).
22 Dr Jessamy Hibberd, *The Imposter Cure: how to stop feeling like a fraud and escape the mind-trap of imposter syndrome* (Octopus, 2019).
23 Studies carried out by Disease Control and Prevention and Kaiser Permanente discovered that people with highly traumatic childhoods – as signified by their scores on the 'Adverse Childhood Experiences' ranking – had significantly higher chances of continual illness, melancholy and attempted suicide. From Vincent J Felitti, Robert F Anda, Dale Nordenberg, David F Williamson, Alison M Spitz MS, Valerie Edwards, Mary P Koss, James S Marks, 'Relationship of Childhood Abuse and Household Dysfunction to Many of the Leading Causes of Death in Adults: the adverse childhood experiences (ACE) study', *American Journal of Preventative Medicine* 14, Issue 4 (1998).
24 Kendra Cherry, 'The Different Types of Attachment Styles', *VeryWell Mind*, June 4 2020, (https://www.verywellmind.com/attachment-styles-2795344).
25 Mimi Wellisch, 'Perfectionism, Attachment and Giftedness', *Tall Poppies* 33, no. 1 (2008).
26 Ann Stoneson, 'What Makes a People-Pleaser?' *Labyrinth Healing*, (https://labyrinthhealing.com/blog/what-makes-a-people-pleaser).
27 *PsychAlive*, 'What's Your Attachment Style?', (https://www.psychalive.org/what-is-your-attachment-style/).
28 Nevelyn Trumpeter, Paul Watson and Brian O'Leary, 'Factors within Multidimensional Perfectionism Scales: complexity of relationships with self-esteem, narcissism, self-control, and self-criticism', *Personality and Individual Differences* 41, no. 10 (2006).
29 Ibid.
30 Claire Bracken, 'Attachment Theory: in what fun ways has your upbringing f*cked you?', *Triple J*, 21 September 2018, (https://www.abc.net.au/triplej/programs/the-hook-up/attachment-theory/10291646).
31 Alice Pung, 28 October 2007, 'Embracing the "F" Word', *The Age* (https://www.theage.com.au/national/its-time-to-embrace-the-f-word-20071028-ge65qk.html).
32 See, e.g. Martin Smith, Vanja Vidovic, Simon Sherry and Don Saklofske, 'Are perfectionism dimensions risk factors for anxiety symptoms? A meta-analysis of 11 longitudinal studies,' *Anxiety Stress & Coping* 31, no. 1 (2018); and Benjamin Dorevitch, Kimberly Buck, Matthew Fuller-Tyszkiewicz, Lisa Phillips and Isabel Krug, 'Maladaptive Perfectionism and Depression: Testing the Mediating Role of Self-Esteem and Internalized Shame in an Australian Domestic and Asian International University Sample,' *Front Psychol* 11 (2020).
33 My own diagnosis is 'generalised anxiety disorder', but I've met high-achieving Yes

Women who have been diagnosed with other anxiety disorders such as social anxiety disorder, panic disorder, obsessive-compulsive disorder, or post-traumatic stress disorder.

34 Thomas Curran, 'Our dangerous obsession with perfectionism is getting worse', November 2018, *TEDMED* 2018. Cited in Sophie Scott, 'The Problem with Striving for Perfection', *ABC Everyday*, Australian Broadcasting Corporation, 10 August 2019, (https://www.abc.net.au/life/the-problem-with-perfect/11396506).

35 Brenda Dolieslager, interview with the author, 2020.

36 Full disclosure: 'Monique' is a made-up character, based on a Reddit thread about feeling like an outsider and perfectionism when attending an elite school on a scholarship. For further reading on being 'caught between social worlds' and feeling like an outsider, see Bea Waterfield, Brenda Beagan and Tameera Mohamed, Tameera, '"You Always Remain Slightly an Outsider": Workplace Experiences of Academics from Working-Class or Impoverished Backgrounds,' *Canadian Review of Sociology/ Revue canadienne de sociologie* 56, no. 1 (2019).

37 Kai Harris, 'Women of Color: Let's Give Ourselves Permission to Do Less', *The Everygirl*, 12 July 2020, (https://theeverygirl.com/women-of-color-lets-give-ourselves-permission-to-do-less/).

38 Kevin Cokley, Shannon McClain, Alicia Enciso and Mercedes Martinez, 'An Examination of the Impact of Minority Status Stress and Impostor Feelings on the Mental Health of Diverse Ethnic Minority College Students', *Journal of Multicultural Counseling and Development* 4, no. 2 (2013).

39 Valerie Young, quoted in Abigail Abrams, 'Yes, Impostor Syndrome is Real. Here's How to Deal With It', *TIME*, 20 June 2018, (https://time.com/5312483/how-to-deal-with-impostor-syndrome/).

40 Pauline Rose Clance and Suzanne Imes, 'The Imposter Phenomenon in High Achieving Women: dynamics and therapeutic intervention', *Psychotherapy Theory, Research and Practice* 15, no. 3 (1978).

41 Samantha Simon, '25 Stars Who Suffer from Imposter Syndrome', *InStyle*, 8 December 2017, (https://www.instyle.com/celebrity/stars-imposter-syndrome).

42 Kirsten Weir, 'Feel Like a Fraud?', *gradPSYCH Magazine*, American Psychological Association, November 2013 (https://www.apa.org/gradpsych/2013/11/fraud).

43 Megan Hull, 'Imposter Syndrome', *The Recovery Village*, 19 September 2020, (https://www.therecoveryvillage.com/mental-health/imposter-syndrome/).

44 Arlin Cuncic, 'What is Imposter Syndrome?', *VeryWell Mind*, 26 February 2021, (https://www.verywellmind.com/imposter-syndrome-and-social-anxiety-disorder-4156469).

45 'The Answer is No', *Ladies, We Need to Talk*, Australian Broadcasting Corporation, 30 June 2020.

46 Susie Orbach, *Fat is a Feminist Issue* (Random House, 1978), 148.

47 Dr Harriet Braiker, *The Disease to Please* (McGraw-Hill Education, 2002).

48 Taylor Swift, cited in Lana Wilson, *Miss Americana*. Netflix (2020).

Chapter 4: Being Nice has a price

1 William Martin, *The Best Liberal Quotes Ever: why the left is right*, (Sourcebooks, Inc., 2004).

2 Jamila Rizvi, *Not Just Lucky* (Penguin, 2018).

3 Yassmin Abdel-Magied, her words, video, 'Yassmin Abdel-Magied on gender stereotypes' (https://www.youtube.com/watch?v=DiNKSa5V6O4).

4 Elizabeth Gilbert, *Big Magic* (Bloomsbury, 2016), 167.

5 Valerie Young, paraphrased in Abigail Abrams, 'Yes, Impostor Syndrome is Real. Here's How to Deal With It', *TIME*, 20 June 2018, (https://time.com/5312483/how-to-deal-with-impostor-syndrome/).

6 Brenda Nguyen, Piers Steel, Joseph Ferrari, 'Procrastination's Impact in the Workplace and the Workplace's Impact on Procrastination', *International Journal of Selection and Assessment* 21, no. 4 (2013); and Timothy Judge, 'The Big Five Personality Traits, General Mental Ability, and Career Success Across the Life Span', *Personnel Psychology* 52, no. 3 (1999).

7 Hugh van Cuylenburg, *The Resilience Project*, 21 May 2018, (https://theresilienceproject.com.au/media-posts/the-resilience-project-founder-hugh-van-cuylenburg-on-the-modern-affliction-of-screen-time-addiction/).

8 Catherine Price, *How to Break Up with Your Phone: the 30-day plan to take back your life* (Ten Speed Press, 2018), 25.

9 Tristan Harris, cited in Jeff Orlowski, *The Social Dilemma*. Netflix, 2020.

10 Catherine Price, *How to Break Up with Your Phone: the 30-day plan to take back your life* (Ten Speed Press, 2018), 10–11.

11 Larry Rosen, *iDisorder: understanding our obsession with technology and overcoming its hold on us* (Palgrave Macmillan, 2012). Cited in Jill Stark, *Happy Never After: why the happiness fairytale is driving us mad (and how I flipped the script)* (Scribe, 2018), 99.

12 I wonder if Alanis was too embarrassed to ask somebody for the true definition of irony when she wrote that song? That would explain a lot.

13 Ellen Winner, *Gifted children* (Basic Books, 1996); and Ellen Winner, 'The Origins and Ends of Giftedness', *American Psychologist* 55, no. 1 (2000).

14 John W Santrock, *A Topical Approach to Life-Span Development* (8th edition), (McGraw Hill Education, 2016).

15 Stefanie Preissner, *Can I Say No?* (Hachette, 2020), 106.

16 Tara Mohr, *Playing Big: find your voice, your mission, your message* (Avery Publishing Group, 2014), 249.

17 'Why Australians are More Stressed Than Ever', *SBS News*, 28 December 2017, (https://www.sbs.com.au/news/why-australians-are-more-stressed-than-ever).

18 Priory, 'Why Stress Levels Among Women 50% Higher Than Men?' *Priory Group Blog*, (https://www.priorygroup.com/blog/why-are-stress-levels-among-women-50-higher-than-men).

19 Ryan Batchelor, 'The Impact of COVID-19 on Women and Work in Victoria: research insights', *The McKell Institute*, August 2020, (https://mckellinstitute.org.au/research/articles/the-impact-of-covid-19-on-women-and-work-in-victoria/).

20 Talha Burki, 'The Indirect Impact of COVID-19 on Women', *The Lancet* 20, no. 8 (2020).

21 Caroline Gurvich, Monash University, email with the author, 2020. Also see: Monash University, Monash Rural Health and Monash Alfred Psychiatric Research Centre, 'Mental Health During COVID-19', 2020 (https://www.monash.edu/medicine/srh/research/projects/mental-health-during-covid-19).

22 Harriet Braiker, *The Type E* Woman: how to overcome the stress of being everything to everybody* (iUniverse, 2002), 16.

23 Dana Harari, Brian Swider, Laurens Bujold Steed, Amy P Breidenthal, 'Is Perfect Good? A Meta Analysis of Perfectionism in the Workplace', *American Psychological Association*, 2018 (https://www.apa.org/pubs/journals/releases/apl-apl0000324.pdf); Handley, AK, Egan, SJ, Kane, RT et al., 'The Relationships between

Perfectionism, Pathological Worry and Generalised Anxiety Disorder', *BMC Psychiatry* 14, 98 (2014); Harari, Swider, Bujold Steed and Breidenthal, ibid at 122, and Enns, M.W., Cox, B.J., 'Perfectionism, Stressful Life Events, and the 1-Year Outcome of Depression', *Cogn Ther Res*, 29, (2005). Cited in Sophie Scott, 'The Problem With Striving for Perfection', *ABC Everyday*, Australian Broadcasting Corporation, 10 August 2019, https://www.abc.net.au/everyday/the-problem-with-perfect/11396506).

24 Dr Fiona Enkelmann; see also Habib Yaribeygi, Yunes Panahi, Hedayat Sahraei, Thomas P. Johnston, Amirhossein Sahebkar, 'The Impact of Stress on Body Function: a review', *EXCLI Journal* 16 (2017).

25 Robert M Sapolsky, *Why Zebras Don't Get Ulcers* (Holt Paperbacks, 1994).

26 Harriet Braiker, *The Type E* Woman:how to overcome the stress of being everything to everybody* (iUniverse, 2002).

27 Robert M Sapolsky, *Why Zebras Don't Get Ulcers* (Holt Paperbacks, 1994).

28 Ibid.

29 McHugh RK, Devito EE, Dodd D, et al. 'Gender Differences in a Clinical Trial for Prescription Opioid Dependence', *J Subst Abuse Treat* 45, no. 1 (2013).

30 MacKenzie Peltier, Terril L Verplaetse, Yann S Mineur et al, 'Sex differences in stress-related alcohol use', *Neurobiology of stress* 10 (2019).

31 *National Institute on Alcohol Abuse and Alcoholism*, 'Alcohol: a women's health issue', 2003, (https://pubs.niaaa.nih.gov/publications/brochurewomen/women.htm).

32 Mary Pipher, *Reviving Ophelia* (Putnam Pub Group, 1994).

33 Julie De Azevedo Hanks, *Assertiveness Guide for Women: how to communicate your needs, set healthy boundaries, and transform your relationships* (New Harbinger Publications, 2016).

34 Ibid.

35 Brené Brown, *I Thought it Was Just Me (but it isn't)* (Penguin, 2007).

36 Ibid.

37 Quote by billionaire Warren Buffett, the chairman and CEO of Berkshire Hathaway. See: Amy Blaschka, 'This Is Why Saying 'No' Is The Best Way To Grow Your Career – And How To Do It', *Forbes*, 26 November 2019 (https://www.forbes.com/sites/amyblaschka/2019/11/26/this-is-why-saying-no-is-the-best-way-to-grow-your-career-and-how-to-do-it/?sh=59004e89479d).

38 Jennifer Lawrence, 'Why Do I Make Less Than My Co-Stars?', *Lenny Letter*, 13 October 2015, (https://www.lennyletter.com/story/jennifer-lawrence-why-do-i-make-less-than-my-male-costars).

39 Tara Moss, *Speaking Out: a 21-st century handbook for women and girls* (Harper Collins, 2016).

40 Kate Wilkinson, *The Modest Mouth: women and modesty in late antiquity* (Cambridge University Press, 2015), 86–116.

41 Helen Lewis, *Difficult Women: a history of feminism in 11 fights* (Jonathan Cape, 2020), 69.

42 Mary Beard, *Oh Shut Up, Dear!*, BBC, 18 June 2018 (https://www.bbc.co.uk/programmes/b03ycql8).

43 Ibid.

44 Fresh Air, 'From Upspeak to Vocal Fry: are we "policing" young women's voices?', *NPR*, 23 July 2015, (http://www.npr.org/2015/07/23/425608745/from-upspeak-to-vocal-fry-are-we-policing-young-womens-voices).

45 Carol Gilligan and Naomi Snider, *Why Does Patriarchy Persist?* (Polity, 2018).

46 Van Badham, her words, video, 'Van Badham: the cost of not speaking up is Donald Trump', video, YouTube (https://www.youtube.com/watch?v=D9uDxacZwAU). Also note that many more men than women are the perpetrators of online abuse, and they attack women more than they attack men. (One academic study put the ratio at something like 30:1 female to male targets.) 'If you venture into traditional male territory, the abuse comes anyway. It's not what you are saying that prompts it, it's the fact you are saying it,' as Mary Beard has noted. Mary Beard, *Oh Shut Up, Dear!*, BBC, 18 June 2018 (https://www.bbc.co.uk/programmes/b03ycql8).
47 Van Badham, her words, video, 'Van Badham: The cost of not speaking up is Donald Trump', 27 August 2017, (https://www.youtube.com/watch?v=D9uDxacZwAU).
48 Soraya Chemaly, *Rage Becomes Her: the power of women's anger* (Simon & Schuster, 2018).
49 Ibid.
50 Tressie McMillan Cottom, 'Dr. Tressie McMillan Cottom: raising really good hell for people who cannot', *Guernica*, 20 March 2019, (https://www.guernicamag.com/dr-tressie-mcmillan-cottom-raising-really-good-hell-for-people-who-cannot/).
51 Laurel Thatcher Ulrich, 'Vertuous Women Found: New England Ministerial Literature, 1668–1735', *American Quarterly* 28, no. 1 (1976), 20–40.

Chapter 5: Busy is best, and other myths we've swallowed

1 Audre Lorde, speech delivered at the Modern Language Association's 'Lesbian and Literature Panel', Chicago, Illinois, 28 December 1977. First Published in *Sinister Wisdom 6* (1978) and *The Cancer Journals* (Spinsters, Ink, 1980).
2 Paul Bennett, 'Are New Yorkers really busy and have no time for socializing?' *Quora*, 2017 (https://www.quora.com/Are-New-Yorkers-really-busy-and-have-no-time-for-socializing).
3 Jenny Odell, *How to Do Nothing: resisting the attention economy* (Melville House, 2019), 70.
4 Ibid.
5 André Spicer, '"Self-care": how a radical feminist idea was stripped of politics for the mass market', *The Guardian*, 21 August 2019 (https://www.theguardian.com/commentisfree/2019/aug/21/self-care-radical-feminist-idea-mass-market).
6 Kenya Foy, 'Six Important Differences between Self-Care and Selfishness', *HelloGiggles*, 7 August 2015 (https://hellogiggles.com/lifestyle/health-fitness/important-differences-self-care-selfishness/).
7 Clementine Ford, *Fight Like a Girl* (Allen & Unwin, 2018).
8 Tara Mohr, 'Why Women Don't Apply for Jobs Unless They're 100% Qualified', *Harvard Business Review*, 24 August 2015 (http://hbr.org/2014/08/why-women-dont-apply-for-jobs-unless-theyre-100-qualified.)
9 Ibid.
10 Voltaire is commonly said to have coined the aphorism "perfect is the enemy of the good". In his *Dictionnaire philosophique* in 1770, he wrote: "*Le meglio è l'inimico del bene*". Source: Susan Ratcliffe *Concise Oxford Dictionary of Quotations* (Oxford University Press, 2011), p. 389.
11 There are books aplenty about the power of embracing failure and imperfection, and I suggest you seek some out. In particular, I highly recommend you read Brené Brown's *The Gifts of Imperfection: let go of who you think you're supposed to be and embrace who you are.*

12 Brené Brown, *I Thought it Was Just Me (but it isn't)* (Penguin, 2007).
13 Adam Ottke, '68 Per Cent of Adults Edit Their Selfies before Sharing Them with Anyone', *Fstoppers*, 30 October 2015, (https//fstoppers.com/mobile/68-percent-adults-edit-their-selfies-sharing-them-anyone-95417).
14 Cited in Sophie Scott, 'The Problem With Striving For Perfection', *ABC Everyday*, Australian Broadcasting Corporation, 10 August 2019, (https://www.abc.net.au/everyday/the-problem-with-perfect/11396506).
15 Mental health issues have skyrocketed since social media became mainstream. We've seen an increase in self-harm and suicide in teen girls – and in older teen girls, suicide rates are up 70 per cent in the US compared to the first decade of the century, according to Jonathan Haidt, a social psychologist at NYU Stern School of Business. That's the same time period in which the use of smartphones became widespread.
16 She's actually talking about those born from the mid-90s, but much of her findings are relevant for those born in the late 80s, like myself.
17 Cited in Catherine Price, *How to Break Up with Your Phone: the 30-day plan to take back your life* (Ten Speed Press, 2018), 43.
18 Brené Brown, *I Thought it Was Just Me (but it isn't)* (Penguin, 2007).
19 Dr Harriet Braiker, *The Type E* Woman: how to overcome the stress of being everything to everybody* (iUniverse, 2002).
20 Ibid.
21 Ibid, 4.
22 Ibid, 412.
23 Zara McDonald and Michelle Andrews, 'In Conversation: Zara McDonald', *Shameless*, 10 September 2020.
24 Tara Mohr, *Playing Big: find your voice, your mission, your message* (Avery Publishing Group, 2014), 223.
25 Helen Lewis, *Difficult Women: a history of feminism in 11 fights* (Jonathan Cape, 2020), 297.
26 Ibid, 315.
27 Yuanyuan Kelly, '15 Inspiring Quotes from Nigerian Author Chimamanda Adichie', *Global Citizen*, 12 August 2015.

Chapter 6: Work out what you want (what you really, really want)

1 Janet Mock, 'Janet Mock: "Unlearn the Things This World Has Thrust Upon You"', *Bust*, June/July 2017 (https://bust.com/feminism/193010-janet-mock-interview.html).
2 Stefanie Preissner, *Can I Say No?* (Hachette, 2020), 60.
3 Ibid, 30.
4 Imi Lo, 'The Non-Conforming Asian Women', *Psychology Today*, 13 July 2018 (https://www.psychologytoday.com/us/blog/living-emotional-intensity/201807/the-non-conforming-asian-women).
5 Ibid.
6 Full disclosure: Thea is a made-up character, based on this article: Anne, 'Loss of Identity and Finding Yourself After Divorce,' *Divorce Magazine*, 20 September 2020, (https://www.divorcemag.com/blog/loss-of-identity-and-finding-yourself-after-divorce).
7 Barbara J Sahakian & Jamie Nicole Labuzetta, *Bad moves: how decision making goes wrong, and the ethics of smart drugs* (Oxford University Press, 2013).
8 Some psychologists – such as Barry Schwartz, author of *The Paradox of Choice: why*

more is less (HarperCollins, 2016) have accordingly argued that eliminating consumer choices can actually reduce anxiety for shoppers.

9 Sheena Iyengar, TED talk, 'The Art of Choosing', TEDGlobal, 2010, (https://www.ted.com/talks/sheena_iyengar_the_art_of_choosing/transcript?language=en).

10 Grace Jennings-Edquist, 'Why Parents are Giving Their Kids "Imaginative" Baby Names', *ABC Everyday*, Australian Broadcasting Corporation, 4 February 2019 (https://www.abc.net.au/life/why-parents-are-giving-their-kids-imaginative-baby-names/10720110).

11 'Millennials and Technology at Home', *Qualtrics and Accel*, no. 5, 2016, (https://www.qualtrics.com/millennials/ebooks/Millennials_And_Tech_At_Home_eBook_All_AK.pdf).

12 Catherine Price, *How to Break Up With Your Phone: the 30-day plan to take back your life*, (Ten Speed Press, 2018).

13 Ibid, 3.

14 Anne Helen Petersen, 'How Millennials Became the Burnout Generation', *BuzzFeed News*, 5 January 2019 (https://www.buzzfeednews.com/article/annehelenpetersen/millennials-burnout-generation-debt-work).

15 Stefanie Preissner, *Can I Say No?* (Hachette, 2020), 120.

16 Bronnie Ware, *The Top Five Regrets of the Dying* (Hay House, 2012).

17 Ibid, 96.

18 Bronnie Ware, 'Seven Ways to Create Space', (https://bronnieware.com/blog/seven-ways-create-space/).

19 Ibid.

20 Brenda Dolieslager, interview with the author, 2020.

21 Dr Lois Frankel, *Nice Girls Don't Get the Corner Office: 101 unconscious mistakes women make that sabotage their careers* (Grand Central Publishing, 2004).

22 Ibid, 176.

23 Christine Armstrong, *The Mother of All Jobs: how to have children and a career and stay sane(ish)* (Green Tree, 2018).

24 Grace Jennings-Edquist, 'Feeling Angry Can Mean Your Mental Health Needs Attention', *ABC Everyday*, Australian Broadcasting Corporation, 18 June 2020, (https://www.abc.net.au/everyday/feeling-angry-can-mean-your-mental-health-needs-attention/12354886).

25 Soraya Chemaly, *Rage Becomes Her: the power of women's anger* (Simon & Schuster, 2018).

26 Krasi Kirova, 'Know Your Boundaries', *Kirova Psychology*, 26 June 2017 (https://kirovapsychology.com.au/2017/06/26/know-your-boundaries/).

Chapter 7: Getting to no

1 Anna Spargo-Ryan, tweet, 11 September 2020, (https://twitter.com/annaspargoryan/status/1304215495873241088).

2 Sahaj Kohli, Instagram post, 14 September 2019, *Brown Girl Therapy*, (https://www.instagram.com/p/B2Xaj51l6jx/).

3 Ibid.

4 This approach came up in several interviews with Yes Women, but is also outlined helpfully in Tim Ferriss, 'How to Say No (#282)' *The Tim Ferriss Show*, 3 February 2018, (https://tim.blog/2018/02/03/the-tim-ferriss-show-transcripts-how-to-say-no/).

5 Byron Katie, 'How to Say No', *The Work*, (https://thework.com/2008/02/how-to-say-no/).

6 Adapted from Marianna Olszewski, quoted in Grace Jennings-Edquist, "Tips for Being Assertive – and Still Likeable – at Work," Spring St, Mamamia Women's Network, 2016, available at *Fairy God Boss* (https://fairygodboss.com/articles/tips-for-speaking-like-boss-lady).

Chapter 8: A friend in need

1 '"Suits" star Meghan Markle talks International Day of the Girl', video, *CityTV/YouTube*, 8 October 2015, (https://www.youtube.com/watch?v=Ape4M6jXw0s).
2 Dr Hannah Korrel, 'Walking on Eggshells: how to know when it's time to ditch a toxic friend', *Sunday Life*, 9 October 2020, (https://www.smh.com.au/lifestyle/life-and-relationships/on-eggshells-how-to-know-when-it-s-time-to-ditch-a-toxic-friend-20201008-p5635q.html).
3 Mark Manson, 'Are You an Emotional Vampire?', (https://markmanson.net/are-you-an-emotional-vampire).
4 Christine Ro, 'Dunbar's Number: why we can only maintain 150 relationships', *Future*, 9 October 2019 (https://www.bbc.com/future/article/20191001-dunbars-number-why-we-can-only-maintain-150-relationships).
5 Stefanie Preissner, *Can I Say No?* (Hachette, 2020), 282.

Chapter 9: Fam, damn

1 Milly Thomas, tweet, 5 February 2020, (https://twitter.com/missmillythomas/status/1224722906883809281).
2 Sarah Knight, *F**k No! How to stop saying yes, when you can't, you shouldn't, or you just don't want to* (Quercus, 2019), 238.
3 Sahaj Kohli, Instagram post, 'Common Growing Pains for Children of Immigrants', *Brown Girl Therapy*, 22 January 2021 (https://www.instagram.com/p/CKUyWb_lUDU/).
4 Sahaj Kohli, Instagram post, *Brown Girl Therapy*, 22 January 2021, (https://www.instagram.com/p/CKUyWb_lUDU/).
5 Melody Beattie, *The Language of Letting Go: daily meditations on codependency* (Hazelden, 1990).
6 Ibid.
7 Sahaj Kohli, Instagram post, *Brown Girl Therapy*, 5 December 2019, (https://www.instagram.com/p/B6d9m0YFZDY/).
8 Kellie Scott, 'Setting Boundaries with Our Parents is Tough. These tips can help', *ABC Everyday*, Australian Broadcasting Corporation, 22 January 2021, (https://www.abc.net.au/everyday/tips-for-setting-boundaries-with-your-parents/12875882).
9 Melody Beattie, *The Language of Letting Go: daily meditations on codependency* (Hazelden, 1990).

Chapter 10: Meet me halfway: give and take in dating and relationships

1 Oprah Winfrey, 'When people show you who they are, believe them', *Oprah's Lifeclass*, Season 1, Episode 13, Oprah Winfrey Network, 26 October 2011.
2 I recounted the start of this date in an old column for Mamamia Women's Network: Grace Jennings-Edquist, 'I Once Went on a Date That I Regretted Almost Immediately', *Mamamia*, 21 May 2014, (https://www.mamamia.com.au/men-who-cant-handle-rejection).

3 Full disclosure: Ari is a made-up character based on several anecdotes on this topic, shared anonymously by friends.

4 David A Frederick, H Kate St John, Justin R Garcia and Elisabeth A Lloyd, 'Differences in Orgasm Frequency Among Gay, Lesbian, Bisexual, and Heterosexual Men and Women in a US National Sample', *Archives of Sexual Behaviour* 47, no. 1 (2018).

5 'Propping up Your Partner', *Ladies, We Need To Talk*, Australian Broadcasting Corporation, 16 June 2020.

6 Domestic Violence Resource Centre Victoria, 'The Signs of Abuse', (https://www.dvrcv.org.au/help-advice/survivors).

7 Roger Wilkins, Inga Lass, Peter Butterworth and Esperanza Vera-Toscano, 'The Household, Income and Labour Dynamics in Australia Survey: selected findings from waves 1 to 17: 2019 HILDA survey: the 14th annual statistical report of the HILDA survey', *Melbourne Institute*, The University of Melbourne (2019).

8 Jean Hailes for Women's Health, National Women's Health survey 2020, (https://www.jeanhailes.org.au/research/womens-health-survey/survey2020).

9 Emma, 'The Gender Wars of Household Chores: a feminist comic', *The Guardian*, 26 May 2017, (https://www.theguardian.com/world/2017/may/26/gender-wars-household-chores-comic).

10 Grace Jennings-Edquist, 'How to Even up Housework with Your Partner', *ABC Everyday*, Australian Broadcasting Corporation, 14 July 2019, (https://www.abc.net.au/everyday/how-to-even-up-housework-with-your-partner/11289272).

11 Eve Rodsky, *Fair Play: a game-changing solution for when you have too much to do (and more life to live)* (Penguin Random House: 2019).

12 Grace Jennings-Edquist, '*Mamamia* Speaks to Annabel Crabb about Kids, Work, and Why All Women Need a "Wife"', *Mamamia*, 6 October 2014, (https://www.mamamia.com.au/annabel-crabb-interview/).

13 Ibid.

Chapter 11: Working 9 to 5 (requires saying nope to all that overtime)

1 Paulo Coelho, tweet, 6 March 2014, (https://twitter.com/paulocoelho/status/441268849871454208?lang=en).

2 Jane Jackson, cited in Grace Jennings-Edquist, 'How and When to Say No at Work,' *ABC Everyday*, Australian Broadcasting Corporation, 18 November 2020, (https://www.abc.net.au/everyday/how-to-say-no-at-work/12821000.)

3 Nancy Beauregard, Alain Marchand, Jaunathan Bilodeau, Pierre Durand, Andrée Demers, Victor Y Haines III, 'Gendered Pathways to Burnout: results from the SALVEO study', *Annals of Work Exposures and Health* 62, no. 4 (2018).

4 Ibid.

5 World Health Organization, 'Burn-out an "occupational phenomenon": International Classification of Diseases', *WHO News*, 28 May 2019.

6 Timothy A Judge, Chad A Higgins, Carl J Thoreson and Murray R Barrick, 'The Big 5 Personality Traits, General Mental Ability, And Career Success Across the Life Span', *Personnel Psychology*, 52, no. 3 (2006). Cited in Peter O'Connor, 'Playing Nice at Work Could Cost You Success', *The Conversation*, 18 April 2018, (https://theconversation.com/playing-Nice-at-work-could-cost-you-success-94744).

7 Dr Lois Frankel, *Nice Girls Don't Get the Corner Office: 101 unconscious mistakes women make that sabotage their careers* (Grand Central Publishing, 2004), 75.

8 Sarah Knight suggests a similar approach (and many other practical, word-by-word examples of what to say) in her book, *F**k No! How to stop saying yes, when you can't, you shouldn't, or you just don't want to* (Quercus, 2019).
9 Imi Lo, 'The Non-Conforming Asian Women', *Psychology Today*, 13 July 2018 (https://www.psychologytoday.com/us/blog/living-emotional-intensity/201807/the-non-conforming-asian-women).
10 Linda Babcock, Maria P Recalde, and Lise Vesterlund, 'Why Women Volunteer for Tasks That Don't Lead to Promotions', *Harvard Business Review*, 16 July 2018, (https://hbr.org/2018/07/why-women-volunteer-for-tasks-that-dont-lead-to-promotions).
11 Ibid.
12 Ibid.
13 Dr Lois Frankel, *Nice Girls Don't Get the Corner Office: 101 unconscious mistakes women make that sabotage their careers* (Grand Central Publishing, 2004).
14 Ibid.
15 *Make It Our Business*, 'Flexibility in the Workplace Can Help Keep More Women in the Workforce', 5 October 2019, (http://makeitourbusiness.ca/blog/flexibility-workplace-can-help-keep-more-women-workforce).
16 Ibid.
17 Linda Duxbury, Christopher Higgins, Rob Smart and Maggie Stevenson, 'Mobile Technology and Boundary Permeability', *British Journal of Management* 25, no. 3 (2013).
18 Melissa A Wheeler and Asanka Gunasekara, 'Forget Work–Life Balance – It's All About Integration in the Age of COVID-19', *The Conversation*, 18 May 2020 (https://theconversation.com/forget-work-life-balance-its-all-about-integration-in-the-age-of-covid-19–137386).
19 Donna Weaver McCloskey, 'Finding Work–Life Balance in a Digital Age: an exploratory study of boundary flexibility and permeability', *Information Resources Management Journal* 29, no. 3 (2016).
20 Will Coldwell, '"Co-living": the end of urban loneliness – or cynical corporate dormitories?', *The Guardian*, 3 September 2019, (https://www.theguardian.com/cities/2019/sep/03/co-living-the-end-of-urban-loneliness-or-cynical-corporate-dormitories).
21 Caroline Leduc, Nathalie Houlfort and Sarah Bourdeau, 'Work–Life Balance: the good and the bad of boundary management', *International Journal of Psychological Studies* 8, no. 133. (2016).
22 Jan De Jonge, Akihito Shimazu and Maureen Dollard, 'Short-Term and Long-Term Effects of Off-Job Activities on Recovery and Sleep: a two-wave panel study among health care employees', *International Journal of Environmental Research and Public Health* 15, no. 9 (2018).
23 The Australian Bureau of Statistics reports that 27 per cent of female employees did not have paid leave entitlements, compared with 23 per cent of men. Source: Australian Bureau of Statistics, 'Gender Indicators, Australia', September 2018, (https://www.abs.gov.au/ausstats/abs@.nsf/Lookup/by%20Subject/4125.0~Sep%202018~Main%20Features~Economic%20Security~4).
24 Ryan Batchelor, 'The Impact of COVID-19 on Women and Work in Victoria: research insights', The McKell Institute, August 2020, (https://mckellinstitute.org.au/research/articles/the-impact-of-covid-19-on-women-and-work-in-victoria/).
25 Jan Dettmers, Stephan Kaiser & Simon Fietze, 'Theory and Practice of Flexible

Work: organizational and individual perspectives. Introduction to the special issue', *Management Revue* 24, no. 3 (2013).
26 Fair Work Ombudsman, 'Protections at Work', (https://www.fairwork.gov.au/employee-entitlements/protections-at-work#coercion).
27 Fair Work Ombudsman, 'When Overtime Applies', (https://www.fairwork.gov.au/employee-entitlements/hours-of-work-breaks-and-rosters/hours-of-work/when-overtime-applies).
28 Jane Caro, 'No, I Can't Be Your Unpaid Mentor', *Women's Agenda*, 17 April 2019, (https://womensagenda.com.au/latest/no-i-cant-be-your-unpaid-mentor-jane-caro).
29 Ruby Hamad, *White Tears/Brown Scars* (Melbourne University Press, 2019), 285.
30 Mikki Kendall, *Hood Feminism* (Viking: 2020), 2.
31 Sana Qadar, 'Hiring Mini-Mes? How to spot similarity bias and encourage diversity at work', *ABC Everyday*, Australian Broadcasting Corporation, 3 April 2019, (https://www.abc.net.au/life/hiring-mini-mes-what-bosses-need-to-know-about-similarity-bias/10883076).
32 Joyce Fletcher, 'The Paradox of Post Heroic Leadership: an essay on gender, power, and transformational change', *The Leadership Quarterly* 15, (2004). Cited in Alison Pullen and Sheena Vachhani, 'Feminist Ethics and Women Leaders: from difference to intercorporeality', *Journal of Business Ethics* (2020).
33 Jackie Ford, Nancy Harding and Mark Learmonth, *Leadership as Identity – Constructions and deconstructions* (Palgrave MacMillan, 2008). Cited in Alison Pullen and Sheena Vachhani, 'Feminist Ethics and Women Leaders: from difference to intercorporeality', *Journal of Business Ethics* (2020).
34 Alison Pullen and Sheena Vachhani, 'Feminist Ethics and Women Leaders: from difference to intercorporeality', *Journal of Business Ethics* (2020).
35 Mikki Kendall, *Hood Feminism* (Viking, 2020), 14.

Chapter 12: Mother, other or martyr?

1 Glennon Doyle, *Untamed* (Dial Press, 2020).
2 Customer reviews, '*The Giving Tree* by Shel Silverstein', *GoodReads*, (https://www.goodreads.com/book/show/370493.The_Giving_Tree#other_reviews).
3 Tenneva Jordan, *GoodReads*, (https://www.goodreads.com/quotes/502972-a-mother-is-a-person-who-seeing-there-are-only).
4 Madeleine Brand, 'Parenting on the Edge: Madeleine Brand casts a critical eye on classic kids' books', *Los Angeles Times*, 16 September 2014, (https://www.latimes.com/la-hm-parenting-ss-htmlstory.html).
5 Lorraine Tulman, Jacqueline Fawcett, Laura Groblewski, Lisa Silverman, 'Changes in Functional Status after Childbirth', *Nursing Research*, 39 (2), (1990). See also: Carol McVeigh, 'Functional Status after Childbirth in an Australian Sample', *Journal of Obstetric, Gynecologic, and Neonatal Nursing* 27, no. 4,(1998).
6 Dr Zoë Krupka on 'Footloose and Childfree', *Ladies, We Need to Talk*, Australian Broadcasting Corporation, June 2019 (https://www.abc.net.au/radio/programs/ladies-we-need-to-talk/footloose-and-childfree/11216364).
7 The last factor is described by Giddens (1992, 2), cited in Rosemary Gillespie, '*Childfree and Feminine*', *Gender & Society* 17, no. 1 (2003), 122–136.
8 Dr Zoë Krupka on 'Footloose and Childfree', *Ladies, We Need to Talk*, Australian Broadcasting Corporation, June 2019 (https://www.abc.net.au/radio/programs/ladies-we-need-to-talk/footloose-and-childfree/11216364).

9 Melissa Graham, Erin Hill, Julia Shelly and Ann Taket, 'Why are childless women childless? Findings from an exploratory study in Victoria, Australia,' *Journal of Social Inclusion* 4, no. 1 (2013).

10 Kristin Park, 'Choosing Childlessness: Weber's typology of action and motives of the voluntary childless', *Sociological Inquiry* 75, no. 3 (2005).

11 Kathryn M Rizzo, Holly H Schiffrin and Miriam Liss, 'Insight into the Parenthood Paradox: mental health outcomes of intensive mothering', *Journal of Child and Family Studies*, 22 (2013).

12 University of California, Irvine, 'Today's parents spend more time with their kids than moms and dads did 50 years ago,' 28 September 2016, *UCI News*, (https://news.uci.edu/2016/09/28/todays-parents-spend-more-time-with-their-kids-than-moms-and-dads-did-50-years-ago/).

13 Aliya Hamid Rao, 'Even Breadwinning Wives Don't Get Equality at Home,' *The Atlantic*, 12 May 2019, (https://www.theatlantic.com/family/archive/2019/05/breadwinning-wives-gender-inequality/589237/).

14 Brenda Parker and Oona Morrow, 'Urban Homesteading and Intensive Mothering: (re) gendering care and environmental responsibility in Boston and Chicago', *Gender, Place & Culture: a journal of feminist geography* 24, no. 2, (2017).

15 Sophie McBain, 'What the New Cult of Perfectionism Means for Motherhood', *New Statesman*, 8 May 2018, (https://www.newstatesman.com/politics/uk/2018/05/what-new-cult-perfectionism-means-motherhood).

16 Sidenote on the name 'attachment parenting': this term borrows from the name 'attachment theory' – an evidence-based foundational principle of psychotherapy – but they're not the same thing. Developmental psychologist Diana Divecha reassures parents that while breastfeeding and co-sleeping have benefits, none are 'actually related to a baby's secure attachment with her caregiver, nor predictive of a baby's future mental health and development'. Source: Diana Divecha, 'Why Attachment Parenting Is Not the Same As Secure Attachment', *Greater Good Magazine*, 2 May 2018, (https://greatergood.berkeley.edu/article/item/why_attachment_parenting_is_not_the_same_as_secure_attachment).

17 Hadley Freeman, 'Attachment Parenting: the best way to raise a child – or maternal masochism?' *The Guardian*, 30 July 2016, (https://www.theguardian.com/lifeandstyle/2016/jul/30/attachment-parenting-best-way-raise-child-or-maternal-masochism).

18 Lisa K Forbes, Margaret R Lamar & Rachel S Bornstein, 'Working Mothers' Experiences in an Intensive Mothering Culture: a phenomenological qualitative study', *Journal of Feminist Family Therapy* (2020).

19 Kathryn M Rizzo, Holly H Schiffrin and Miriam Liss, 'Insight into the Parenthood Paradox: mental health outcomes of intensive mothering', *Journal of Child and Family Studies*, 22 (2013).

20 Ibid.

21 Jordana K Bayer, Ann V Sanson and Sheryl A Hemphill, 'Parent Influences on Early Childhood Internalizing Difficulties', *Journal of Applied Developmental Psychology*, 27, (2006). Cited in Kathryn M Rizzo, Holly H Schiffrin and Miriam Liss, 'Insight into the Parenthood Paradox: mental health outcomes of intensive mothering', *Journal of Child and Family Studies*, 22 (2013).

22 See Jordana K Bayer, Ann V Sanson and Sheryl A Hemphill, 'Parent Influences on Early Childhood Internalizing Difficulties', *Journal of Applied Developmental Psychology*, 27 (2006); William R Beardslee, Jules Bemporad, Martin B Keller and

Gerald L Klerman, 'Children of Parents with Major Affective Disorder: a review', *American Journal of Psychiatry*, 140 (1983); and E Mark Cummings and Patrick T Davies, 'Maternal Depression and Child Development', *Journal of Child Psychological Psychiatry*, 35 (1994). Cited in Kathryn M Rizzo, Holly H Schiffrin and Miriam Liss, 'Insight into the Parenthood Paradox: mental health outcomes of intensive mothering', *Journal of Child and Family Studies*, 22 (2013).

23 Pratyusha Tummala-Narra, 'Contemporary Impingements on Mothering', *The American Journal of Psychoanalysis*, 69 (2009). Cited in Kathryn M Rizzo, Holly H Schiffrin and Miriam Liss, 'Insight into the Parenthood Paradox: mental health outcomes of intensive mothering', *Journal of Child and Family Studies*, 22 (2013).

24 Helen Lewis, 'The Next Battleground for Feminism is Simple: women's time', *Penguin*, 4 March 2020 (https://www.penguin.co.uk/articles/2020/mar/helen-lewis-on-whats-next-for-feminism.html).

25 Christine Armstrong, *The Mother of All Jobs: how to have children and a career and stay sane(ish)* (Green Tree, 2018).

26 Helen Lewis, 'The Next Battleground for Feminism is Simple: women's time', *Penguin*, 4 March 2020 (https://www.penguin.co.uk/articles/2020/mar/helen-lewis-on-whats-next-for-feminism.html).

27 Brigid Schulte, *Overwhelmed: work, love, and play when no one has the time* (Macmillan, 2015), 50.

28 Ibid, 49.

29 Jennifer Lynn Barnes, tweet, 23 January 2020 (https://twitter.com/jenlynnbarnes/status/1220182162118451200).

30 Ibid.

31 Dr Brigid Jordan, 'An Overview of Attachment Theory', *Community Paediatric Review* 17, no. 2 (2009).

32 Melissa A Milkie, Kei M Nomaguchi, Kathleen E Denny, 'Does the Amount of Time Mothers Spend With Children or Adolescents Matter?' *Journal of Marriage and Family* 77, no. 2 (2015).

33 Mary Beth Ferrante, 'How Intensive Mothering Is Hurting Working Parents', *Forbes*, 30 August 2018, (https://www.forbes.com/sites/marybethferrante/2018/08/30/how-intensive-mothering-is-hurting-working-parents/).

34 Grace Jennings-Edquist, 'How Much Attention Does Your Toddler Really Need When You're Working from Home?' *ABC Everyday*, Australian Broadcasting Corporation, 8 June 2020 (https://www.abc.net.au/everyday/how-much-attention-do-toddlers-need-when-youre-working-from-home/12307736.)

35 Melissa Milkie and Catharine Warner, 'Status Safeguarding: mothers' work to secure children's place in the social hierarchy', 66–85, in Linda Rose Ennis (editor), *Intensive Mothering: the cultural contradictions of modern motherhood* (Demeter Press, 2014).

36 Grace Jennings-Edquist, 'How Much Attention Does Your Toddler Really Need When You're Working From Home?' *ABC Everyday*, Australian Broadcasting Corporation, 8 June 2020 (https://www.abc.net.au/everyday/how-much-attention-do-toddlers-need-when-youre-working-from-home/12307736).

37 Deborah Cole, a senior social worker and family counsellor at not-for-profit Drummond St Services in Melbourne. Cited in Grace Jennings-Edquist, 'How Much Attention Does Your Toddler Really Need When You're Working From Home?' *ABC Everyday*, Australian Broadcasting Corporation, 8 June 2020 (https://www.abc.net.au/everyday/how-much-attention-do-toddlers-need-when-youre-working-from-home/12307736).

38 Glennon Doyle in interview with Marie Forleo, 'How to Rediscover Your Wild Untamed Heart W/ Glennon Doyle', *MarieTV*, March 2020, (https://www.marieforleo.com/2020/03/glennon-doyle-untamed/).

Chapter 13: Are you saving the world yet?

1 Emmeline Pankhurst, *Suffragette: the autobiography of Emmeline Pankhurst* (CreateSpace, 2016), cited in Helen Lewis, *Difficult Women: a history of feminism in 11 fights* (Jonathan Cape, 2020).

2 Annie Kelly, '"Virtually Entire" Fashion Industry Complicit in Uighur Forced Labour, Say Rights Groups', *The Guardian*, 23 July 2020 (https://www.theguardian.com/global-development/2020/jul/23/virtually-entire-fashion-industry-complicit-in-uighur-forced-labour-say-rights-groups-china).

3 Malcolm Moore, 'Apple Admits to Using Child Labour', *The Sydney Morning Herald*, 2 March 2010 (https://www.smh.com.au/technology/apple-admits-using-child-labour-20100301-pbzz.html).

4 Peter Singer, *The Most Good You Can Do: how effective altruism is changing ideas about living ethically* (Yale University Press, 2015).

5 Alden Wicker, 'Conscious Consumerism is a Lie. Here's a Better Way to Help Save the World', *Quartz*, 1 March 2017 (https://qz.com/920561/conscious-consumerism-is-a-lie-heres-a-better-way-to-help-save-the-world/).

6 'The Impact of a Cotton T-Shirt,' *WWF*, 16 January 2013 (https://www.worldwildlife.org/stories/the-impact-of-a-cotton-t-shirt) and Michael Mobbs, '23 Years Off Grid for Water in the Centre of Sydney – What the Data Says,' *Sustainable House* (https://www.sustainablehouse.com.au/michaels-blog/2019/4/2/23-years-off-grid-for-water-in-the-centre-of-sydney-what-the-data-says).

7 Mintel, 'The Eco Gender Gap: 71% of Women Try to Live More Ethically, Compared to 59% of Men', 27 July 2018 (https://www.mintel.com/press-centre/social-and-lifestyle/the-eco-gender-gap-71-of-women-try-to-live-more-ethically-compared-to-59-of-men).

8 Ibid.

9 Glenn, 'Who Are Australia's Volunteers? (The 2019 update)', *Informed Decisions*, 26 March 2019 (https://blog.id.com.au/2019/population/demographic-trends/who-are-australias-volunteers-the-2019-update/).

10 Mintel, 'The Eco Gender Gap: 71% of Women Try to Live More Ethically, Compared to 59% of Men', 27 July 2018 (https://www.mintel.com/press-centre/social-and-lifestyle/the-eco-gender-gap-71-of-women-try-to-live-more-ethically-compared-to-59-of-men).

11 Janet K Swim, Ashley J Gillis & Kaitlynn J Hamaty, 'Gender Bending and Gender Conformity: the social consequences of engaging in feminine and masculine pro-environmental behaviors', *Sex Roles*, 82 (2020).

12 Professor Laura Wright, lecturer in English at Western Carolina University, and author of *The Vegan Studies Project*, which launched the new academic field of vegan studies, cited in Dr Alex Lockwood, 'Why Aren't More Men Vegan?', *Plant Based News*, 21 February 2018 (https://www.plantbasednews.org/opinion/why-arent-more-men-vegan).

13 Aaron R Brough, James EB Wilkie, Jingjing Ma, Mathew S Isaac, David Gal, 'Is Eco-Friendly Unmanly? The green-feminine stereotype and its effect on sustainable consumption,' *Journal of Consumer Research* 43, no. 4 (2016).

14 Jonas Anshelm & Martin Hultman, 'A green fatwā? Climate change as a threat to the masculinity of industrial modernity', *International Journal for Masculinity Studies* 9, no. 2 (2014).

15 Jessica Kennedy, Mary-Hunter McDonnell and Nicole Stephens, 'Does Gender Raise the Ethical Bar? Exploring the punishment of ethical violations at work', Vanderbilt Owen Graduate School of Management, Research Paper No. 2770012 (25 April 2016).

16 Ibid.

17 Ashley Madison, 'The Good Wife Study: a report on female sexuality and cheating habits', 2019 (https://www.ashleymadison.com/female-infidelity-statistics/).

18 Andy Ricketts, 'Nine in 10 Charity Workers Have Felt Stress, Overwhelm or Burnout over the Past Year, Survey Shows,' *The Third Sector*, 20 January 2021 (https://www.thirdsector.co.uk/nine-10-charity-workers-felt-stress-overwhelm-burnout-past-year-survey-shows/management/article/1705083).

19 Cheryl Scott Williams, Combating Teacher Burnout, *THE Journal*, 3 November 2011 (https://thejournal.com/articles/2011/11/03/teacher-burnout.aspx).

20 Waguih William Ishak, Sara Lederer, Carla Mandili, Rose Nikravesh, Laurie Seligman, Monisha Vasa, Dotun Ogunyemi & Carol Bernstein, 'Burnout during Residency Training: a literature review', *Journal of Graduate Medical Education* 1, no. 2 (2009).

21 Gary Morse, Michelle P Salyers, Angela L Rollins, Maria Monroe-DeVita & Corey Pfahler, 'Burnout in Mental Health Services: a review of the problem and its remediation', *Administration and Policy in Mental Health* 39, no. 5 (2012).

22 Christianna Silva, 'Black Activist Burnout: "You Can't Do This Work If You're Running on Empty"', *NPR*, 10 August 2020 (https://www.npr.org/2020/08/10/896695759/Black-activist-burnout-you-can-t-do-this-work-if-you-re-running-on-empty).

23 Paul Gorski, 'Relieving Burnout and the "Martyr Syndrome" Among Social Justice Education Activists: the implications and effects of mindfulness', *The Urban Review* 47, no. 4 (2015).

24 Grace Jennings-Edquist, 'How to Stay Energised and Take Care in the #MeToo Era', *ABC Everyday*, Australian Broadcasting Corporation, 22 October 2018 (https://www.abc.net.au/everyday/how-to-stay-energised-and-take-care-of-yourself-in-the-metoo-era/10387412).

25 Newcastle-based psychotherapist Rita Barnett. Cited in Grace Jennings-Edquist, 'How to Stay Energised and Take Care in the #MeToo Era', *ABC Everyday*, Australian Broadcasting Corporation, 22 October 2018 (https://www.abc.net.au/everyday/how-to-stay-energised-and-take-care-of-yourself-in-the-metoo-era/10387412).

26 Paul Gorski, 'Relieving Burnout and the "Martyr Syndrome" among Social Justice Education Activists: the implications and effects of mindfulness', *The Urban Review* 47, no. 4 (2015).

27 Jess Sims, 'Four BIPOC Women on the Power of Saying "No" – And Why It's Essential for Self Care', *Health*, 4 August 2020 (https://www.health.com/mind-body/bipoc-women-power-of-saying-no).

28 Timothy Devinney, 'Do Consumers Really Care? The Myth of the Ethical Consumer,' *The Modern Cynic,* 27 February 2012 (https://modern-cynic.org/2012/02/27/do-consumers-really-care-the-myth-of-the-ethical-consumer/).

29 Peter Singer, *The Most Good You Can Do: how effective altruism is changing ideas about living ethically* (Yale University Press, 2015), 4.

30 Ibid, 39.

Chapter 14: Pretty (tired)

1 Erin McKean, 'You Don't Have to Be Pretty', *A Dress A Day*, 20 October 2006.

2 Asma Nigar and Irum Naqvi, 'Body Dissatisfaction, Perfectionism, and Media Exposure among Adolescents', *Pakistan Journal of Psychological Research* 34 (2019).

3 Angela S Cain, Anna M Bardone-Cone, Lyn Y Abramson, Kathleen D Vohs, and Thomas E Joiner, 'Refining the Relationships of Perfectionism, Self-Efficacy, and Stress to Dieting and Binge Eating: examining the appearance, interpersonal, and academic domains', *International Journal of Eating Disorders* 41, no. 8 (2008).

4 Clementine Ford, *Fight Like a Girl* (Allen & Unwin, 2018).

5 Jessica DeFino, 'How White Supremacy and Capitalism Influence Beauty Standards', *Teen Vogue*, 19 October 2020 (https://www.teenvogue.com/story/standard-issues-white-supremacy-capitalism-influence-beauty).

6 Itisha Nagar and Rukhsana Virk, 'The Struggle Between the Real and Ideal: impact of acute media exposure on body image of young Indian women', *SAGE Open* 7, no. 1 (2017).

7 Ahmed Zambarakji, 'Fighting for diversity within beauty', *Raconteur*, 24 November 2016 (https://www.raconteur.net/fighting-for-diversity-within-beauty/).

8 Maria Denardo, 'New York Fashion Week Fall 2015 Wasn't as Diverse as You Might Think', *The Fashion Spot*, 25 February 2015 (https://www.thefashionspot.com/runway-news/547137-diversity-report-for-new-york-fashion-week-fall-2015/).

9 Ibid.

10 United States Census, 'Race and ethnicity makeup of NYC', American Community Survey, 2018 (https://www.census.gov/acs/www/data/data-tables-and-tools/data-profiles/2018).

11 Maisha Z Johnson, '10 Ways the Beauty Industry Tells You Being Beautiful Means Being White', *Everyday Feminism*, 3 January 2016 (https://everydayfeminism.com/2016/01/when-beauty-equals-white/).

12 Cordelia Tai, 'Report: 2019 Was Not a Good Year for Diversity on Magazine Covers', *The Fashion Spot*, 19 December 2019 (https://www.thefashionspot.com/runway-news/850787-diversity-report-fashion-magazine-covers-2019/).

13 Ibid.

14 Maisha Z Johnson, '10 Ways the Beauty Industry Tells You Being Beautiful Means Being White', *Everyday Feminism*, 3 January 2016 (https://everydayfeminism.com/2016/01/when-beauty-equals-white/).

15 Dana Oliver, 'Iman Opens up About Deeply Upsetting Career Moment', *Huffington Post*, 10 September 2015 (https://www.huffpost.com/entry/iman-racism-fashion-industry_n_55f02b31e4b002d5c0775000).

16 Breanne Fahs, 'Dreaded "Otherness": Heteronormative Patrolling in Women's Body Hair Rebellions', *Gender and Society* 25, no. 4 (2011).

17 Kendra Hodgson, Media Education Foundation Study Guide, 'Killing Us Softly 3: advertising's image of women' (http://www.mediaed.org/assets/products/206/studyguide_206.pdf).

18 Sophia Rosenbaum, 'New Study Finds Models are Woefully Underweight', *News*, 11 June 2016 (https://www.news.com.au/lifestyle/beauty/face-body/new-study-finds-models-are-woefully-underweight/news- story/3f9b5b531e899080da20c817e073a79b).

19 Luxury Activist, 'Top Models Body Mass Index – Red Health Alert!', 8 January 2017 (https://luxuryactivist.com/fashion/top-models-body-mass-index-health-red-alert/).

20 Kate Fox, 'Mirror, Mirror: a summary of research findings on body image', Social Issues Research Centre, 1997, (http://www.sirc.org/publik/mirror.html).

21 Hollie McKay, 'Pills, Injections and Plain Starvation: the dangerous extremes models go to for the fashion week runways', *Fox News*, 5 September 2012 (https://www.foxnews.com/entertainment/pills-injections-and-plain-starvation-the-dangerous-extremes-models-go-to-for-the-fashion-week-runways).

22 Jen Selter, Instagram post, 23 August 2017 (https://www.instagram.com/p/BYHkHhEhdaW/?hl=en).

23 Zan Romanoff, 'How The Kardashians Reflect Changing Ideas Around Plastic Surgery,' *BuzzFeed News*, 15 September 2017 (https://www.buzzfeednews.com/article/zanromanoff/how-the-kardashians-reflect-changing-ideas-around-plastic).

24 Grace Jennings-Edquist, 'A Parent's Guide to Talking about Body Editing Apps For Instagram', *ABC Everyday*, Australian Broadcasting Corporation, 16 July 2018 (https://www.abc.net.au/life/talking-to-daughter-about-body-editing-apps-instagram/9771928).

25 Lily Robinson, Ivanka Prichard, Alyssa Nikolaidis, Claire Drummond, Murray Drummond, Marika Tiggeman, 'Idealised Media Images: the effect of fitspiration imagery on body satisfaction and exercise behaviour', *Body Image*, 22 (2017).

26 I could give countless examples here: from university courses on personal branding (https://www.coursera.org/learn/personal-branding), to articles in mainstream publications about 'building your personal brand as a female professional', (https://www.theguardian.com/careers/personal-brand-female-professional-women-work), to university guides to personal branding for students and graduates (https://www.northeastern.edu/graduate/blog/tips-for-building-your-personal-brand/) and endless blogs on the topic by online marketing entrepreneurs (https://neilpatel.com/blog/personal-branding/).

27 Claire Charles, *Elite Girls' Schooling, Social Class and Sexualised Popular Culture* (Routledge, 2013).

28 Jia Tolentino, 'Athleisure, Barre and Kale: the tyranny of the ideal woman', *The Guardian*, 2 August 2019 (https://www.theguardian.com/news/2019/aug/02/athleisure-barre-kale-tyranny-ideal-woman-labour).

29 Sarah Marsh, 'The Pressure of Perfection: five women tell their stories', *The Guardian*, 14 October 2016 (https://www.theguardian.com/commentisfree/2016/oct/14/perfect-girls-five-women-stories-mental-health).

30 Jacqueline Howard, 'Cosmetic Skin Fillers Rise in Popularity, and Complications', *CNN*, 21 December 2017 (https://edition.cnn.com/2017/12/21/health/dermal-lip-filler-injections-risks-study/index.html/).

31 Kelly Allen, 'There's Been a Massive Increase in Anal Bleaching Because of Porn and Reality TV', *Glamour*, 6 December 2017 (https://www.glamourmagazine.co.uk/article/anal-bleaching-demand-up-due-to-porn).

32 Jessica Bursztynsky, 'Instagram Vanity Drives Record Numbers of Brazilian Butt Lifts as Millennials Fuel Plastic Surgery Boom', *CNBC*, 19 March 2012 (https://www.cnbc.com/2019/03/19/millennials-fuel-plastic-surgery-boom-record-butt-procedures.html).

33 Susruthi Rajanala, Mayra B C. Maymone and Neelam A Vashi, 'Selfies – Living in the Era of Filtered Photographs', *JAMA Facial Plastic Surgery*, 20 (2018).

34 Jessica Bursztynsky, 'Instagram Vanity Drives Record Numbers of Brazilian Butt Lifts as Millennials Fuel Plastic Surgery Boom', *CNBC*, 19 March 2012 (https://www.cnbc.com/2019/03/19/millennials-fuel-plastic-surgery-boom-record-butt-procedures.html).

35 Jia Tolentino, 'Athleisure, Barre and Kale: the tyranny of the ideal woman', *The*

Guardian, 2 August 2019 (https://www.theguardian.com/news/2019/aug/02/athleisure-barre-kale-tyranny-ideal-woman-labour).

36 Rachel M Calogero, 'Objectification Theory, Self-Objectification, and Body Image', In: Thomas F Cash, editor, *Encyclopedia of Body Image and Human Appearance*, Vol. 2 (San Diego: Academic Press, 2012), 574–580.

37 Barbara Fredrickson and Tomi-Ann Roberts, 'Objectification theory', *Psychology of Women Quarterly* 21, no. 2 (1997).

38 Jasmine Fardouly, Brydie K Willburger, Lenny R Vartanian, 'Instagram Use and Young Women's Body Image Concerns and Self-Objectification: testing mediational pathways', *New Media and Society* 20, no. 4 (2017).

39 Igor Pantic, 'Online Social Networking and Mental Health', *Cyberpsychology Behavioural and Social Networking* 17, no. 10 (2014).

40 William Barnhill, 'The Cellulite Myth', *The Washington Post*, 6 March 1985 (https://www.washingtonpost.com/archive/lifestyle/wellness/1985/03/06/the-cellulite-myth/661b5726-da95–43ec-9459-dfabb505bbcf/).

41 Mikki Kendall, *Hood Feminism* (Viking, 2020), 104.

42 Ibid, 101.

43 'Research Suggests Bias Against Natural Hair Limits Job Opportunities for Black Women', *Fuqua Insights*, Duke University, 12 August 2020 (https://www.fuqua.duke.edu/duke-fuqua-insights/ashleigh-rosette-research-suggests-bias-against-natural-hair-limits-job).

44 Ahmed Yussuf, 'The young women of colour redefining Australian beauty standards,' *ABC News Breakfast*, 10 March 2021 (https://www.abc.net.au/news/2021–03–10/young-women-of-colour-redefining-australian-beauty-standards/13229946).

45 Maria Thattil, 'People are saying I'm "not Australian enough" to be our Miss Universe,' *Mamamia*, 3 February 2021 (https://www.mamamia.com.au/miss-universe-australia-maria-thattil/).

46 Yumi Stynes for *Ladies, We Need to Talk*, 'Yumi Stynes on How Coronavirus Isolation Transformed the Way She Thinks About "Beauty"', *ABC Everyday*, Australian Broadcasting Corporation, 7 June 2020 (https://www.abc.net.au/life/yumi-stynes-on-the-gender-beauty-gap/12312244).

47 Katie Cunningham, 'My beauty regime was obsessive. But in isolation, I have been liberated from caring', *The Guardian*, 11 June 2020, (https://www.theguardian.com/commentisfree/2020/jun/11/my-beauty-regime-was-obsessive-but-in-isolation-i-have-been-liberated-from-caring).

48 Yumi Stynes for *Ladies, We Need to Talk*, 'Yumi Stynes on How Coronavirus Isolation Transformed the Way She Thinks About "Beauty"', *ABC Everyday*, Australian Broadcasting Corporation, 7 June 2020, (https://www.abc.net.au/life/yumi-stynes-on-the-gender-beauty-gap/12312244).

49 Caryl Rivers and Rosalind C Barnett, *The New Soft War on Women: how the myth of female ascendance is hurting women, men – and our economy* (Penguin, 2015).

50 Naomi Wolf, *The Beauty Myth* (Vintage, 1993), 217.

51 Caryl Rivers and Rosalind C Barnett, *The New Soft War on Women: how the myth of female ascendance is hurting women, men – and our economy* (Penguin, 2015).

52 Jill Stark, *Happy Never After: why the happiness fairytale is driving us mad (and how I flipped the script)* (Scribe, 2018), 87.

53 Sarah Marsh, 'The Pressure of Perfection: five women tell their stories', *The Guardian*, 14 October 2016 (https://www.theguardian.com/commentisfree/2016/oct/14/perfect-girls-five-women-stories-mental-health).

54 British sociologist and feminist cultural theorist Rosalind Gill has written that one significant way in which media culture changed in the 21st century has been the shift from sexual 'objectification' of women towards the representation of women as 'empowered' confident sexual subjects. Today's 'post-feminist' media culture is characterised by a hyper-intensive focus on women's bodies, under the guide of 'empowerment' rather than victimisation, she writes. From: Rosalind Gill, 'From Sexual Objectification to Sexual Subjectification: the resexualisation of women's bodies in the media', *Feminist Media Studies* 3, no. 1 (2003).

55 Claire Charles, *Elite Girls' Schooling, Social Class and Sexualised Popular Culture* (Routledge, 2013), building on Gill's work in ibid.

56 Jill Filipovic, 'How Kim Kardashian Killed the Term "Empowerment"', *Cosmopolitan*, 10 March 2016 (https://www.cosmopolitan.com/entertainment/a55017/kim-kardashian-naked-selfie-empowerment/).

57 Ibid.

58 Mikki Kendall, *Hood Feminism* (Viking, 2020), 110–111.

59 Sonya Renee Taylor, TED talk, 'Bodies as Resistance: claiming the political act of being oneself', TEDx Marin (8:50), 19 October 2017 (https://www.youtube.com/watch?v=MWI9AzkuPVg).

60 Lisa R Rubin, Carol J Nemeroff and Nancy Felipe Russo, 'Exploring Feminist Women's Body Consciousness', *Psychology of Women Quarterly* 28, no. 1 (2004).

61 Hannah M Borowsky, Marla E Eisenberg, Michaela M Bucchianeri, Niva Piran and Dianne Neumark-Sztainer, 'Feminist Identity, Body Image, and Disordered Eating', *Eating Disorders* 24, no. 4 (2016).

62 Taryn Brumfitt, *Embrace* (New Holland Publishers, 2015), 77.

63 Jameela Jamil, Instagram post, 17 March 2018, *jameelajamilofficial*, (https://www.instagram.com/p/BgY7nmeld40/?taken-by=jameelajamilofficial)

Chapter 15: Preparing for pushback and driving change

1 bell hooks and Emma Watson, 'In conversation with bell hooks and Emma Watson', *Paper*, 18 February 2016 (https://www.papermag.com/emma-watson-bell-hooks-conversation-1609893784.html).

2 Audre Lorde, 'The Transformation of Silence into Language and Action' – a short paper delivered at Chicago's Modern Language Association in 1977, later included in Lorde's anthology *Sister Outsider: essays and speeches* (Crossing Press, 1984).

3 Helen Lewis, *Difficult Women: a history of feminism in 11 fights* (Jonathan Cape, 2020), 300.

4 Ibid.

5 Ben Raue, 'Australians Voted in Massive Numbers for Marriage Equality and a Fair Go', *The Guardian*, 16 November 2017 (https://www.theguardian.com/australia-news/2017/nov/16/australians-voted-in-massive-numbers-for-marriage-equality-and-a-fair-go).

6 Geoff Gilfillan and Chris McGann, 'Trends in Union Membership in Australia', Parliament of Australia, Parliamentary Library, 15 October 2018 (https://www.aph.gov.au/About_Parliament/Parliamentary_Departments/Parliamentary_Library/pubs/rp/rp1819/UnionMembership).

7 Erin Delmore, 'This is How Women Voters Decided the 2020 Election', *Know Your Value*, 14 November 2020 (https://www.nbcnews.com/know-your-value/feature/how-women-voters-decided-2020-election-ncna1247746).

8 Arianna Huffington, 'The Third Women's Revolution: a look at how far we've come', *Thrive Global*, 9 March 2017 (https://medium.com/thrive-global/the-third-womens-revolution-daad613d95ad).
9 Liv Little, 'Women's Equality Still Doesn't Centre on Women of Colour – and It Needs To', *The Guardian*, 13 January 2018 (https://www.theguardian.com/lifeandstyle/2018/jan/31/2010s-why-shocked-see-michaela-coel-tv).
10 Kate Manne, *Down Girl: the logic of misogyny* (Penguin Books, 2018).
11 'It wasn't just the wages,' Fredrickson said. 'It was the lack of benefits and access to credit, childcare, paid sick days, and time off, and it was the indignities of harassment and misogyny,' she said.
12 Arianna Huffington, 'It's Time to End Perfectionism Anxiety Once and For All,' *Thrive Global*, 11 June 2019 (https://thriveglobal.com/stories/how-to-stop-perfection-anxiety-tips-arianna-huffington/).
13 Imi Lo, 'The Non-Conforming Asian Women', *Psychology Today*, 13 July 2018 (https://www.psychologytoday.com/us/blog/living-emotional-intensity/201807/the-non-conforming-asian-women).

Resources and further reading

Resources

If this book has raised issues for you, or if you need help, please get in touch with one of the support services below.

- **1800 RESPECT:** 1800 737 732. Free, 24-hour national sexual assault, family and domestic violence counselling line for any Australian who has experienced, or is at risk of, family and domestic violence and/or sexual assault.
- **Beyond Blue:** 1300 224 636 or web chat at https://online.beyondblue.org.au/. Support for people affected by anxiety, depression and suicide.
- **Butterfly Foundation:** 1800 33 4673 or web chat at https://butterfly.org.au/get-support/chat-online/. Phone, web-chat and email support for those experiencing eating disorders, as well as friends, family, carers and professionals.
- **Gidget Foundation:** https://gidgetfoundation.org.au/get-support/. Support services for new and expectant parents.
- **Lifeline:** 13 11 14 or web chat at https://www.lifeline.org.au/crisis-chat/. Confidential, 24/7 crisis support for people who are having difficulty coping or staying safe.
- **MindSpot:** 1800 61 44 34 or online assessments at https://mindspot.org.au/. Free, anonymous assessment and treatment for adults experiencing stress, anxiety, depression, obsessive-compulsive disorder, post-traumatic stress disorder and chronic pain.
- **Perinatal Anxiety and Depression Australia** (PANDA): 1300 726 306. Free, national helpline service for those affected by perinatal mental illness. Offers counselling, support, information and referrals.
- **QLife:** 1800 184 527 or web chat at https://qlife.org.au/. Anonymous and free LGBTQI peer support and referral for people in Australia wanting to talk about sexuality, identity, gender, bodies, feelings or relationships.

- **Relationships Australia:** 1300 364 277. Offers family and relationship counselling as well as a range of specialist counselling services.
- **SANE Australia:** 1800 18 7263 or web chat at https://www.sane.org/counselling-support/sane-support-services. Counselling, information, and referrals for adults who identify as having complex mental health issues, complex trauma or high levels of psychological distress.
- **Suicide Call Back Service:** 1300 659 467 or web chat at https://www.suicidecallbackservice.org.au/phone-and-online-counselling/. National 24/7 telehealth provider for people affected by suicide, including anyone who is feeling suicidal.

Further reading

Looking for additional information about feminism or finding your voice? Here's a selection of books I found useful in my research or that have informed my thinking.

Adichie, Chimamanda Ngozi, *We Should All Be Feminists,* Harper Collins, London, 2014

Benn, Melissa, *What Should We Tell Our Daughters?: The pleasures and pressures of growing up female*, Hodder & Stoughton, London, 2013

Braiker, Harriet, *The Disease to Please: curing the people-pleasing syndrome*, McGraw-Hill Education, New York, 2002

——, *The Type E* Woman: how to overcome the stress of being everything to everybody*, iUniverse, 2002

Brown, Brené, *I Thought It Was Just Me (but it isn't),* Penguin Random House, New York, 2007

Chemaly, Soraya, *Rage Becomes Her: the power of women's anger*, Simon & Schuster UK, London, 2018

de Beauvoir, Simone, *The Second Sex,* Knopf, New York, 1949

Dent, Georgie, *Breaking Badly: how I worried myself sick*, Affirm Press, Melbourne, 2019

Filipovic, Jill, *The H-Spot: the feminist pursuit of happiness*, Bold Type Books, New York, 2018

Friedan, Betty, *The Feminine Mystique*, W. W. Norton, New York, 1963

Gay, Roxane, *Bad Feminist,* Harper Perennial, New York, 2014

Hamad, Ruby, *White Tears/Brown Scars*, Melbourne University Press, Melbourne, 2019

hooks, bell, *Ain't I a Woman: black women and feminism*, South End Press, Boston, 1981

———, *Feminist Theory: From Margin to Center*, South End Press, Boston, 1984

Kendall, Mikki, *Hood Feminism: notes from the women that a movement forgot*, Viking, New York, 2020

Knight, Sarah, *F**k No!: how to stop saying yes, when you can't, you shouldn't, or you just don't want to*, Quercus, New York, 2019

Lewis, Helen, *Difficult Women: a history of feminism in 11 fights*, Jonathan Cape, London, 2020

Lorde, Audre, *Sister Outsider: essays and speeches*, Crossing Press, New York, 1984

Mohr, Tara, *Playing Big: practical wisdom for women who want to speak up create and lead*, Avery, New York, 2015

Moreton-Robinson, Aileen, *Talkin' Up to the White Woman: Indigenous women and feminism*, University of Queensland Press, Brisbane, 2000

Odell, Jenny, *How to Do Nothing: resisting the attention economy*, Melville House, 2019

Petersen, Anne Helen, *Can't Even: how millennials became the burnout generation*, Houghton Mifflin Harcourt, Boston, 2020

Rizvi, Jamila, *Not Just Lucky*, Penguin, Sydney, 2018

Rodsky, Eve, *Fair Play: a game-changing solution for when you have too much to do (and more life to live)*, Hachette, Sydney, 2019

Rugg, Sally, *How Powerful We Are: behind the scenes with one of Australia's leading activists*, Hachette, Sydney, 2019

Schulte, Brigid, *Overwhelmed: work, love, and play when no one has the time*, Macmillan, New York, 2015

Shraya, Vivek, *I'm Afraid of Men*, Parallax, Berkeley, 2018

Stark, Jill, *Happy Never After: why the happiness fairytale is driving us mad (and how I flipped the script)*, Scribe, Melbourne, 2018

Tolentino, Jia, *Trick Mirror: reflections on self-delusion*, HarperCollins, London, 2019